A Vision Betrayed

功成十堡血成溪　百文恩流分自西
身列四橋丰夜路　徒方三背兩番鷄
五千鞭撻寸膚裂　六尺懸垂二盜旁
捧功八侯警九品　七言一畢万灵啼

录康熙诗

王神荫

一九八八年九月二十七日

A Vision Betrayed

The Jesuits in Japan and China
1542–1742

ANDREW C. ROSS

ORBIS BOOKS

Maryknoll, New York 10545

The Catholic Foreign Mission Society of America (Maryknoll) recruits and trains people for overseas missionary service. Through Orbis Books, Maryknoll aims to foster the international dialogue that is essential to mission. The books published, however, reflect the opinions of their authors and are not meant to represent the official position of the society.

Copyright ©1994 by Andrew Ross

Published by Orbis Books, Maryknoll, New York 10545, U.S.A.

Manufactured in the United Kingdom

Library of Congress Cataloging-in-Publication Data

Ross, Andrew (Andrew C.)
    A vision betrayed : the Jesuits in Japan and China, 1542–1742 / Andrew C. Ross.
        p.   cm.
    Includes bibliographical references and index.
    ISBN 0–88344–991–9
    1. Jesuits—Missions—Japan—History.   2. Jesuits—Missions—China—History.   3. Japan—Church history—To 1868.   4. China—Church history.   I. Title.
    BV3447.R67   1994
    266'.252—dc20
                                                            94–10623
                                                            CIP

Contents

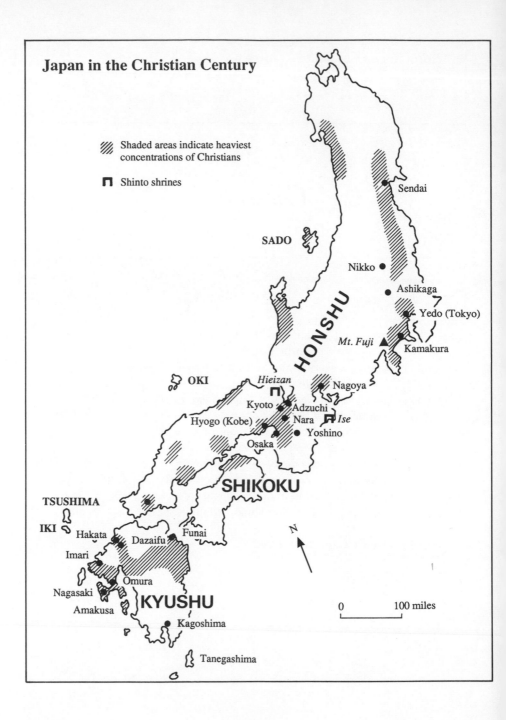

Japan in the Christian Century

///// Shaded areas indicate heaviest
concentrations of Christians

⊓ Shinto shrines

SADO

Sendai

Nikko

Ashikaga

Yedo (Tokyo)

HONSHU

Mt. Fuji

Kamakura

OKI

Hieizan

Nagoya

Kyoto

Adzuchi

Hyogo (Kobe)

Nara

Ise

Yoshino

Osaka

SHIKOKU

TSUSHIMA

IKI

Hakata

Funai

N

Dazaifu

Imari

Omura

100 miles

Nagasaki

Amakusa

KYUSHU

Kagoshima

Tanegashima

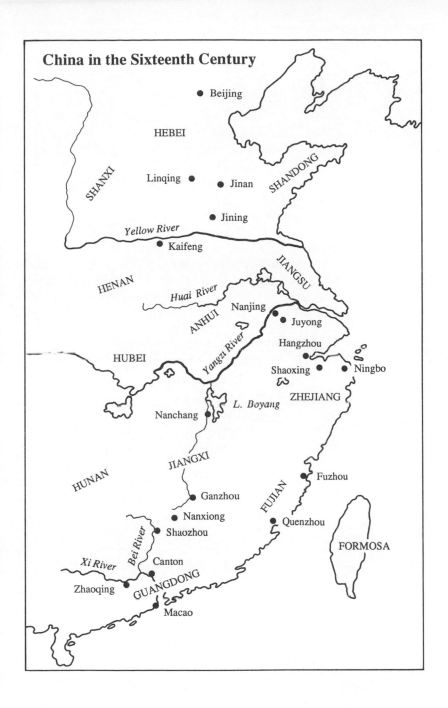

China in the Sixteenth Century

Beijing

HEBEI

SHANXI

Linqing   Jinan

SHANDONG

Jining

Yellow River   Kaifeng

JIANGSU

HENAN

Huai River

ANHUI   Nanjing

Juyong

Hangzhou

HUBEI   *Yangzi River*   Shaoxing   Ningbo

ZHEJIANG

L. Boyang

Nanchang

JIANGXI

HUNAN

Fuzhou

Ganzhou

Nanxiong   FUJIAN

Bei River   Shaozhou   Quenzhou

FORMOSA

Xi River   Canton

Zhaoqing   GUANGDONG

Macao

To the memory of the six members of
the Society of Jesus, and their two faithful
attendants, martyred in San Salvadore on
16 November 1989

Amando López Quintana
Ignacia Ellacuría
Juan Ramón Moreno Pardo
Joaquín Lopez y López
Ignacio Martín-Baró
Segundo Montes Mozo
Celina Maricet Ramos
Elba Julia Ramos

Acknowledgements

In attempting to write a synoptic history of the mission of the Society of Jesus in Japan and China from the arrival in Asia of Francis Xavier to Benedict XIV's constitution *Ex quo singulari* of 1742, I have depended upon the army of scholars American, European, Japanese and Chinese who have published in this field. In addition, there are a number of people to whom I owe particular thanks.

I must thank for their help Fr Willi Henkel of the Library of the Pontificia Universitas Urbaniana in Rome, the staff of the Library of Dartmouth College, Ms Martha Smalley and her colleagues in the Day Missions Library of Yale University, and the ever helpful librarians of New College, University of Edinburgh.

My thanks are also due to Professor Richard Gray, lately of the School of Oriental and African Studies at the University of London, and Fr Albert Chan sj of the University of San Francisco for their careful reading of the completed manuscript and the good advice and information they offered me. I hope they will overlook the places where I have not heeded them sufficiently.

At the Edinburgh University Press Penny Clarke and Jonathan Price have been supportive and encouraging and Dr Ian Clark has provided a very careful editing of the whole text 'con il modo soave' — for which I am most grateful.

Introduction

As the sixteenth century was drawing towards its close and the august Dynasty of the Chinese Ming had run more than two-thirds of its course, there came to China one of the most remarkable men of the age. His name was Matteo Ricci and he was a Jesuit priest. Of all the Europeans who attempted the task of understanding the Chinese and their civilisation he was the most talented, the most important. Among all the Westerners who sojourned in China, he was the only one to whom the Chinese accorded unreservedly their respect as a scholar in their own language and literature.[1]

Nigel Cameron's tribute to Matteo Ricci is echoed by many scholars including the greatest European authority on Chinese history and culture, Joseph Needham.[2] Many scholars have written about the extraordinary achievement of the Italian priest and intellectual who was accepted as one of themselves by the highest ranks of the academic elite, the Confucian literati, who had administered China for centuries even as different dynasties came and went.

How did this extraordinary Italian come to be in China at all? He was there because he had been chosen to join another Italian Jesuit, Michele Ruggieri, in the inaugural mission of the Society of Jesus to China. The mission was planned by Alessandro Valignano, Visitor to the East of the Society who had already reformed the Jesuit mission in Japan which had been inaugurated by St Francis Xavier.

Valignano reformed the mission in ways that broke fundamentally and decisively with the approach to the propagation of the Christian faith by missionaries under the authority of the Spanish and Portuguese crowns. When, midway through the fifteenth century, the Portuguese began the massive Iberian expansion over the whole world by reaching India via the Cape of Good Hope, they did so with the blessing of the Papacy. After Columbus' discoveries, the Spanish joined the game and expanded their authority over vast areas of the Americas with astonishing rapidity.

In those extraordinary last decades of the fifteenth century the leaders of the two kingdoms and the officials of the Papal curia still perceived the world in conventional medieval terms. Thus, in a series of Papal Bulls and in treaties between the two kingdoms and between them and the Holy See, the two crowns were given the right to rule over lands 'discovered' by them. In turn they had to undertake the costs of christianising them. In this way the Spanish and Portuguese crowns extended, into the new colonies, the rights they had in Europe of choosing who should be appointed to all senior ecclesiastical posts. Indeed, the power they achieved was such that the Pope was almost as removed from any effective authority over the Churches in the Iberian colonies as he was to be later in Henry VIII's England. The process began with Pope Nicolas V's Bull *Romanus Pontifex* of 1454 which dealt with Portuguese privileges in the East, and ended with the agreement in 1508 between the Holy See and the Spanish crown which went so far as to forbid the bishops, abbots and other senior Church officials in the Spanish colonies from communicating with the Pope save through the crown and vice versa. The crown had the right to decide whether the letters should go any further in either direction. In the Portuguese dominions the sytem of royal control of the Church was known as the Padroado.

The dynamic drive of the Spanish and Portuguese was such that eventually the two powers met on the Pacific rim, with the Portuguese in their trading post of Macao on the Chinese shore and the Spanish conquistadors looking for new lands to conquer from their new imperial province of the Philippines. In very clear and dramatic contrast with this whole movement, the Jesuit leader in the East, Alessandro Valignano, was adamant that Japan and China were not lands to be conquered, and he insisted that any attempt at such an adventure would be to the detriment of the missionary outreach of the Church.

So nervous was he of the influence of the Spanish 'conquistador' understanding of the expansion of Christianity that he sought Papal authority to forbid even Jesuits from coming to Japan or China via New Spain, as Mexico was then called, and the Philippines. In a long letter to the General from Japan in December 1579,[3] Valignano insists that Japan was not like Mexico or Peru. He believed that the Spanish could not conquer Japan, and even if they did so temporarily they could never hold the country. He repeats this with regard to China also, in his *Apologia* of 1598 to warn off, as it were, the Spaniards in the Philippines.[4]

This understanding of the situation was in marked contrast with the thinking of many Spaniards in both Manila and Mexico City, who, at one time, contemplated the invasion of China in order to impose Christianity. The whole crusading experience of recent Spanish – and to a lesser degree Portuguese – history meant that it was difficult for Spaniards or Portuguese to conceive of an expansion of Christianity that did not mean the expansion of Iberian political authority and Iberian culture. In contrast, Valignano insisted that both Japanese and Chinese culture contained elements of truth and morality upon which Christian faith could build. The creation of a truly Japanese and Chinese Church was his aim, and he viewed the imperial pretensions of both Portugal and Spain as a threat to that end, not an aid.

Wherever Christian missions had gone under the authority of the Portuguese or Spanish crown, the converts had had to become Spanish or Portuguese as well as Christian. The traditional missionary Orders – and, it must be noted, also at times the leadership of the Portuguese Province of the Jesuits – seemed incapable of distinguishing between the incidentals of European culture and the essential elements of the Christian faith. This was so even when they struggled for justice for the native Americans, as the Dominicans did so nobly on many occasions.[5]

Despite this emphasis on the convert accepting European cultural norms as an essential part of his or her new life, in neither empire was there any serious or prolonged attempt to transmit European 'high culture' to the indigenous people. In stark contrast, the Jesuit mission led by Valignano in Japan and China, while seeking to understand and, to an astonishingly large degree, to conform to Japanese and Chinese ways, also sought to offer to their hosts the best of European intellectual culture. Ricci came to be recognised as a genuine Confucian scholar by the Confucian elite, but he also taught the new mathematics he had learned under Clavius in Rome and translated Euclid into Chinese.

The Society of Jesus, the creation of Ignatius Loyola, was a product of Catholic renaissance humanism as it was also a product of revived Catholic piety and devotion. This great Basque, who was both a mystic and a brilliant organiser, went through a deep religious experience after a serious wound had ended his career as a diplomat and soldier. After a while spent in seeking his way forward in the Christian life, he decided that spirituality and asceticism were not enough and he needed education. As a mature man he went back to school and then to university, creating meanwhile a new guide to help men and women develop themselves for the service of God, the *Spiritual Exercises*. In August 1534, Ignatius Loyola and six companions, including Francis Xavier and Jaime Laynez, took vows of poverty and charity and committed themselves to going together on a mission to Jerusalem. If this intention failed then they would offer themselves, as a group, to the Pope to serve him in any way he saw fit to the 'Glory of God'. This phrase in Loyola's thought always implied service to one's neighbour and the propagation of the faith; and this small beginning led to the formal recognition of the Society of Jesus as a new religious Order for men in 1541. New members of the Society all went through the profound spiritual formation brought about by being taken through Loyola's *Spiritual Exercises*. It has often been claimed that this rigorous training, together with the Society's emphasis on obedience, left the Jesuits as well drilled servants of the Society's Superior General, while others have described their training as if it were some kind of brain-washing. However, it can also be argued that the training was so rigorous and profoundly effective that it enabled individual Jesuits to be secure psychologically and spiritually. Indeed, far from being well drilled automata, they came to have such tremendous confidence in their judgement and ability to decide what they must do 'for the Glory of God' that they would pursue the way they were called to go to fulfil the task given them by the General or the Pope, even when it meant going against the local establishment of Church or state. The ability to make choices was one of the key elements in the spiritual formation that was to be engendered by undergoing the *Exercises*.[6] Indeed, in order to be free to act in this way, the constitution of the Society liberated its members from many of the traditional patterns of the 'religious life'.

As well as a profound spirituality and devotion to the service of the Church through its head the Pope, the Society also laid great emphasis on the education of the laity and of the priesthood – which was certainly badly in need of reform in the sixteenth century. As a result of this the Roman College of the Society, the later Gregorian University, soon became one of the centres of Catholic humanist learning and renaissance science.

At this point it is important to point out that, from its inception, the Society of Jesus had problems with Spain which were to last for centuries. The Spanish Church was inextricably involved with the Spanish crown. The Spanish Inquisition had become a royal institution despite its technical ecclesiastical status and a most important tool of royal policy and control over the newly united and reconquered Spain. Its authority was extraordinary and it did not recognise any actual spiritual authority beyond itself – not even that of the Pope, although nominally recognising the authority of Rome. During his time as a student, the ex-soldier Ignatius Loyola had fallen foul of it on occasion. After his Society was recognised as an Order, it was still suspect in Spain. The spirituality of the *Exercises* was held to be related to earlier forms of Spanish mysticism condemned by the Royal Inquisition. Most important of all, however, was its profound objection to the Jesuit claim, the very basis indeed of their constitution – of a direct and special relationship to the Pope. This special relationship, the Jesuits insisted, meant that they were not subject to the Spanish Inquisition. This was an assertion that the Royal Inquisition could not tolerate, so a powerful campaign began, headed by the Spanish Dominicans who staffed the Royal Inquisition, to bring the Jesuits to heel.[7] Dominican and Spanish suspicion of the Society of Jesus is thus built into the story of the Society from the beginning. The conflict is part of the background to the history of the Jesuit mission in the East and, though rooted in Europe, constantly affects judgements made about the nature of the Christian missionary task outside Europe.

The conflict with Spanish royal authority over the Church was a slightly more extreme example of a fundamental problem facing the Catholic Church with regard to its autonomy. Throughout the sixteenth and seventeenth centuries the Catholic Monarchs of Portugal, Spain and France, as well as more petty Catholic rulers, attempted to control the Church in their dominions, and loyalty to the Pope as head of the Church was always shaped by the de facto control of the crown. The commitment of the Society of Jesus to go wherever the Pope might send them for the extension of the faith symbolised an understanding of the autonomy of the Church that cut across the control of the altar by the throne – in practice total in the Spanish dominions and nearly so in the Portuguese.

In Alessandro Valignano these two Jesuit traditions of deep piety and humanist culture came together in a peculiarly dynamic way. It should also be noted that this proud man was born and raised in Chieti, a city that was under Spanish domination like the rest of southern Italy. He could not have been unaware as he grew up that Spanish officers often referred to Italians as the 'indios' of Europe. It was this Italian who guided the Society in the East into a style of mission that attempted to break free from both European political imperialism and, what was even more powerful and longer lived, Europeanism – the belief that the European experience is the Christian experience and is definitive for all humanity. This was not a philosophy that was ever named but it was the unspoken assumption of so much thought. It outlived the period of Iberian expansion and dominated Protestant missionary activity when it burst upon the rest of the world in the last decade of the eighteenth century, as well as the revived missionary activity of the Roman Catholic Church in the mid-nineteenth century. In the last decade of the twentieth century, Europeanism is still alive and well, flourishing in western intellectual circles which reject European political imperialism and Christianity yet still unquestioningly assume the experience of western European humanity to be definitive, and that since secularism followed industrialisation and urbanisation in western Europe, it will inevitably do so in Africa and Asia.

Valignano, when he became Jesuit Visitor to the East, was able to direct the shape of developments in Japan only within certain limits. These limits had been created by the experience of the mission in Japan after its foundation by St Francis Xavier. However, in China the mission was initiated by the Visitor who, in Matteo Ricci, found the perfect instrument to carry out and indeed lead and develop his programme. The two worked together in closest accord at all times, and those who have tried to explain Ricci without Valignano inevitably present an incomplete picture of the Jesuit effort.

Under Valignano's leadership genuinely Japanese and Chinese Churches came into being. In Japan this finally provoked a crisis when the new Tokugawa Shogunate came to believe by 1614 that it could not tolerate any institution that insisted that there was a loyalty beyond that which was owed to the state. Thousands of Japanese Christians died rather than give up their faith until the Tokugawas had to create a special religious police to uproot them and to close Japan to all outsiders as well as forbid all Japanese, on pain of death, from travelling abroad. So Japan became the 'Closed Land' until the middle of the nineteenth century.

In China the growth in numbers of Christians was not so large or so fast as in Japan, but Christianity, as interpreted by the Jesuits, gained a place among a significant group of the Confucian literati, as well as people of other ranks. The Jesuits lived and behaved as literati, the academic elite who had administered the Chinese Empire for a thousand years, and were so successful in achieving a Confucian–Christian synthesis that they were accused by members of other Orders who were eventually allowed into China, of creating a Christian veneer under which Confucianism still flourished. For a time they were able to convince Rome of the orthodoxy of what they were doing. However, because of political and intellectual conflicts in Europe that had nothing to do with China, Jesuit policy in China was finally condemned as heterodox. At the same time the great Qing Emperor, Kangxi, issued a formal imperial endorsement of Christianity giving it a new status in China similar to the status given to Christianity by Constantine the Great in the Roman Empire. Rome was adamant in its judgement, however, despite this extraordinary event, and the way of Valignano and Ricci was condemned. In turn, Kangxi furiously insisted that it was only the Christianity of Li Madou (Ricci) that was approved. As a result of this, Christianity, in a tragically short time, went from being a respected possible option for Chinese of all ranks to being a fringe sect for people on the margins of society. This was not because 'the gospel preference for the poor' could not be accepted by Chinese society at that time, but because the eighteenth-century Church could not shake itself free of Europeanism.

There are a number of good studies of the Christian Century in Japan, notably that by C. R. Boxer, and George Elison's *Deus Destroyed*; and there are a large number of monographs on individual Jesuits in China during this period, particularly on Matteo Ricci. George Dunne's magisterial *Generation of Giants* covers a large part of the history of the Jesuits in China but ends, regrettably, with the 1660s. Outstanding among the biographies of Ricci are Vincent Cronin's old but still very useful *Wise Man from the West*, and the recent and outstanding *Memory Palace of Matteo Ricci* by Jonathan Spence.

There has been recently an upsurge in interest in the philosophic problems surrounding the possibility of the kind of integration of Confucianism into Christianity in the way that Aristotle was assimilated in Medieval Europe. This theological and philosophical problem is not one that I attempt to deal with. Scholars like Paul Rule, who thinks assimilation possible, J. D. Young who is not sure and Jacques Gernet who is certain it is impossible, have produced work of great interest, style and scholarship and must be read to pursue that topic in depth. As an historian I can only observe that a leading Confucian scholar of the Ming era, a Grand Secretary of the Empire, Xu Guangqi, believed in the actuality of this integration, while another devoted Confucian scholar of the same period, Yang Guangxian, insisted on the fundamental incompatability of Christianity and Confucianism.

Despite the recent growth in the publication of studies of individuals or of specific problems associated with the Jesuit mission and of special periods of the story, there is no one book which attempts to outline and discuss the whole. It was, after all, one story, that of one missionary effort that had its root and essential shape in the thinking of a group of Italian Jesuits led by Alessandro Valignano. To tell that story is what I have attempted in this book. In trying to describe and analyse this extraordinary episode in the history of Christianity and of east–west relations I acknowledge my massive dependence upon the original research of the many scholars, American, European, Japanese and Chinese, whose works are listed in the bibliography.

NOTES

1. Cameron, *Barbarians and Mandarins*, p. 149.
2. Needham, *Science and Civilisation in China*, vol. 1, p. 148.
3. Moran, 'Letters from a Visitor to Japan, 1579'.
4. Moran, *The Japanese and the Jesuits*, pp. 80–2.
5. See Friede and Keen, *Bartolomeo de las Casas in History*.
6. Ganss (ed.), *Ignatius of Loyola*, pp. 50–1.
7. Wright, *The Counter-Reformation*, pp. 17 ๑๑.

CHAPTER ONE

Japan and China
Before the Expansion of the
Iberian Sea-borne Empires

B efore the expansion of the Iberian Sea-borne empires, the two great empires at each end of the Eurasian land mass, Rome and China, knew very little about each other, but Graeco-Roman culture and Chinese culture each shared the belief that they were the civilised centre of the world and beyond their borders was barbarism. In the period of the Roman empire there developed both in Rome and China knowledge that far away on the edge of the world another empire existed, so that in China there was acknowledgement of the existence of 'the Land of the Far West', and in the Mediterranean world they talked of 'the Land of Silk'. However, they knew very little about each other, and what they knew had no relevance to anything of importance. Thus the acknowledgement of the existence of this other did not affect the self understanding of each empire that it was the civilised centre of an otherwise barbarian world.

When the great Mongol Khans created an empire that included China (1279) and reached to Poland, there was some direct contact between the two cultures. During this time the Venetian Polo family acted as ambassadors in each direction. It was in their reports that the West first heard of Japan, referred to as Zipangu by Marco Polo. In this period Franciscan Fathers also travelled to China and founded a small but flourishing western Catholic Church in China. The Franciscans found Nestorian Christian congregations already in existence there. From the middle of the seventh century missionaries of the Nestorian Church, whose base was Mesopotamia, began to enter China and a Nestorian community grew there and flourished for two hundred years. How far this form of Christianity took root among Chinese people proper and how much among the many immigrant groups which were in China in that period cannot now be known, but the end came when in 845 a ferocious persecution erupted which appears to have wiped the Church out, although it continued to flourish among some Mongol tribes and so re-entered China in the train of the Great Khan.

However, with the fall of the Mongol empire (1368) the fragile connection between the West and the East was broken and what knowledge there was in each of the other was soon forgotten, in China as in Europe. For example the first Franciscans to enter China in the seventeenth century appear to have had no knowledge of their predecessors in that land, though some had held bishoprics there. When the Portuguese maritime expansion first brought news to Europe of Japan and its neighbouring powerful empire, China, these were seen as totally new 'discoveries'. Where there was knowledge of Polo's writing no connection was made between his Cathay and Zipangu and the 'newly discovered' China and Japan.

It was the great Portuguese conquistador, Alfonso de Albuquerque, who captured the important Chinese trading base of Malacca on the Malayan peninsula in 1511 and thus made the first contacts between the Portuguese and the Chinese. Using Malacca as their base a number of individual Portuguese reached the Chinese coast, but it was not until 1517 that an official Portuguese embassy was sent to China. The behaviour of the Portuguese during these first contacts was such that their status as barbarians was only too definitely confirmed. The official visitors flew their flags inside Chinese territory, fired cannon inside the harbour of Canton, in Chinese eyes inexcusable even if in salute, and they also refused to kou tou, the fundamental gesture of polite and formal greeting throughout Chinese society. At the same time other Portuguese captains behaved more like pirates than traders along the Chinese coast.

Eventually in 1521 the Portuguese were excluded altogether from Chinese territory. However the trade they provided was too profitable to be banned permanently and in 1530 it reopened; and then, in 1557, the Portuguese were allowed to make a small settlement on an uninhabited island connected to the mainland by a narrow causeway at the mouth of the Pearl River close to Canton – this was Macao. Macao was not seen as being under Portuguese sovereignty. It was not a stronghold from which they dominated both the neighbouring rulers and the trade of the area as they did from Malacca or Calicut or Goa. In Macao they were utterly at the mercy of the Chinese authorities, restricted in their movements, unable to enter China except on a certain number of limited occasions that suited the Chinese. Macao was more a trading ghetto than 'a foothold in China'. Indeed in Chinese law the Portuguese in Macao were being treated exactly in the way the imperial authorities treated the aboriginal southern hill tribes that had not accepted Chinese culture but had accepted Chinese suzerainty.

In 1542 or 1543 – historians are not agreed – three Portuguese traders, who were involved in illegal trade on the Chinese coast, were blown ashore on the small Japanese island of Tanegashima. They were well received and their firearms aroused a great deal of interest and excitement. These were soon being replicated on Kyushu and later Honshu, the two main islands of

Japan. Soon after this the Portuguese became the middlemen in a thriving trade between China and Japan. The Ming Dynasty had forbidden any direct trade with Japan because of the terrible depredation wrought by Japanese pirate raids on the Chinese coast. However, Japan wanted China's silk and China wanted Japan's silver and the barbarian traders appeared to be a useful channel through which this trade could continue without any need for direct contact between the Chinese and the Japanese.

We should now consider in some more detail these two great civilisations which Francis Xavier, founding member of the Society of Jesus and its pioneer missionary, set out to conquer in spiritual warfare.

JAPAN

When Europeans first reached Japan, the Emperor on the throne was Go Nara, the one hundred and fifth Emperor descended from the Sun Goddess, Amaterasu. Japan had become a united kingdom by AD 400, and it rapidly became such a powerful state that it dominated the Korean peninsula for a time. (Japan did not include Hokkaido, which did not become Japanese until the nineteenth century.) The Japanese state from its inception had a close relationship with China, sometimes directly, sometimes via Korea. The two oldest written sources for Japanese history were both written using Chinese ideograms, the *Kojiki* (Record of Ancient Matters) 712, and the *Nihonshoki* (Chronicle of Japan) 720. However in this same period there appeared an extraordinary volume containing several thousand poems written by men and women drawn from almost all ranks of Japanese society, the *Manyoshu*. This was written in the 'kana' syllabary, the root of the modern Japanese script and held by many authorities to be, of all the early texts, the most truly expressive of Japanese life and thought. Some authorities believe that it is vital still to any attempt to understand late twentieth-century Japan.

The indigenous religion of Japan was Shinto, that is the way of the kami, the divinities. These were spiritual beings, but, in addition, humans and natural objects could also be or become kami. Shinto had two main forms. One was clan based. Each clan had a central shrine where the clan divinity was honoured, these communal rituals helping to bind the clan together. The kami of the imperial clan was Amaterasu, the Sun Goddess. The second pattern of Shinto was a form of religious activity centred upon a shaman or charismatic individual through whom kami spoke amd who might become kami after death. Shinto was inextricably related to clan headship and political authority, indeed some offices, including that of Emperor, were seen as themselves bestowing charismatic power and authority upon their holders.

China, during the Tang Dynasty (AD 626–910), developed a particularly powerful influence on Japan, artistically, religiously and to a lesser degree politically. The Confucian classical writings were brought to Japan in this era although Confucianism did not become a widespread and deep influence in

Japanese life. Its influence, while important, was restricted to a narrow group
within aristocratic and academic circles. It was Buddhism in its Chinese form
that was the foreign influence which had a deep as well as widespread impact
on Japan. Not only were a number of the Chinese Buddhist schools exported
to Japan where they gained influence in aristocratic and court circles but the
Japanese also created new Buddhist schools or sects as Buddhism became
indigenised in aristocratic culture. Eventually, in what is called the Kamakura
period of Japanese history (1192–1333), Buddhism came to permeate all of
Japanese life, shaping it and in turn being shaped by it.

Buddhism first entered Japan because of the close connections with China
and Korea and because of the numbers of Chinese and Korean families who
came to Japan and became 'naturalised'. However, it was only after Buddhism
was formally patronised and supported by Prince Shotoku (573–621) that it
came to dominate the religious life of the court and the aristocracy and became
integrated with clan Shinto in those circles. The common people received nothing from this new religious development, and as a result they all the more turned
to charismatic individuals for guidance and spiritual comfort. But Buddhist
influences penetrated even into this area of Japanese life and so there developed a particularly Japanese form of Buddhism, called by Kitagawa and other
scholars, shamanistic Buddhism. How far this can be judged as an expansion
of Buddhism and how far it was rather the adaptation of certain Buddhist ideas
and rituals into what was still essentially popular Shinto is a matter of debate
among scholars.

What is clear is that the worship of the official Shinto shrines and official Buddhism were both associated with the authority of the state and the prestige and
power of the upper ranks of society. The imperial state patronised Buddhism
and absorbed it as an alternative form of the state cult. The state built Buddhist
temples and monasteries and even laid down formal ecclesiastical laws for the
regulation of the Buddhist clergy, monks and nuns.

Buddhism became much more widespread in its impact and appeal from the
beginning of the ninth century (794–1185 is called the Heian Period in Japanese
history) with the rapid growth of two new schools of Buddhism introduced
from China, the Tendai and Shingon schools. All levels of society were now
permeated by Buddhist concepts and ideas, but there was no single enforced
orthodoxy so these ideas and beliefs were varied and led at times to direct
conflict between groups of believers. Also popular shamanistic Buddhism still
flourished with groups of common people looking to particular charismatic
leaders rather than the official clergy of any of the sects. These movements
were particularly open to other influences from China and various forms of
magical practice from Daoist and other Chinese traditions entered into the
religious mix.

Despite the syncretism or perhaps because of it, this was a period when the
imperial authorities laid down very clear regulations for Shinto clergy in charge

of certain nationally important shrines, about twenty in all. These regulations provided for their support as well as rules for their behaviour and even for their liturgical rituals. These Shinto clergy and shrines were explicitly separate from the Buddhist ecclesiastical structures, which were also state supported, and the many other forms of popular religious activity of the period.

In the thirteenth century, known as the Kamikura period (1192–1333) of Japanese history, official Buddhism became so deeply involved in the political affairs of the nation that many people felt disillusioned by it. New charismatic figures arose to meet the spiritual needs of the people. They were not outside traditional Buddhism as the leaders of shamanistic Buddhism had been in the earlier period. They came from within the traditional Buddhism and their impact was such that some scholars have seen this period in Japanese Buddhist history as similar to the Reformation in Western Christianity. Their followers formed into new schools or sects. Three of these, Jodo, Shin and Ji, were all forms of Pure Land Buddhism, that is schools that focused on the heavenly paradise that could be reached by devotees of Amida Buddha, the compassion-ate saviour. The other two were the Zen school and the Nichiren school, though sect is probably the better word since they all rapidly developed autonomous ecclesiastical structures and organisations.

These new sects played a very important role in Japanese society. The Pure Land and Nichiren sects were very successful in appealing to the common peo-ple and providing them with a sense of personal worth and a set of explicitly Buddhist religious beliefs that were geared to their existence. This was in direct contrast with the older sects with their focus on the state and the security of the government. The Nichiren sect went further and often actively opposed the authorities on behalf of the common people and threatened to become a permanent opposition to the central authority of the state.

With their mass popular followings, which the older sects had never suc-ceeded in producing nor indeed had they been interested in producing, the new sects became powerful popular religious societies. This was a new type of religious authority in Japan. The older Buddhist sects had built up power and authority within the traditional power structure of the state. Their great monastic settlements of Mount Hiei, Mount Koya and Nara had long played an important role in affairs but they had never developed a mass popular fol-lowing. The new sects became mass religious movements arousing passionate devotion among the common people in both the towns and the countryside.

However, these new movements which had been brought into being in a spiritual revolt against the worldliness of official Buddhism, gradually came to be themselves important forces in the political life of Japan. Like the abbots of the old sects some of the leaders of the new sects would on occasion gather monk armies together and make their monasteries into fortresses. What was new was that some of the Pure Land and Nichiren abbots could, in addition, call on devoted popular support among the ordinary people.

It was also in the Kamikura period that the peculiar Japanese parallel to European knighthood developed, the samurai, with their strict code of honour in which complete loyalty to the superior was the supreme virtue. This code was profoundly influenced by the new revival of Buddhist piety and philosophy.

The samurai code of loyalty to the lord and the passionate devotion aroused by the new sects all played their part in the break-up of Japanese unity. Down the centuries the Emperor, the Son of Heaven, had continued on the throne, a symbol of a continuing unity of the state even though real authority very often lay with others. In particular from the end of the twelfth century effective authority was in the hands of the Shogun, the leader of the military aristocracy with their attendant samurai. Despite disputes from time to time among great families over who should hold the office of Shogun, Japan was still a unified state under the system of Shogunal rule. However in 1467 a civil war, called the Onin War, began which heralded a period of Japanese history called Sengoku Jidai (the age of the country at war). The great lords (daimyo), based in their fortified castle-towns and using their samurai armies, each sought to aggrandise the power of his own family. What made the situation more complex was that the powerful leaders of both old and new sects of Buddhism also entered the fray. As Kitagawa says,

> Towards the latter part of the sixteenth century Japan was divided not only among the semi-independent feudal lords (daimyo) but also among equally powerful and fanatic followers of religious societies. That is why the task of unification of the nation...involved religious as well as political measures.[1]

It was into Japan in this period of conflict that the Portuguese arrived and contributed to the fray the new technology of firearms. Daimyo eagerly sought the visit of Portuguese vessels to their harbours to profit from the trade and thus increase their financial and political power.

It was into this complex situation, too, that Francis Xavier and his Jesuits came in 1549. As we shall see, he soon came to believe that the very success the Society was having in Japan necessitated his going to China. This was partly because he believed this large and sophisticated empire was clearly the next necessary objective of Christian mission. It was also because he believed success in China was necessary for real success in Japan. Major religious and philosophical ideas had so often come to Japan from China that again and again he had been asked in Japan why, if what he taught was so old and true, was it not known in China?[2]

CHINA

By the year 1600 BC there was in existence a culture in the valley of the Yellow River which is in direct continuity with the culture of China today. Already the oldest form of writing in the world was in existence, the Chinese ideogram. There followed in the era of the Chou Dynasty (1100–256 BC) a flowering of

Chinese culture, a surge of both prose and poetry expressing an astonishing variety of social, political and religious philosophies. It was, however, in the brief period of the Qing Dynasty (221–206 BC) that the empire was firmly united, occupying the land which has ever since been seen as China proper. From this time, although there were periods of division often into a number of small kingdoms, the belief in the oneness of the Middle Kingdom was fundamental to Chinese politics and philosophy.

It was in the succeeding dynastic period of Han, 202 BC to AD 200, that one of the most striking features of the history of the Middle Kingdom developed. This was the manning of the central and provincial administration of the empire by men chosen for their ability rather than their aristocratic birth or connection. Although in this period there was not yet the consistently organised system of examinations with an elaborate system of education to prepare candidates for entry to the service which was to develop later, examinations of various kinds did take place. For example, from time to time, candidates, however powerful their patrons, had to submit essays on set topics to the authorities to test their suitability for appointment. The basis of the future system was laid by the creation of what can only be called the first national university, founded in 124 BC as the apex of the existing system of schools and which taught students to interpret the classic Confucian texts.

From this beginning there developed the system that was brought to completion in the eighth century AD during the period of the Tang Dynasty. Entry to the civil service was by a formally structured and organised examination system, and an elaborate system of schools was developed to prepare candidates for these examinations. Although the system was not totally egalitarian initially, and often was temporarily modified by forms of patronage, over the centuries it achieved an astonishing ability to allow men of talent from very modest backgrounds to reach the highest ranks in the service of the empire. Military and civil services were shaped by this system in which the civil was always the more prestigious branch, in marked contrast with any system produced in the West until the nineteenth century.

What is equally important to note is that as dynasties came and went the administration of China was always in the hands of the civil service produced by the examination system, the literati, as the Jesuits called them. This was so even during the period of rule by the Great Khans when China was part of a much larger empire. Even as part of this Mongol empire, China was still administered separately by the literati. The Khan was treated as Emperor of China and the Mongols accepted this and gave themselves a Chinese dynasty name, Yuan.

The literati are also sometimes referred to in English as 'mandarins', sometimes as 'scholar-administrators', but literati is probably the best word to express who they were. All who passed the examinations were of the dignity or status of literati with a specific form of dress reflecting their place in Chinese society. Not all literati, however, entered the civil or military service, and those who did sometimes retired for a time and then re-entered the service; thus all civil or military officers were literati but not all literati were in the imperial service.

There were three levels of examination. Candidates who successfully passed the first, the xiucai (flowering talent or government student), achieved scholar status. However they were under considerable strain because they could not be admitted to even a minor civil service post until, after further examination, they moved up through the five ranks within the xiucai status. In the fifth rank they had what we would call tenure. All members of the xiutsai aimed at succeeding in passing the examinations so as to be awarded the rank of zhuren (recommended man).

Those who achieved this second level did not have to undergo re-examination and could be appointed to a variety of intermediate level jobs in the administration or the army. All the most senior positions in the civil and military services were reserved for those who passed the third level examinations and so became jinshi (presented scholar), sometimes referred to by the Jesuits as those who had received their doctorate. These men were a small exclusive intellectual elite. The examinations for this third level were held every three years and though thousands qualified to attempt the test only a few were deemed good enough. This number varied over the centuries between a low of thirty-two and a high of 472.

In the era of the Ming Dynasty the central government of China was divided into a number of units, sometimes referred to in English as Boards but probably better translated as Ministries, subordinate to the imperial Secretariat. The number of Grand Secretaries varied at the will of the Emperor and there was usually one who was thought of as 'The' Grand Secretary.

The Ministries were six in all, each headed by a triumvirate of very senior mandarins holding the offices of president with two vice-presidents. The Ministries were first, that of the Civil Service which oversaw the mandarins in the provinces; second, the Ministry of Finance; third, Ministry of Rites, one of whose branches was responsible for all foreigners within the empire; fourth, the Ministry of War; fifth, the Ministry of Criminal Justice; and finally the Ministry of Public Works. There was one sub-division of the Ministry of Rites of enormous importance: that was the office sometimes called in English the Calendar Office, sometimes the Board of Astronomy. This office had a staff of mathematicians, some of whom followed ancient Chinese mathematical principles and another group who followed mathematics brought to China in the time of the Mongol Khans from the Islamic schools of Mesopotamia. Its task was to prepare the imperial Calendar each year which had to forecast accurately any possible lunar or solar eclipses, however partial. Any failure to do so would indicate a disjunction between heaven and earth: an indication of a possible withdrawal of the Mandate of Heaven from the Emperor. The importance of that office can hardly be exaggerated.

The overwhelming majority of Chinese were commoners divided into three groups, farmers, artisans and merchants. Above and beneath the literati and the commoners were two small groups of Chinese people. At the top, enjoying wealth and social prestige but no political power were the members of the imperial clan and members of other ancient aristocratic families. At the bottom was another marginal element in society, made up of what might be called outcaste groups whose status was hereditary, prostitutes, entertainers, certain fishing groups and in addition the non-hereditary slaves. However, the overwhelming majority of Chinese were neither aristocrats nor outcastes. It is vital to remember that the literati who ran government and officered the army were the product of educated ability and not a hereditary caste such as ruled western Europe through most of its history. Aristocats and commoners could all attempt the examinations to become literati; only those of the outcaste groups were forbidden this opportunity.

On what was this vital examination system based? It focused on a series of texts associated with the thinker Confucius (Kongfuzi, 551–479 BC). He lived in an era of very lively and varied intellectual and spiritual activity in Chinese society, but it was the texts associated with Confucius which became the basis of the examination system and the intellectual orthodoxy of the imperial state and not writings from any of the many other schools of thought of the period.

The examination syllabus was based on a series of texts referred to as *The Four Books (Sishu)* and *The Five Classics (Wu Ching)*. The *Five Classics* were the key texts. The *Four Books* were what students began with and had to master before embarking on the *Five Classics* which were the *I Ching* (Classic of Changes), the *Shih Ching* (Classic of Poetry), *Shu Ching* (Classic of History), *Li Chi* (Classic of Rituals), and the *Chun Qiu* (Spring and Autumn Annals). These had to be supplemented by the book of Confucius himself, the *Analects (Lun yu)*, and by the book of his most prominent follower Mencius, the 'Second Sage' of China, the *Mencius (Meng Zi)*.

Confucius' teaching centred on the human being and human society and attempted to construct a moral code and life style for the good man and a truly humane and just society. Jen, which can be translated virtue, love, or magnanimity, and is possibly best translated as love, was the supreme virtue which would encompass the traditional Chinese values of righteousness (yi) and even filial piety (xiao) held by others to be the supreme virtue. However, although Confucius did not take part in any kind of metaphysical speculation nor anything that could be called theology, he was intensely interested in and laid very firm emphasis upon Li, which can mean simply decorous behaviour but in Confucius explicitly included performing religious ceremonies correctly and appropriately. It seems clear that Confucius, while spending no time on any kind of religious or theological teaching, accepted the existence of 'tian', literally 'heaven', a cosmic spiritual authority with a profound moral concern.

The ruler ruled by the Mandate of Heaven, and if that was withdrawn then another ruler could rightly replace him.

Equally important was the teaching of Confucius that the ruler ruled because of his virtue and wisdom, and that authority should not need to be maintained by force. The ruler's task was to create peace and harmony in society so that earth accorded with heaven. Confucius was dismissive of much of the religious activity of his day from which, however, he exempted the formal honouring of the ancestors and the necessity for the ruler always to seek the Mandate of Heaven by the performance of all appropriate rituals as well as by virtuous behaviour.

Of the many other philosophical and religious developments in the Chou period the only important long term tradition other than Confucianism was Daoism. In Chinese 'dao' is the 'way', so the Confucian way is the way of the virtuous man. However, Daoism usually refers to a religious tradition said to have begun with the teaching of Lao Tzu who lived in the sixth century BC. It is both a philosophic school and a religious tradition. The religious strain in Daoism developed a priestly hierarchy and congregations of devout believers together with a body of sacred scripture. Some scholars see this as a response to the impact of Buddhism upon Chinese society in the period from the third to the seventh centuries AD.

The Daoist priesthood held themselves to be superior to the shamanistic exorcists and mediums of popular religion and shared with the Confucian state antagonism towards what they held to be unauthorised religious activity. The Confucian took this view because such religious activity was seen as dangerous to the good order of society, the Daoist because it endangered the individual worshipper involved. This highlights one of the key differences between Confucianist and Daoist: Confucianism is fixed upon the good of society, Daoism on the salvation of the individual.

It was during the third century of the Christian era that Buddhism began to enter China. It was brought by missionaries from India and Tibet and one of their most effective means of propagating the faith was the printed word. China was already a society in which the book was central to the transmission of knowledge and ideas. The missionaries and their early converts spent a great deal of time and effort translating classic Buddhist texts into Chinese. When, even after bursts of persecution by Daoist or Confucianist rulers, Buddhism began to have a mass following, its Chinese leaders were not content to accept teaching translated from other sources but began to produce their own Chinese Buddhist theology. So, as time went by, new and specifically Chinese schools of Buddhism developed, some of which, as we have seen, had an important impact on Japan.

During the Tang Dynasty (AD 589–845) the Emperor directly ruled a vast area beyond the boundaries of China proper, Manchuria, Mongolia, Tibet, northern Korea and at times parts of central Asia and Indo-China. In this period, which was very cosmopolitan and outward looking, Islam, Judaism and Christianity all entered the Middle Kingdom. The Christians were merchants and missionaries from the Nestorian Church of Mesopotamia. They first arrived in 635 led by a bishop Alopen. Much of what we know of them comes from the so-called Nestorian Stone, a large stone inscribed with a history of the mission erected by the Church in 781 in the capital of the empire which was then Changan. In 845 the Emperor Wu Zong, a very strict Confucian, began a ferocious attack on all monastery-based religious organisations. As we have already noted the Nestorians, who had only a few hundred monasteries compared with the thousands of Buddhist houses, did not survive the imperial purge in China proper, as Buddhism did. Nestorian Christianity did hold out among the sinicised tribes in the Mongolian frontier areas.

The Yuan Dynasty, that is the period of rule by the Mongol Khans, was another time of cosmopolitanism in China and was the era when the first direct contact between China and western Europe occurred. This cosmopolitanism was, however, not a development stemming from Chinese initiative nor on Chinese terms as it had been under the Tang, it was a function of rule of the Mongol Khans.

In 1368 the Mongol garrison of Khanbalic, as the Great Khan called the city that was to become Beijing, fell before Chinese forces, and the Yuan Dynasty of the Mongol Khans ended and the Ming Dynasty began. When Mongol rule ended both the Latin and the Nestorian Christian Churches disappeared, the vast majority of the Christians would seem to have been Mongol or Alan subjects of the Yuan Emperors and not Chinese proper.

The first ruler of the new dynasty, the Hung Wu Emperor, began an expansionist policy not unlike that of the Tang Dynasty, sending armies deep into Mongolia and, for a time, occupying the ancient Mongol capital of Karakorum.

The Yung Lo Emperor, the third of the dynasty, took the expansionist policy further than any Chinese ruler has ever done by carrying out the only period of overseas political expansion in Chinese history. He organised massive seaborne expeditions which regularly collected tribute from the sultans in what are now Indonesia and Malaysia, as well as from the rulers of Sri Lanka and the trading towns on the East African coast. After his reign which ended in 1424, the expansionist policy of the early Ming ceased and the newly created navy was allowed to decay. Ming China turned to what can only be termed an isolationist policy. This was based on the traditional presumption of the centrality of the Middle Kingdom in a world of barbarians, but there now developed a sense of suspicion and antagonism toward the outside world that most authorities see as new. Contact with the barbarians was always to be carried out on Chinese terms only and trade was allowed only when it was clearly to China's advantage. Embassies from the barbarian peoples were allowed but their visits were always temporary; there could not be anything like a modern permanent diplomatic presence. Indeed the ambassadorial visit was deemed to be a privilege granted to the barbarians allowing them briefly to taste the greatness and beauty of Chinese culture. For the Chinese literati nothing the barbarian had or thought could be of any interest or importance. China had become xenophobic in a way that Chinese society had not been in the great dynastic periods of Sung and Tang before the Mongol invasions.[3]

It was while seeking vainly to be allowed to enter the isolationist and somewhat self-satisfied China of the Mings that Francis Xavier died.

NOTES

1. Kitagawa, *Religion in Japanese History*, p. 130.
2. This whole section is based primarily upon Kitagawa, op. cit., and Sansom, *A History of Japan*.
3. Sebes, 'A Bridge Between East and West', p. 561.

CHAPTER TWO

Francis Xavier and the Mission to Japan

The very pious King of Portugal, John III, was deeply concerned about the spiritual welfare of his subjects. He was acutely aware that the number of clergy serving in the overseas possessions was woefully inadequate for the pastoral oversight of the Christians, let alone for missionary outreach to the non-Christians within his dominions. As a result he was constantly seeking out volunteers to swell their ranks, and since he knew that Portugal alone could not supply an adequate number, he looked abroad. Yet looking abroad for clergy to serve under the bishops of the Padroado raised problems for the King and his advisers. Was it possible to balance the King's genuine desire to serve the Church's mission in the world with the need to ensure that this Church would still be the Portuguese Church of the Padroado? John tried to reconcile these two desires by setting up a scheme which, in essence, lasted for centuries. All priests and other religious going to serve in the Portuguese territories in the Indies or Brazil had to leave from Lisbon only. During their stay in Portugal they had to learn Portuguese and they had to travel to their posts only in Portuguese ships. In the field all missionaries served under the authority of the bishops of the Padroado. In addition all their mail, even that intended for the eyes of the heads of religious orders in Rome, even letters for the Pope himself, had to come back on Portuguese vessels to Lisbon first. This last rule inordinately delayed the mail from the missions in China and Japan when they were begun. From Macao mail via the Philippines and Mexico could reach Europe in around eight months. A letter from Macao going on the legal Portuguese route via Malacca, Cochin and Goa usually took from eighteen months to two years, but if connections were missed then it could take three years. This was because sailings were entirely controlled by the prevailing monsoon winds.[1]

In his continual search for volunteers to serve in his overseas possessions, John III turned to the Portuguese academic, Diogo de Gouvea, the principal of the Collège de Sainte-Barbe in the University of Paris. In 1538 Diogo drew the

King's attention to Ignatius Loyola and his followers whose activities in Rome were becoming well-known. Loyola himself, Xavier, Le Favre and Rodriguez were, after all, alumni of Sainte-Barbe. Le Favre replied to a query from de Gouvea that all the members of the Company would be willing to go to the Indies if the Pope so wished since they had dedicated themselves to obey his wishes. How many would be free was another matter since, as we have seen, by 1538 the Pope was already using Ignatius and his Company as if they were the established religious Order completely at his disposal which they were later to become. After hearing this from de Gouvea, King John formally requested the Pope to obtain volunteers from Loyola's Company to serve the Church in the Portuguese Indies. At that time the Company consisted of ten members, and after some discussion the Pope and Ignatius agreed that two members should go. Ignatius chose Simon Rodriguez and Nicolas Bobadilla, and Rodriguez left Rome by sea for Lisbon with some of the Portuguese ambassador's entourage early in March 1540. The other member was to go with the Portuguese ambassador who was returning by land. Unfortunately, Bobadilla returned very ill from a special trip to Naples undertaken on behalf of the Pope. There was no way he could set off for Lisbon. Loyola was very disconcerted because all the others were either away on Papal service or ill. This only left his closest friend, Francis Xavier, who was acting as his secretary in the exhausting campaign to overcome the opposition of Cardinal Guidiccioni and his supporters to the constitution of the Society of Jesus. There was no alternative, and so it was Francis who, on 15 March 1540, left Rome with the Portuguese ambassador Dom Pedro de Mascarenhas on the long weary horseback ride to Lisbon. Thus the pioneer of the Jesuit mission to the East set off on his task before the Society of Jesus formally existed.

Xavier's closeness to Loyola and the decisive nature of going 'to the missions' which was literally a life sentence, is very clear in a poignant passage from Xavier's much quoted letter to Loyola from Bologna a fortnight later: 'for what is left of this life, I am well assured, it will be by letter only that we shall be together – in the other we shall embrace face to face'.[2]

The desperate problems of communications which will dog the Jesuit mission throughout its existence are highlighted in this first part of Xavier's journey. He left Rome on 15 March and arrived in Lisbon in June 1540. He then had to wait in Lisbon for the next sailing of the Indies fleet which was due in March of 1541, though in fact they did not get away until 7 April. During his stay in Lisbon he as usual took up residence in a local hospital where he worked caring for the sick when he could. He was also a chaplain to the King's pages and used this court appointment to gain the support of the King and his advisers for the struggle with Cardinal Guidiccioni. In addition he decided to dedicate his Mass every alternate day to the cardinal for his change of heart. More than two years later, in India, he was still saying Masses for the cardinal. Then he got the news, at last, that the cardinal had given way in July 1540 and the Bull

Regimini militantis ecclesiae, had been promulgated on 27 September 1540, more than five months before he left Lisbon!

The journey to Goa was, like all sea journeys of that time, exceedingly unpleasant. When Alessandro Valignano made the same journey in 1574 it took five months and sixteen days; Xavier's journey took one whole year and twenty-nine days. This included six months on Mozambique island while the fleet waited for the return of the south-east monsoons to take them across the Indian Ocean. The delay in leaving Lisbon had meant they lost the previous period of suitable winds to make the crossing. The new Governor decided he could wait no longer and took Xavier with him on a single craft which tacked up the African coast, then along the Arabian coast before sailing south to Goa. Xavier thus arrived in Goa months before the rest of the original fleet. These delays, to modern eyes appalling, were an integral part of the extraordinary experience that was sailing to and from the Indies. Valignano in his brief *Life of Saint Francis,* lists six 'incomodidades' and six 'peligros'.[3] One of the 'inconveniences' was that the water became so bad that it had to be drunk through a linen sieve and one 'peril' was that it was expected that a majority of the passengers would die. Although Xavier did not embark on such a long voyage again, he and his great successor Valignano spent an enormous amount of time moving around India and between India, Indonesia and Japan on Portuguese ships and Chinese junks in conditions not dissimilar to that initial voyage, although blessedly shorter.

During the many months spent getting to Mozambique and during his months on that island, Xavier passed much time with the sick and the dying. People welcomed him and were both comforted and charmed by him. Indeed this charm, which brought reassurance to the frightened, restored faith to the cynic, and gained affection and respect from the many who could not share his faith, was a characteristic of Xavier's which is attested again and again in the records. This personal charisma, call it what you will, may go a long way to explain his later evangelistic success. Among Indians, Indonesians and Japanese he attracted many to Christianity, not the tens of thousands of legend, but many; and it could hardly have been through his preaching. This he had always to do through interpreters who often were not competent, or by reading from prepared texts in the local language that were translated so badly that occasionally a paragraph would make no clear sense at all. His feats were massively exaggerated even before he died and this has continued in some of the literature into the twentieth century. But his achievements were substantial nevertheless, and the need to explain them may lie at the root of one inaccurate claim constantly made about him, that he was a brilliant linguist, picking up local languages almost instantly. Francis himself always complained he was a bad linguist, Latin, Castillian and Portuguese were the only languages he ever commanded effectively other than his native Basque, and he probably learned Castillian along with Basque in childhood. The stories have persisted and both their invention and persistence may be partially explained by the need to account for his missionary success across so many language barriers. Although he was not a linguist, Xavier always insisted that the communication of the Christian message did depend on translation. He strove to ensure that priests should get to know as well as possible the language of the people among whom they worked. This was a small but significant change from what had been going on before he arrived in the East. Hitherto the pressure was for local people to become Portuguese as well as Christian, so why translate?

On his arrival at Goa, Xavier took up residence in the hospital which had been built by the great conquistador, Albuquerque. In the adjacent church he began daily teaching sessions. He gained his audience for these by an approach that he would use in a variety of forms for the rest of his life. He went through the streets with a handbell calling out that all who wanted to learn the faith should follow him to the church, and crowds did, particularly children. During these sessions he taught the duties of the Christian life and tried to communicate a pattern of piety, using well-known Portuguese catechetical texts. However, he adapted the texts into rhyming verses which he set to popular tunes. He taught the people to sing their lessons. He also set a number of prayers to music so that, he hoped, they would become part of the mental furniture of the person who learned the songs. The prayers he held to be essential were the Our Father, the Hail Mary, the Salve Regina, the Confiteor. Using music as a tool in this way, to bind people together in a common cause and with a common set of ideas and rituals, has since been used by evangelists, both religious and political many times – from the Wesleys to the Sandinistas. It was new in the Catholic missions to the East.

After only five months in Goa, Xavier went, at the request of the Governor, Affonso de Sousa, to the Parava Christians of the Coromandel coast opposite the north-west coast of Sri Lanka. There a pearl-fishing community of very low caste had become Christians. They had done so primarily in the hope of getting Portuguese protection from local rulers who exploited them and from Arab sea-raiders. Although baptised by Franciscans sent from Cochin they had not been instructed in the faith to any extent and had no resident priests or catechists. Francis travelled there by sea with three Indian priests who were Tamil speakers. The Paravas also spoke Tamil, the principal ancient language of south India. This was as well since Francis had not a word of it. However, with the help of the Tamil priests, in each of the Parava villages in turn, he began his technique of teaching basic truths and the essential prayers of the Church set to music. He attracted the children to the point that he says, 'then the young boys would never let me say the office, or eat, or sleep till I had taught them some prayers. It made me understand for the first time "of such is the kingdom of heaven".'[4]

Xavier spent nearly two years among the Paravas and had prepared a Tamil version of the Ten Commandments and the Creed with brief commentary on each point. These he taught throughout the villages in addition to the material he had had prepared for the children. The translations were bad, because the Tamil-speaking priests simply did not have the theological and linguistic sophistication to make good translations, but it was the Christian Gospel in Tamil for the Paravas. The very attempt to translate is an attempt to cross cultural frontiers and to adapt. Francis then went back to Goa, taking some promising Parava boys to be educated at the college of St Paul there. It was then, November 1543, that he heard with joy that the Bull formally creating the Society of Jesus had been promulgated.

He now returned to the Paravas with two priests, one Spanish, one Indian, and a Portuguese layman, to continue the work there. During 1544 he faced many difficulties and setbacks, indeed he was almost heart-broken by the fact that he could not protect the Paravas in a series of violent conflicts between local Indian princes in which the Portuguese traders of south India and the one Royal Officer for the area simply sought a profit even when it led to the Paravas suffering.

During the year, Xavier attempted to go from the Parava lands by foot round Cape Comorin to Cochin. On the way he found another fisher people of 'untouchable' caste, the Macuas of Travancore. He stayed among them for a time and they asked to be baptised and a mass conversion ensued. Arriving at Cochin he set in motion the arrangements for obtaining priests for them and the financial resources for some kind of elementary school. Meanwhile one of the priests working among the Paravas had gone to a small fishing community of related peoples a few thousand strong, who lived along the chain of islands that connect the south-east coast of India to north-west Sri Lanka. Like the Macua of Cape Comorin, this group asked for baptism and became a Christian community in effect.

It has been hard for people in the highly individualistic West of the nineteenth and twentieth centuries to understand communal conversion, though it was how a great deal of Europe was converted to Christianity. However doubtful of its reality we may be, the sincerity of the Corea people was soon tested because the Raja of Jaffna demanded that they abjure their faith and six hundred died rather than do so. It is difficult for a western person of the late twentieth century to understand, but they did choose to die, and that is hard evidence that communal conversions could be a matter of real change and the creation of genuine new loyalties. This massacre horrified Xavier particularly because, yet again, there was Portuguese complaisance, if not involvement, at an official and commercial level.

His experience in Portuguese India up to this point drove Xavier into a bitter condemnation of the Portuguese who came east. Throughout his life there were Portuguese, both officials and merchants, who helped Xavier and his Jesuits greatly, something which he was always ready to acknowledge. However, these terrible events in the south together with the behaviour of many in Goa explain his bitter complaint to Rodriguez and sadly were only too typical of the Portuguese empire. In a letter to the only Portuguese of the original six of Montmartre, and his dear friend, the confidant and personal adviser to King John, he wrote

> Do not allow any of your friends to be sent to India with the charge of looking after the finances and affairs of the King. To such persons we may most truly apply which is written 'Let them be blotted out of the book of the living, and let their name not be written among the just.' However great may be your confidence in any one whom you know and love, trust my experience and oppose him on this point... There is here a power which I may call irresistible, to thrust men headlong into the abyss, when besides the seduction of gain, and the easy opportunities of plunder, their appetite for greed will have been sharpened and there will be a whole torrent of bad examples and evil customs to overwhelm them and sweep them away.[5]

This letter to Rodriguez was one of three he sent at this time. The others were to Loyola himself and one to the rest of the Society in general. In these he appealed for a massive effort to be made by the Society to find men for the mission in the Indies. However, while still in Cochin his spirits were lifted and he was again enthusiastic and full of hope and optimism, a state more typical of Xavier than depression and bitterness. He was excited by the arrival of Portuguese merchants from the Moluccas who said two important chiefs in the islands wanted priests to come to baptise them and their people.

Here was a new challenge. Xavier worked hard to make sure that the communities he had begun among the Paravas and Macua would be maintained and developed and then he took off for the East. More accurately one ought to say he started yet another of those ghastly sea voyages, this time from Cochin to Malacca. Malacca, on the south-west coast of Malaya, was the main entrepot of trade in south-east Asia. It was a Portuguese possession but the neighbouring Malay people were Muslim.

In Malacca, Xavier made his home in the Casa Misericordia (a charitable institution for the care of the sick and homeless) and immediately plunged into his usual effort to set up regular teaching of the essentials of the faith and of piety. He attempted to gain audiences in his usual 'Pied Piper' manner and again set about having translations prepared of the Creed, with commentary on each article, the essential prayers and the Ten Commandments. Again he tried to have them set to singable chants. His days followed his usual exhausting round. Crowds came to demand he hear their confessions, he preached daily as well as holding a daily instruction class for the children, and he always made time to visit the sick and dying, which he held as fundamental to his priestly office. From his arrival in Malacca in September 1545, for the next two years, Xavier travelled in what is now Indonesia. He rallied the clergy in the Portuguese garrisons, he revived the faith of many Portuguese and nominal 'Prangui' type converts.[6] Above all he reached out to the indigenous peoples by this technique of drawing people from the highways and byways to be taught sung versions of the Creed and the key prayers of the Church, all translated into their language.

During all this time he also wrote regularly, first to Goa to try to ensure that his orders were being carried out for the care of his fledgling churches, also to Lisbon and Rome, reporting what was happening but above all begging the Society to find more men for the missions. As with the letters he sent to Lisbon and Rome on the eve of his departure from Cochin, he is quite clear that there is no need to seek out the most highly trained and most academically able candidates, physical strength, stamina and simple piety are the essentials. His opinion was still, as he had written to Loyola in January, that he should send those of the Society who were not very good as confessors or preachers but who were strong and of a deep faith.[7]

It was during these two years in Malaysia and Indonesia that Xavier first heard of China and Japan. China was first to be drawn to his attention. In a confidential insertion in a letter to the Society in general, written at Amboina on 10 May 1546, he reported that he had met a Portuguese merchant who had come back from China, a very great land. He speculated a great deal about this land and its peoples. He reported that it was said that St Thomas had gone there after India and baptised many people. He regretted not having much hard information but should he learn more he would report it. It is clear that he in no way connected this land with the Cathay of Marco Polo and John of Montecorvino. He speculated about the possibility of it being the kingdom of Prester John or even of the lost tribes of Israel, but he did not mention Cathay.[8]

Xavier's contact with Japan was much more positive, indeed it was decisive both for him and for the Society of Jesus. It was decisive because it took him beyond the Portuguese Padroado; and in Japan he took the decisive step of trying to understand Japanese culture, which, together with his first initiative of insisting upon translation from Portuguese into the indigenous language, gave Alessandro Valignano the base upon which to build the radical mission theory and practice of the later Jesuit mission in Japan and China.

Until he went to Japan, Xavier was an outstandingly effective charismatic evangelist in an apparently entirely traditional mould – apparently, but not quite. Before 1547 Xavier expresses nothing but antagonism and contempt for Hinduism, Islam and the primal religion of the Indonesian tribal people. That is the classical 'tabula rasa' approach: everything religious in the local culture had to be swept away and a new start made. Yet, as we have seen, his insistence on translation meant that the Christian communities brought into being by him were not simply the 'Prangui' Christians of Goa. A skeleton liturgical pattern and a basic understanding of the faith was articulated in their own language and that meant, though Xavier did not consciously intend or perceive this, at least before he got to Japan, that adaptation had begun. The work of many theologians from the so-called Third World has, in the last third of the twentieth century, pointed to the profound transformation translation brings to any set of ideas. No word of any serious philosophical or theological meaning carries with it the same background of nuance and reference as the equivalent word in a non-related language. As a Tamil-speaker tried to work with Xavier on translating the Creed from Portuguese, the very act of trying to find the most appropriate word in Tamil was the first step in making Christianity Tamil and already different, even if only slightly, from Portuguese Christianity.

The fundamental issue is what happens to philosophical and theological ideas when the words representing them in one language are translated into another? Perhaps the best discussion of this so far is *Translating the Message* by Lamin Sanneh of Yale. When Sanneh's understanding of what happens in translation is brought to bear on the work of Xavier his work can be seen in a new light. From this point of view Francis, although showing so many of the characteristics of the 'tabula rasa' approach, had already broken with it decisively when, among the Paravas, he composed his badly translated Christian catechism and prayers for the people. Badly translated though they were, they were translated, the ritual prayers were in their own language, not Portuguese.

The great Jesuit scholar H. Bernard-Maître talked of Xavier's 'deux manières', his two styles of mission, and sees the new style coming into being through his contact with the people of Japan.[9] Professor Treadgold, on the other hand, sees no innovation coming from Xavier; instead he sees the creative, adaptive style of the later Jesuit mission to Japan and China taking shape only after Alessandro Valignano became the Visitor to the East.[10] Both these scholars wrote before the new work on translation had developed. Sanneh's understanding of the nature of translation would seem to challenge both of the more usual interpretations of Xavier's role in developing the Jesuit approach to mission in the East: the seed of all that was to happen later was planted by Xavier when he insisted on translation into the vernacular.

It does not appear Xavier himself was aware that this concern for the vernacular was any kind of decisive step, yet he must have realised, one would think, that this move broke decisively with the practice heretofore of making anyone who wanted to be a Christian also a Portuguese. There is, however, no record of his having articulated this in any extant document. Perhaps he was simply carrying over into the mission the existing Jesuit rule (though Ignatius was probably thinking only of Europe at that time) that a Jesuit should always try to become fluent in the language of the people among whom he was sent. There is no doubt, however, that contact with Japan did make a difference to Xavier's perception of the nature of the Christian mission. Bernard-Maître would appear correct in asserting that it was in Japan that Xavier made changes in his approach to mission deliberately and consciously.

In December 1547 Xavier was brought face to face with the challenge of Japan. Marco Polo had referred to Japan, calling it a rich and mysterious land, though he had not seen it. We are aware of this but the people of Xavier's day were not. Neither Xavier nor the Portuguese merchants and seafarers who had landed on Japan for the first time only four years previously, knew that their China and Japan were Polo's Cathay and Chipangu. Xavier was now told that a Japanese in his mid-thirties had come to Malacca, accompanied by his two servants, expressly to see Xavier. Even someone a lot less concerned about what he believed God was calling him to do than Xavier was would have seen this as a 'call'.

The story began when a great admirer of Xavier's, a merchant adventurer, George Alvares, was in the Japanese port of Yamaguchi. A samurai called Yajiro had sought refuge on his ship because he had killed a man and it was better that he should not be around for a bit. Alvares and the samurai got on very well and Yajiro appears to have unburdened himself to Alvares. He felt burdened by guilt from which he wished to be free. This is how Xavier described it later, but what Yajiro and Alvares actually said to each other in their confusing combination of bad Japanese and bad Portuguese, it is impossible now to say. Whether Yajiro was expressing the desire to be free from guilt in the sense a sixteenth-century Catholic would have understood it is highly unlikely, but he clearly was seeking some sort of spiritual comfort or renewal. Alvares recommended that since Yajiro wanted to leave Yamaguchi for a time anyway, he should sail with him to Malacca and talk with Father Francis. Yajiro agreed and accompanied by his two servants came to Malacca only to find that Xavier was elsewhere. After waiting some time, the three Japanese took ship to return home. When approaching Japanese waters, their ship was caught in a severe storm and had to take shelter in a safe anchorage off the China coast. There Yajiro met another Portuguese captain who assured him that if Yajiro returned with him to Malacca, this time he would find Xavier there.

Thus, in December 1547 Xavier and Yajiro met, and the 'Apostle of Japan' began to learn about the land that was to have such an impact on him and on the Society of Jesus. He was so taken by Yajiro and so excited by what he learned of Japan that he invited Yajiro and his companions to go to Goa to learn more of the Christian faith and prepare to be ready to accompany a Jesuit mission to their land. On his way to Goa with them he stopped at Cochin to catch the fleet so as to send off four letters. These letters mark a new start to his mission, and on 20 January he despatched them to Europe. Two were short, one to Rodriguez at the Portuguese court, the other to the General in Rome, and they were supplements to the two other longer letters. The first of these was to the King. In many ways it is an extraordinary document. In it Xavier explains he has been long torn as to whether he should write thus to the King or not. If he did not tell the King of the lack of commitment to the propagation of the faith displayed by his servants in the East, then before God, John would not be guilty because of ignorance. However, in the end, Xavier felt he had to write because he could do no other without sin, though he is sorry he has thus increased the King's burden before the Lord's tribunal! He begged the

King to make the royal administration responsible for the propagation of the faith and for the protection of the indigenous Christians. He was not asking for a Portuguese version of the Spanish Royal Inquisition, but for an end to the situation where Portuguese officials were implicated in the exploitation and even massacre of Indian converts. Significantly he adds:

> I have not yet, Sire, fully made up my mind whether I shall go to Japan; but a great motive for my inclining to the plan of going to that country is added by this fact, that I am very much without hope that here in India I shall find that true and efficient support from the officials which is necessary to increase our holy faith and to preserve the Christians already made.[11]

This makes clear that apart from the attractive possibilities which Japan offers, he sees it as a way of escaping the bad influence of the Portuguese presence. He is still traditionalist enough to want a strong Portuguese presence if it is the ideal one he outlines in his letter to the King, but if it is not, then perhaps it would be better without it at all. Whether Xavier had at this time conceived of the Gospel spreading outwith the authority of Christendom is by no means certain. Too much weight should not be placed on one short paragraph, in what was, for him, a bitter and angry letter. What is certain is that he is planning a Jesuit mission to Japan which is certainly beyond the authority or protection of the Portuguese representatives of Christendom, and outwith the bounds of the Padroado.

The second long letter is to the Society of Jesus in general and is a lengthy report on the activities of the Society in the East and a compelling plea for the Society to send him more men to serve with him.

Very soon after this, Xavier decided that he should lead the mission to Japan himself. In writing to tell Loyola about this, he indicates that as things are in India at this time, neither the Church nor the Society of Jesus could be kept going by Indian Christians alone. Reinforcements would have to continue to come from Europe. He was doubtful of the potential of Indians for growth into maturity and responsibility in the faith, but apportions some of the blame for this on the Portuguese.

> Certainly, if the Portuguese were more remarkable for their kindness to the new converts, a great number would become Christians; as it is the heathen see that the converts are despised and looked down upon by the Portuguese, and so, as is natural, they are unwilling to become converts themselves.[12]

He then goes on to explain that from all the information he has received from Yajiro he has high hopes for a mission in Japan. He therefore plunged with all his vigour into organising the centres in India and Indonesia so that work would continue effectively in his absence. In the midst of all this he went to spend some months with the Paravas and the Christian fishing communities of Cape Comorin. These people, despised and exploited by the Portuguese as they were also by higher caste Indians, seem always to have had a high place in his affections. He was deeply distressed to find that all his complaints in his letter to the King from Cochin were amply confirmed on this visit. The new Portuguese official 'protector' of the Paravas was even more unjust and dishonest than the previous one. Xavier complained again to the Governor in Goa and to Lisbon. The difference now was that he could plan to have Jesuits resident with the Parava and Macua communities which might help them.

It was the coming of a steady stream of Jesuit recruits that enabled Xavier to take up the challenge of Japan. By the end of 1548 he had enough Jesuit missionaries to place a few in each Christian community. He aimed at having four in the Moluccas, two at Malacca, six among the Parava and Macua Christian communitites in South India, and two each at Quilon and Bassein. He also hoped that four would go to serve the ancient Monophysite Christian community on Socotra.[13] There were twelve other Jesuits who were to work in Goa, under the authority of the first Jesuit Rector of St Paul's College. He was Antonio Gomez, a brilliant young Portuguese preacher and protégé of Simon Rodriguez. Initially Xavier was delighted at his arrival since he had long begged Rodriguez to send some good preachers to awaken and uplift the Portuguese in the East. However, Gomez and St Paul's which had now passed under Jesuit authority for the first time – though Jesuits had already been teaching there – constituted the one big problem Xavier had to leave unresolved at his departure for Japan. Gomez created the problem by deciding St Paul's should become the centre of academic and theological study for the Portuguese in the East. The existing body of students, Ethiopians, Mozambiquans, Malgaches, Indonesians and Indians from many provinces, were not the kind of students he had come to teach. When Xavier came to realise what a mistake Gomez' appointment was, he could do nothing about it. After all Gomez was chosen by the King's special adviser and head of the Portuguese province of the Society, Simon Rodriguez, and he was himself a favourite of the Portuguese court. All Xavier could do was to appoint Superiors over every other group of Jesuits, responsible to him as Visitor, leaving only the Jesuits in Goa itself under Gomez. This was a foretaste of the problems Valignano was to have with the senior Jesuits at the royal court in Lisbon and illustrates that provinces of the Society could, under a certain style of leadership, become as 'national' as any other Order.

Xavier took special week-long retreats with many of the newly arrived men and also wrote them very careful instructions, emphasising the great care and love they should lavish on the children. He also again and again insisted that penances should not be of the extreme ascetic kind favoured by Rodriguez; it was better to make the penitent work in the Casa de Misericordia, or the Hospital or prison. There is a clear difference in style between Jesuits nurtured in Portugal under the influence of Rodriguez and the style of missionary that Xavier wanted to cultivate. There was not yet the open confrontation that was to come after Valignano was appointed Visitor to the East, but almost from

the beginning the Jesuit leadership in Portugal had accepted royal authority in
a way that set them apart from the rest of the Society.

It is worth noting the presence of two Jesuits of Jewish ancestry among
the thirty-two members of the Society serving under Xavier at this time.
One, Affonso de Castro, was to be martyred in Indonesia, the other, Henry
Henriques, was a brilliant linguist and the first Jesuit, perhaps the first westerner, to study the classic texts of Hinduism. They were forerunners of the many
Jesuits of Jewish ancestry that Valignano was to recruit for the missions and
which caused him difficulties with the Portuguese authorities both ecclesiastical
and secular.[14]

On 15 April 1549, accompanied by the three Japanese Christians, Yajiro,
John and Antonio and two Jesuits, Father Cosme de Torres and Brother Juan
Fernandez, Xavier left Goa, travelling to Cochin and on to Malacca en route
for Japan.[15] In Malacca, where they arrived after an uneventful seven week
voyage, Xavier was very pleased to see the work being done there by his newly
appointed staff. However, the new Japanese mission now ran into travel difficulties. Although the Portuguese were barred from trading with China by the
imperial authorities, some illegal trading still went on and many Portuguese
ships went to China illegally and then on to Japan. Portuguese traders were
willing to take Xavier and his five comrades to Japan but only if the missionaries would winter with them on the China coast. They were unwilling to
change their schedules to help Xavier. However, a Chinese trader nicknamed
the 'Pirate' said he would take them to Japan and they left Malacca aboard his
junk on 24 June bound for Japan. The journey was very slow and on a number
of occasions it looked as if the 'Pirate' was going to try to winter on the China
coast like the Portuguese. However a combination of the fear of other pirates
and the pleas and threats of his passengers kept him going. So on 15 August
1549 the Jesuit mission arrived at Kagoshima, home town of Yajiro and capital
of Satsuma province on Kyushu, the southernmost of the three main islands of
Japan.

The people of Kagoshima were very excited at the return of Yajiro to his
home accompanied by these strange visitors. The three Jesuits and Xavier's
Indian body-servant and constant companion all appear to have stayed at
Yajiro's home. On 5 November Xavier sent to the brethren at Goa perhaps
the longest report he ever wrote.[16]

Francis Xavier came to Japan with the idea that it was a united 'Empire' and
that therefore his primary task was to obtain an audience with the Emperor and
gain his permission to preach the Gospel throughout his dominions, this being
the impression he had obtained from Yajiro and from Portuguese reports on
Japan. It was as mistaken, as we shall see, as his understanding of the meaning
of the key religious terms in the Japanese language also obtained from Yajiro.

At this time Japan was far from united, and was in the throes of the Sengoku
Jidai as this period of baronial strife was called. It was a situation not unlike

those experienced at various times in medieval Europe when kings looked on helplessly as great feudatories fought each other for land and power. The Emperor of Japan, referred to as 'Dairi' in the European records of the time, still lived in the capital, Kyoto, in close association with ancient noble families who constituted a court of sorts. However, the Emperor had no political, administrative or military authority whatsoever, except that formal titles, still very important in Japanese life, could only be awarded by him, the true descendant of the sun goddess, Amaterasu. This had been the case for at least four hundred years, although the unity of the nation had been maintained throughout most of those centuries by the Shogun. The Shoguns had become the de facto rulers of Japan, just as the Carolingian family had, as Mayors of the Palace of the Merovingian kings, ruled the Frankish Kingdom in eighth-century Europe.

The decade 1467–77, the period of the Onin wars, marks the break-down of central authority in Japan and the great lords, daimyo, each ruled their domains autonomously with their armies of 'knights', the samurai. This was the beginning of the period of conflict, Sengoku Jidai, when the lords competed for power and land. The situation was made more complex by the role of the abbots of some of the great Buddhist houses. These men built up armies of monks and became players in the wars, so much so that some provinces were dominated not by a daimyo but by the abbot of a Buddhist house. This style was particularly true of the True Pure Land sect of Buddhism, known in Japanese as Jodo Shinshu or Ikkoshu.[7] Their monasteries were fortresses and the towns that grew around them were no different from the fortified 'castle-town' of a daimyo. The rest of the Japanese people who were neither monks, samurai nor of the 'nobility', were firmly classified in one of three categories, merchants, artisans and peasants.

It was into this bitterly divided Japan of constant conflict that Xavier came. It was excusable that in these first weeks at Kagoshima, Xavier did not recognise this situation. In the province of Satsuma at that time there was order and peace under the authority of the daimyo, Shimazu Takahisa. The latter received Xavier kindly and gave him permission to preach within his lordship. This was all very fine but Xavier wanted to get on and go to Kyoto and greet the Emperor and obtain his permission for the Society of Jesus to preach throughout the whole empire. Takahisa, who wanted the Portuguese ships to come to his ports which would bring him much needed revenue, managed to keep the missionaries within his domains for a year, hoping thus to guarantee the Portuguese connection. Things changed dramatically, however, when the Portuguese ships arrived in 1550 but did not come to his ports. Angrily he expelled the foreign priests though he did not demand recantation of their faith by the newly baptised Japanese Christians within his fiefdom.

So it was in the August of 1550 that Xavier and his companions left Kagoshima and went to Hirado where the Portuguese ship had arrived. Here they were again well received by the local authorities, without any doubt because of their association with the profitability of having the Portuguese ships come to the local ports.

Brother Fernandez had made some progress in mastering spoken Japanese by this time and he preached often in the streets of Hirado with Xavier standing beside him, praying for his comrade's words to strike home to the hearts of their hearers. A small group did become associated with the Fathers and about 100 were baptised. Matsuura Takunobu, the local daimyo, did not try to detain Xavier when he decided the time was ripe to make the long journey to Kyoto and the Emperor. He left Father Torres at Hirado to look after the small flock of Christians they had gathered there. This might explain the difference in behaviour between Takunobu and Takahisa since it is possible that Takunobu let Xavier go so readily because he saw Torres as a hostage.

Xavier set off with Fernandez and the converted ronin (i.e. lordless samurai) who had been given the name Bernardo. They travelled on foot, as simple pilgrims, begging the necessary help to pay for the long sea-journey across the inland sea. The journey thus undertaken in winter entailed much physical suffering. They often had to sleep in wet clothes, and although in some places they were well received and were given letters of introduction to merchants or even daimyo further along the way, they were also at times scornfully turned away or laughed at when seeking hospitality and occasionally were even stoned. Eventually they arrived at Kyoto which proved a desperate disappointment to the missionaries. There they learned that the Emperor had no real power and very little wealth and that the Shogun was now no more than a local daimyo controlling the territory around the capital. Xavier had heard of a great 'University' close to the capital, which was, in fact, a collection of Zen monasteries at Hieizan that were famous throughout Japan as centres of learning. Try as he might he was not allowed admission to interview anyone of importance there because he was seen as someone of no significance.

This journey was a very painful one but it was also an important learning experience. The Jesuit leader learned about the political reality of Japan and in addition he discovered that his whole style of 'apostolic poverty' was a barrier to being taken seriously by Japanese people, and indeed constituted a barrier to being received at all in many situations in Japan. Xavier had by this time come to see that it was through the support of the daimyo alone that the Society would be able to operate effectively in Japan. It was therefore very important that these daimyo be cultivated and if possible converted or at least brought into sympathy with the Society and its mission.

On the journey to the imperial court, Xavier and his companions had been kindly received by the daimyo of Yamaguchi, Ouchi Yositaka. After his return to Hirado, Xavier felt that such an opportunity should not be passed by, and set out to win the daimyo over. This decision also marked another change in tactics. The poor beggar dependent on charity was clearly not the way to gain entry to Japanese society, so it was not only to whom the approach was to be made that was changed but also the style of the approach. Xavier now dressed in the finest clothes he had available and those who were to accompany him to Yamaguchi did the same. They also took with them valuable presents of western artefacts, including a large clock and a three-barrelled musket, as well as illuminated parchment letters from the Viceroy in Goa and the Archbishop of Goa. These had been held in reserve for eventual presentation to the Emperor had Xavier's original approach failed. Now they were brought into use in an attempt to gain the support of this important and sympathetic daimyo.

Yoshitaka was suitably impressed, and in April 1551 he not only gave Xavier permission for the Society to preach the Gospel within his dominions but he also gave the Jesuits an old Buddhist temple as their headquarters. In the next six months Xavier, Fernandez and Bernardo prosecuted their mission in Yamaguchi. Xavier spent a great deal of time in discussion with the many Buddhist monks in the city and in particular with those of the Shingon sect. Only a small number of monks became Christians but one made a widespread impact. He had been trained at the great Buddhist centre of learning, Ashikaga Gakko, and was highly regarded as a scholar. He was an important convert because of his ability to teach the Jesuits about Buddhism and Japanese culture in general and his ability to communicate effectively with other Japanese. An equally important conversion for the future of the mission made at that time, was that of a wandering professional minstrel. This extraordinary man, who had severely impaired sight, did not simply become a Christian but also an ardent and eloquent evangelist. Later he was accepted into the Society of Jesus as its first Japanese member, a lay Brother, who chose for his religious name Lourenço.[18]

He played a vital role in the conversion of many people and it is important to note this since so often the growth of Japanese Christianity is written off as simply the product of authoritarian actions by daimyo. Lourenço was a popular and effective communicator so that even great men like Oda Nobunaga, the initiator of the movement to again unite Japan under one authority, sought him out. Lourenço knew no Latin and had only minimal Portuguese. He learned his faith from Xavier. Within Lourenço himself, therefore, the process of translation was going on constantly. As he composed his Christian songs he was creating the skeleton of an indigenous Christianity. He had had no training at all in any form of western thought so that his evangelistic message, which had a very widespread effect, had to be Japanese in form. He was not simply a singer but a brilliant debater and took part regularly in debates with Buddhist monks and other learned men, some of whom were converted to Christianity through him. For most of his lifetime there was no Jesuit with mastery enough of Japanese to record the detail of these debates for us with any accuracy.

This form of popular grass-roots indigenisation, often unplanned by missionaries, is too often ignored by historians and missiologists who tend to concentrate on the written records of the educated elites who accepted or rejected Christianity. Popular Christianity is much more difficult to discuss after such a lapse of time because it leaves few written sources. Yet such popular religion was and is fundamental to the life of any Christian community, and Japan during 'the Christian century' was no different.

Xavier had, as we have seen, from the beginning insisted on the importance of the Japanese language and that becoming a Christian was not to be linked inextricably to becoming Portuguese. However, his attempts to reach out and find Japanese words and groups of words to express the Christian doctrine were such a disaster that they created a long term problem for the mission of the Society in Japan. As we shall see later, Alessandro Valignano attempted to shape the work and style of the Society into a Japanese form, insisting that members of the Society should do all things in a Japanese way if possible; they were to wear Japanese clothes, eat Japanese food, follow Japanese ways of politeness and be ruled by their rules of etiquette. But the ability to translate the Christian message into Japanese thought-patterns and the Japanese spirit was profoundly handicapped by decisions taken before Valignano arrived in Japan; these were initiated by Xavier to correct the wrong impression created by the first attempts to translate Christian ideas into Japanese thought forms.

From the very beginning Xavier wanted to communicate effectively with the mind of the Japanese people, and he used Yajiro for this task. The young converted samurai was to be the creator of the tools necessary for effective communication of the Gospel to the Japanese mind. This choice was the root of the problem that broke over Xavier's attempts at translation. Yajiro had been a good student at St Paul's in Goa, but he had never been a student in Japan. He had been a samurai, he could only read the kana syllabary not the Chinese script and had no knowledge in depth of Buddhist theology or philosophy. This is not surprising; after all, some time before, that Christian samurai, Ignatius Loyola, after his transforming spiritual experience, knowing how ignorant he was of theology, had had to start a long learning process before he could become a priest let alone a theologian. As far as Buddhist theology was concerned Yajiro was in the situation of the newly devout Loyola; he knew about Buddhist theology just what the average knight of that time in Navarre or Castille would know of Christian theology and philosophy. The first attempts by the Jesuits to find Japanese equivalents for Christian theological terms were a disaster. It is important to see that this was an attempt by Xavier genuinely to cross over into the Japanese thought world and find Japanese expressions to express Christian ideas. He tried too hard and too early before he, or anyone in the Society, was equipped to do the task. It is on this point that one must disagree with Professor Treadgold when, in an otherwise brilliantly suggestive summary of the Jesuit mission in China initiated by Valignano and his chosen agent Matteo Ricci, he says 'The forceful personality and impressive character of the "Apostle of the Indies" left an inspiring example, but Xavier's approach was essentially pre-Jesuit'.[19] By 'pre-Jesuit' Treadgold presumably means pre-Valignano, since obviously Xavier could not be pre-Jesuit literally.

Since his first experience of cultural challenge among the Parava, Xavier had firmly grasped that translation into the vernacular had to take place if any effective communication of the Christian message was to occur. This was the basic idea on which Valignano was to build a dramatic new missionary approach. The tragedy was that Xavier's attempt was too impetuous, it went wrong because there had not been careful enough preparation. The resulting shock and embarrassment caused him to retreat into the mind set which provoked Treadgold's remark.

Xavier had depended on Yajiro for producing the appropriate terms in Japanese for the translation of the Christian message and the latter chose them from his own Shingon Buddhist background in ways that were singularly unhelpful. For God he chose Dainichi, for heaven or paradise the word was jodo; jigoku was the word he chose for hell and for angels, tennin. Xavier was furious when, after using it for some time in public preaching, he discovered that Dainichi was a particular manifestation of the wisdom which illuminates the universe worshipped by Shingon Buddhists. It could also refer to a particular statue of the Buddha, but what the word could not in any way convey was the idea of a personal Creator. It is arguable, at least, that some of the other terms could have been adopted and, with care, filled with Christian meaning. After all that was a process which Paul had initiated and the Fathers completed with the Greek language, and the Christians did it again with Latin and Armenian, and later missionaries carried through the same translation process among the Celts and the Germans.

The Dainichi embarrassment was such that Xavier and the other early Jesuit leaders in Japan recoiled from the whole attempt. They developed a series of key terms which were in fact modified Latin words. God becomes Deusu from the Latin *Deus*, and various other classic Latin terms were given Japanese pronunciations and became the key theological expressions in the catechism, the liturgy and Scripture, for example anima, sacramento, eucaristia. So the heritage that Xavier left was one which already blocked off one channel of translating Christianity into Japanese forms.

Meanwhile, in September 1551 a Portuguese vessel put into the port of Funai which was part of the domain of the daimyo of Bungo, Otomo Yoshishige. Through this Portuguese connection Xavier was invited to Bungo and talked with the daimyo who became a lifelong supporter of the Society and of Christianity. Xavier was, by this time, worried about the work of the Society in the rest of the vast field for which he was still responsible and about which he had heard nothing for two years. He therefore took the opportunity provided by the Portuguese ship to try to get back to Goa to deal with his responsibilities there. Not only that but it would allow him to begin to plan his new move which was to attempt to initiate a mission to China. Again and again in conversation with Buddhist bonzes and others, he had been asked why, if the Gospel was true and of such great antiquity, it was not known to the Chinese. The Japanese love–hate relationship with China did not prevent them perceiving China as the cultural centre of the world. Thus Xavier had come to see China as a country to which the Gospel should be taken in its own right, and also as a route for achieving the conversion of the Japanese. If China became Christian, Japan would be sure to follow! The captain of the vessel in the port at Funai was Duarte da Gama who promised to take Xavier at least part of the way back towards Goa.

Having decided to return to Goa, Xavier then received shattering news that at Yamaguchi, Yoshitaka, the sympathetic daimyo had been overthrown and had taken his own life and that of his son to prevent their falling into their enemies' hands, a usual practice for Japanese lords at that time. The two Jesuits that Xavier had left there, Torres and Fernandez, had had to go into hiding but were safe. The news had come, in fact, through letters from the two missionaries. They were protected throughout this whole difficult period by Naito Okimori and his wife who were devoted patrons of a number of Buddhist monasteries and were one of the richest families in Japan. When things were at their worst, Lady Naito took the two Jesuits into her women's quarters where they were completely safe from the rebels. Torres assured Xavier that they could renew their work with safety once things had calmed down. With their letters to him they also included letters to be sent to Europe to encourage new volunteers for service in Japan from among the members of the Society.[20]

Then, to the surprise and delight of Xavier, a delegation from the victorious rebels of Yamaguchi arrived at Funai and offered their lordship to Haruhide, the brother of Otomo Yoshishige, the daimyo of Bungo and a good friend of the Society. Haruhide accepted the offer and promised Francis to protect the work of the Society and the small Christian community as the deposed daimyo had done.

Xavier now believed that he could leave Japan and try to deal with the rest of his vast responsibilities before attempting to enter China. When he was waiting on Sancian island off the coast of China for another ship to take him on to Malacca en route for Goa, he heard of the plight of a number of Portuguese who were being held by the Chinese authorities in Canton. The plight of these Portuguese, who, people said, would never be freed unless someone spoke on their behalf to the Emperor, touched him deeply. Their predicament helped to make him decide that even before returning to Japan he must attempt to enter China and gain an audience with the Emperor. He would seek permission for the Society to propagate the faith in the empire and petition for the release of the Portuguese captives.

He eventually arrived back in Goa on 24 January 1552. After a few brief months seeing to the affairs of the Province, he set off for China and before the end of the year was back on Sancian island at the mouth of the Pearl River. He was unable to get permission to enter China. The Portuguese merchants who went to the island annually to do some illegal trade with the toleration of local magistrates would not risk that privilege by landing him illegally. When they left again, Xavier stayed on alone but for his Chinese servant, hoping to get ashore by other means. On 5 December 1552 Francis Xavier died on the tiny uninhabited Chinese island, still waiting to enter China and begin the Jesuit mission there.

NOTES

1. A full description of these problems, together with a list of the sailing schedules, can be found in Schutte, *Valignano's Mission Principles*, vol. 1, Appendix II.
2. *Monumenta Xaveriana*, p. 208, my translation.
3. The whole list can be found in *Monumenta Xaveriana*, pp. 10–13.
4. Coleridge, *Life and Letters of St Francis Xavier*, vol. 1, p. 146.
5. Ibid., pp. 277–8.
6. Prangui was the word used for a Portuguese in western and southern India. It was also used for a Christian, whether Indian or Portuguese, since to all intents and purposes under the Padroado in India, to become a Christian was to become a Portuguese.
7. Coleridge, op. cit., vol. 1, p. 272.
8. Ibid., pp. 377–9.
9. Bernard-Maître, 'St François Xavier et la mission du Japon' in Delacroix, *Les Missions des Origines au XVIe Siècle*.
10. Treadgold, *The West in Russia and China*, vol. II, p. 7.
11. Xavier to King John III, 20 Jan. 1549, in Coleridge, op. cit., pp. 6–14. All four letters can be found in *Monumenta Xaveriana*, pp. 424–59.
12. Xavier to Loyola, 14 Jan. 1549, in Coleridge, op. cit., pp. 67–76.
13. In the end they were unable to get there since Muslim domination of the surrounding waters prevented any Portuguese ships going there for some years.
14. See Chapter 3.
15. Yajiro was baptised Paul and his two companions, John and Antonio, by the Archbishop of Goa on 20 May 1548.
16. Coleridge, op. cit., vol. 22, pp. 237–60.
17. Elison, *Deus Destroyed*, p. 119n.
18. Ebisawa, 'Irmao Lourenço', *Monumenta Nipponica*, (1942) pp. 225–33.
19. Treadgold, op. cit., p. 7.
20. The full text of all these letters can be found in Schurhammer, *Francis Xavier*, vol. 4, pp. 267–90.

CHAPTER THREE

Alessandro Valignano

F rancis Xavier initiated the Christian mission in Japan and died attempting to enter China and begin the mission there. He did not realise the land he was trying to enter was the Cathay to which the Venetian Polos had travelled in search of trade and profit and where the Franciscans had gone as pioneers of Christianity only to find that the Nestorians had begun that work centuries before.

Xavier's life and vision links the Jesuit mission in these two ancient eastern civilisations, but it was Alessandro Valignano who shaped the mission in both those countries and made them a massive challenge to the 'Christendom' understanding of Christianity as incarnated in the Portuguese Padroado and the Spanish patronato. In modern terms he shaped the missions in such a way as to challenge the Eurocentric understanding not only of Christianity but of history and culture.

When Valignano arrived in the East as Visitor, the work of the Society in Japan was already established and significant decisions had been made. So in Japan he had to work with what was already in being, reshaping attitudes and structures as best he could, but with room for manoeuvre in certain areas, limited, as we shall see, by the firm decisions taken by Xavier. However, that experience of Xavier's as well as his own in Japan, helped prepare him for directing the work of the Society in China when at last it was permitted to begin, a mission that was his from the beginning.

Fathers Matteo Ricci, John Adam von Schall and their Jesuit companions have been called by the Jesuit historian George Dunne 'A Generation of Giants', but their brilliant and controversial apostolate of science, philosophy and Christian faith in China would not have been conceived and carried out but for the insight, imagination and determination of Alessandro Valignano.

He was born in February 1539 in the Italian city Chieti in the Abruzzi, at that time under Spanish rule. His family was a distinguished one in the area, its members often holding the senior office of Camarlengo, perhaps best translated 'treasurer', in the administration of the city. Some authorities suggest that the Valignano family was close to Gian Pietro Carafa, bishop of Chieti from 1504 to 1524, later Pope Paul IV. The connection has been disputed by the leading authority on the life and thought of Valignano[1] though most authorities, even Schutte, allow that the young Alessandro, after distinguishing himself as a law student at Padua, was sent to Rome by his father, hopeful that the Carafa connection, whatever form it took, would start him off on a prosperous career.

When Valignano graduated in 1557 his father prepared him for his career in a way typical of the unreformed pre-Tridentine medieval Church. In May 1557, Alessandro was tonsured by the bishop of Chieti and was then granted the abbacy of San Stefano del Casale. In 1559, just before going off to Rome, the young man was also made a canon of the cathedral. Thus the young Alessandro went off suitably endowed. However, when he got to Rome, Paul IV had died and with him Alessandro's hope of advancement. It is not clear what the young man then did, though it is recorded a little later that he gave up his canonry and went back to Padua as a student. Surprisingly, when he next appears, it is in the criminal records of the Republic of Venice in which Padua was situated. Valignano was arrested and imprisoned during the last weeks of 1562 and was not released until March 1564. This imprisonment, it would appear, could have lasted much longer but that the influence of Cardinal Carlo Borromeo was brought to bear on the Venetian authorities to bring the young man's case to a rapid conclusion. The Venetian magistrates had imprisoned Valignano and had then brought him into court on a number of occasions but had failed each time to decide on his guilt or innocence on a charge of slashing a young woman's face with his sword. As a result of the intercessions of his distinguished protector the case was finally brought to a conclusion and Valignano released after nearly sixteen months in gaol. In all the documents in the case the young swordsman is referred to as a student not as a cleric.

Again Valignano disappears from view only to re-appear at the Papal court in the service of Cardinal d'Altemps. Then, suddenly, this only too conventional young aristocrat who appeared to be using the Church, somewhat cynically but for the time not untypically, simply as a means of advancement, turned up in May 1566 seeking to enter the Society of Jesus as a novice. We have no record of what went on in the mind of Valignano in these years. Clearly a profound change in attitude took place, but a discussion or reflection on the nature of this conversion is not to be found and Valignano himself has left no record of his dramatic transformation.

After a year in the novitiate in the Jesuit House of Sant'Andrea in Rome, Valignano was transferred to the College of Rome, as the future Gregorian University was then called, to begin his further studies. He included in his Arts curriculum, Physics and Mathematics under Clavius, who was later also to teach Matteo Ricci, the standard-bearer of what has been called the Jesuit 'scientific apostolate' in China.[2] Valignano took the three vows of a 'religious' on 12 February 1570 and was then ordained priest in the Lateran by William Chisholm, the Scottish bishop who was the viceregent of Cardinal Sabelli, Administrator of the diocese of Rome, on 25 March 1571.

He then served briefly as the novice-master of Sant'Andrea where he supervised the early months of the novitiate of Matteo Ricci. In September of the next year Valignano went to Macerata as Rector of the Jesuit College there, so far a not unusual career for an able younger man in the Society.[3] In August 1573, however, something quite extraordinary happened.

Everard Mercurian, who had recently been elected General of the Society, summoned Valignano to Rome. Arrangements were made by the new General for Valignano to make his 'Solemn Profession', a ceremony which includes the famous Fourth Vow of the Society. This made him one of the elite. The 'professed' alone could hold senior office and they alone could vote in the election of a new General. Many outstanding Jesuits have had to wait years after their entry to the Society before they were permitted to take the Fourth Vow; indeed many scholarly and pious Jesuits even after they had been ordained priest have still had to wait many years before achieving that status. Of course many who enter the Society do not attain to the status of 'professed' at all.

Valignano made his Solemn Profession at the church of Sant'Andrea in Quirinale on 8 September 1573, a date only just within the legal minimum time permitted by the Constitutions of the Society to elapse between entry and taking this solemn step. This decision of the General's was surprising and caused murmuring, but his next decision on Valignano's future was astonishing. The young priest, only thirty-four years old, who had been one of the 'professed' for a few days only, was now appointed Visitor to the East. He was to be in sole charge of all the Jesuit missions and missionaries in the vast area stretching from Mozambique to Japan.

None of the authorities on the history of the Jesuits in general, nor of the Jesuit missions in particular, give any explanation of why Mercurian took this extraordinary and very risky decision.[4] Clearly, however promising Valignano's abilities appeared to the new General, he was untried, so new that it would have been a bold decision to make him Provincial of a small well-established Jesuit Province in Europe, yet the General made him Visitor to the East, one of the two or three most important positions within the Society.

There is no doubt that Mercurian had a very high regard for the tall Italian aristocrat and intellectual. The General certainly communicated this trust to the young Visitor and made clear he was expecting him to carry out a new policy in the East. From the moment he set off from Rome, Valignano was planning developments contrary to the accepted ways of the Portuguese authorities in Lisbon, both royal and ecclesiastical. Indeed from the moment he arrived in Lisbon he did not hesitate to enter into direct face-to-face conflict with the most powerful figures in Portugal, powerful in the Church, in the Society and at the royal court at Lisbon. All of the General's official advisers in Rome expressed uneasiness about the appointment except, strangely, Pedro Fonseca the General's Assistant for the Portuguese territories. Fonseca's support, it has been suggested, was simply to be explained because he believed that such a young man would be readily amenable to guidance from the Portuguese superiors in Lisbon and India.[5] This is no more than intelligent speculation on Schutte's part, since there is no hard evidence to back it, save perhaps for Fonseca's grave displeasure, evinced within a few months of the appointment, at Valignano's determined insistence on pursuing the policies he believed to be right, irrespective of what the Portuguese authorites in Lisbon, royal and ecclesiastical, thought.

Mercurian's complete trust in Valignano is shown unambiguously in his formal instructions for the Visitor. There are no copies of these extant but there are copies of Valignano's suggested amendments which he sent to Rome from Genoa on his journey to Lisbon, and there are also copies of his letter to the General acknowledging receipt of the final version with which he expresses himself well pleased. Fundamentally then the instructions gave Valignano the power the General himself would have had were he to be in the East. The original seems to have given somewhat less than that as we can see from Valignano's suggested amendments sent from Genoa:

> After Article 7 add: 'He can send back to Europe any member of the Society, if, after consultaton, it seems good in the Lord to do so'.
> In Article 8 where it says 'except the (solemnly) professed', it had better read 'also the (solemnly) professed, but only in cases of persistent disobedience'.[6]

He also insisted on authority to divide the East into two Provinces if that appeared expedient and also the explicit authority to begin novitiates for the Society where they did not already exist.

There is no doubt that the untried young Italian Visitor arrived in the Iberian peninsula with a very clear picture of what he was to do and with absolute assurance as to its rightness and necessity. Clearly a new start had been planned. The General and his new Visitor had agreed that Valignano should take with him to the East the unprecedented number of as many as fifty-five new Jesuits; indeed, on his long journey to the field, Valignano continued to try to persuade the General to agree to send a similar number of new recruits within the next few years. In addition, other things that they had decided only emerge when Valignano reached Lisbon and began discussions with the Jesuit and royal authorities there. The radicalness of the size of what came to be called the 'Great Mission of 1574' can be seen when one realises that every assistant to the General wrote him a minute objecting to the number of men Valignano was being allowed to take with him. In Lisbon, as we shall see, the size of his party was only one of a long list of objections to Valignano's plans.

The new Visitor travelled overland from Rome to Genoa then by sea to Alicante then overland to Lisbon. He used the opportunity the overland journey gave him to visit many Jesuit establishments in Spain and recruit men for his mission. This recruiting campaign was greatly assisted by the fact that the Jesuit superiors of Toledo and Castille travelled with him as far as Spain. At Alicante, where he arrived on 10 November 1573, he sent his seven Italian recruits straight off to Lisbon while he used his contacts with the Spanish superiors to travel round Jesuit Colleges selecting and examining recruits. All went well in Spain but when this energetic, confident, some have said arrogant, young man got to Lisbon he ran into trouble, but trouble he appeared to expect and was prepared to overcome.

According to the terms of the Padroado, Valignano had to get the agreement of the Portuguese crown and the Portuguese Province of the Society both for his travel plans, which they would finance, and for the size of his party and the details of their preparation. In Lisbon the royal authorities and the senior members of the Society were as one. Here the Society did not disturb in any way the Christendom tradition of the union of 'crown and altar' enshrined in the Padroado. At the King's palace at Almeirim, Valignano negotiated with the Portuguese Superior and his two advisers. These three together presented a massive weight of seniority in the Society of Jesus over against the new Visitor and his seven-year membership. Jorge Serrao the Portuguese Superior was himself a very senior figure, but more significantly he brought along with him to these negotiations two men who were of outstanding stature both in the Society and within the counsels of the Portuguese throne. This was a move that appears to have been specifically mounted to overawe Valignano and make sure he conformed to Portuguese authority.

The two men whom Serrao brought were cousins. They had known Loyola, Xavier and the other original members of the Society when they were all together as students in Paris, though the two Portuguese cousins had not joined the Society until after it was officially approved. The first was Leao Henriques, who had been Rector of the University of Coimbra and was currently confessor to the Cardinal Infante of Portugual, Dom Henrique. The other was Luis Gonçalves da Câmara, who was the King's confessor and to whom Ignatius Loyola had dictated his memoirs.

Valignano had written to them, while still in Spain, warning them of his aim to take as many as fifty-five new recruits to the East. For their part the Portuguese leaders had completely disregarded Valignano's plans and asked the crown for passages to the East for fifteen Jesuit missionaries only. The rest, they had decided, would go to Brasil or, if they were to go to the East, it would only be after a long period of testing under their supervision in Portugal. Câmara and Henriques, who prided themselves, as we shall see, on being totally loyal to the true 'Ignatian way', had built the Portuguese Province of the Society into the Portuguese establishment, making it an arm of the Portuguese branch of Christendom. The fact that they called Valignano to meet them in the royal palace was indicative of their perception of the place of Christianity and the Christian mission.

At the Almeirim meeting the three Portuguese leaders made their position clear to the appalled Italian, and further they drew his attention to the fact that a majority of those whom he had chosen to accompany him were Spaniards which was likely to be unacceptable to the King, but worse, a majority of these Spaniards were of Jewish extraction and this made them utterly unacceptable to the King, the Cardinal Infante and to the Portuguese authorities in the East. In any case, they asserted that Valignano had misunderstood the General, who wanted the majority of these volunteers to go to Brasil and be thoroughly tested in Portugal before they went anywhere.

Valignano showed the Portuguese his written instructions from the General and also insisted that he had understood perfectly well all that had been said to him by the General. There was a series of hard-hitting meetings between the four men and several letters were sent from both sides to the General in Rome. It was the Visitor who won the first victory in the matter of numbers. The Portuguese accepted that they would have to find room for and pay the passages of as many men as Valignano finally chose to go with him, even if they were Spaniards of Jewish ancestry. However, there were still another two battles to be fought before Valignano could settle down with his men and prepare them for their long voyage to Goa and their new tasks.

The first was over the form of preparation the Jesuits missionaries were to undergo. The three Portuguese Fathers wanted Valignano's men to be divided among various Jesuit establishments in Portugal under their control and for them to remain in those houses while being spiritually prepared for their missionary task during the months of waiting for the the departure of the royal fleet for the East. This Valignano refused to accept for two reasons. First, he wanted to use the time they had to wait in Portugal as a time for sifting out any that were unsuitable from among his volunteers and to prepare the others in the way he thought best. Second, he wanted all his men together under his authority because he believed that the spirit of the Society in Portugal was a wrong and harmful one under the de facto leadership of Gonçalves da Câmara.[7]

This clash over the spirit and style of leadership of the Society was not just a matter of these weeks of waiting in Portugal but was fundamental to any understanding of Valignano's missionary policy and his style of leadership in all his years in Asia.

Luis Gonçalves had, for many years, used his personal contact in the past with Ignatius Loyola to insist that he knew better than anyone the true 'Ignatian way'. On the basis of this connection he successfully insisted on a rigorous authoritarian style of leadership of the Society in the Portuguese Province. There was no intimacy between superiors and juniors and he insisted that it was by the external discipline of severe punishment that virtue was developed. He was passionately opposed to what he referred to as the 'Roman' way which the previous General of the Society, Francis Borgia, had personally introduced to Portugal but which Gonçalves had reversed as soon as Borgia's appointed Visitor had gone. As Schutte points out, Valignano's letters to the General on this matter show how close the link was between the General and his protégé.[8] Valignano did not hesitate to give the General advice on how to deal with what he considered the badly misguided leadership of the Society in Portugal. He did not restrict himself to the specific problems of the new mission but criticised the Portuguese Jesuit style in general.

Valignano won this battle. He was allowed to keep his men together and put them through a careful spiritual training of the kind he believed appropriate. He also saw to it that those who had not yet completed their philosophical or theological studies continued their academic training throughout the whole period. He also used this time to winnow out unsuitable, if enthusiastic, volunteers and so reduced his party to forty. He also took advantage of this time to have a number of meetings with the pious young King, Sebastian III. Through these meetings he won the King over so that he became a supporter of his 'Great Mission' and confirmed royal support for all the volunteers to travel with the fleet to the East.

Throughout this period of preparation, the style of leadership and the spirit it was used to inculcate was what Gonçalves da Câmara called the 'Roman' way; but it was the style which Valignano always referred to – and it was one of his favourite phrases throughout his life – as 'il modo soave' or 'il spirito soave'. Valignano's fondness for this phrase, which certainly did describe his style, has led the distinguished historian, George Elison, to slip into a rather vituperative play on words while discussing Valignano's later opposition to the entry of the Mendicant Orders to Japan and China: 'The Jesuit masquerading as a Zen choro could ill admit fraternity to the barefoot Franciscan beggar. The virtue of apostolic poverty is little honored in Japanese eyes, sibilates the suave Valignano'.[9]

The last challenge the Visitor to the East had to present to the Portuguese establishment was, in some ways, the most important. It was certainly the most revealing of the intention of the General and Valignano to disengage the Jesuit mission in the East from the stranglehold in which it had been held hitherto by the Portuguese establishment. This hold had been achieved by interpreting the meaning and intention of the Padroado so as to make the Superior of the Portuguese Province and his allies, Henriques and Gonçalves so close to the throne, the final authority over the Jesuit mission in the East rather than the General in Rome or the Pope. This was achieved by ruling that all correspondence from Jesuits in the field was opened and dealt with by the authorities in Lisbon. Only those letters they thought appropriate were sent on to Rome, other than the very very few special letters marked 'personal to the General'. This procedure represented most fully the restrictions upon the Society within the orbit of the Padroado which kept it, no matter the interior attitude of its members, a vehicle of the Portuguese crown rather than an arm of the Church.

For the modern observer this distinction is for them not only clear but taken for granted yet, to the vast majority of European Christians in 1574, including the leaders of the Portuguese Jesuits, the distinction was by no means obvious.

As we shall see, in Japan and China, Valignano initiated a missionary strategy which attempted to break Christianity free from this understanding, not only in practice but at the deepest theological and philosophical level. At that moment in Lisbon, it would appear that that was what Valignano, under authority from Mercurian, was trying to do − or was it?

There is no doubt that Francis Xavier had begun to work in practice as independently as possible of Portuguese royal authority, though he still slipped back into using it from time to time when it suited his purposes. In these moves that Valignano was making, he made no reference to Xavier's ambiguous attitude towards the Padroado nor to any formally articulated theory of the mission. What was happening was much simpler. It was a struggle to assert a minimum of ecclesiastical autonomy in one of the two Iberian empires where the Church was normally so fully under royal authority that even the ultimate authority of the Pope only received lip-service. In other words, this was simply a continuation of the kind of struggle that had often occurred within medieval Christendom between the claim of an all-embracing authority by the crown and the assertion of ecclesiastical autonomy.

From its inception, the Society of Jesus was committed both to its own auton-omy and to that of the Church. However, as we have seen, the leadership of the Portuguese Province of the Society had allowed that Province to conform completely to the Padroado. Mercurian had appointed a young, able, Italian leader to make sure that the Jesuits in the East would be as free as was realis-tically possible to carry out the mission as seemed best to them, as opposed to what suited the Portuguese authorities. In terms of the hard political realities of the time, this had to be done without seriously antagonising the Portuguese crown, otherwise the way to the East could have been cut off to the Society.

Valignano moved on two fronts to achieve a measure of independence. The first was his insistence on taking such a large number of recruits to the East against the wishes of Serrao and his allies, and in particular, his choosing so many Spanish and Italian members of the Society to be in the party. When accused of being pro-Spanish and anti Portuguese, he insisted that he was Italian through and through and the fact of Spanish suzerainty over Chieti did nothing to enamour Spain in his eyes. Why he chose the team of men that he had was because the missions of the Society in the East needed a massive new injection of men of talent and it was unfair to ask the Portuguese Province, from its limited resources, to bear this burden alone. As we have seen he got away with this, but the second prong of his attack provoked another bitter clash with Serrao, Gonçalves and Henriques.

Valignano now asserted that the General wanted a Jesuit Procurator ap-pointed to hold office in Lisbon. This official was to deal with all the necessary business for supplying the Jesuit missions in the East and the transporting of the missionaries to the field. In addition, the Procurator was to receive all letters from Jesuits in the East and deal with them himself, making sure that the General was kept fully in touch with what was happening there and with what the members of the Society there were doing and thinking. The privilege of the Portuguese Provincial receiving and opening this mail was to cease forthwith. The first Procurator was to be Alessandro Vallareggio, then present in Lisbon and another Italian. Naturally the Portuguese Superior and his allies were very upset at this. Valignano showed them the clear written instructions from Mercurian of which they demanded a copy, presumably to help them confirm its authenticity and have something upon which to base an appeal against this decision. However, they had no alternative but to give way.

Finally on 21 March 1574, the 'Indian' fleet set out from Lisbon after two false starts so typical of the difficulties of travel in that era. After a comparatively straightforward voyage, Valignano landed at Goa on 6 September 1574. For the next five years the Visitor spent his time getting to know the situation of the Society in the countries we now know as India, Indonesia and Malaysia. As he came to understand the situation so he also began a process of re-invigoration and reorganisation of the work of the Society.

Before he went to Japan for the first time, Valignano wrote some very important reports to Rome which give us an insight into his thinking about the future of the Jesuit missions in the East at this early stage in his career. The principal report he prepared during this period raises a very serious problem which the historical authorities on the Jesuit missions in Asia make no attempt to resolve. In some ways what is more surprising is that most of the literature does not even notice that there is a problem at all.

How is it possible to reconcile Valignano's recruitment of so many Jesuits from Spain who were 'confessi', 'New Christians' that is, of Jewish ancestry, with his recommendation in his major report to Mercurian in this period that the Society should not recruit any such 'confessi' in the East? Remember he had taken these Jesuits of 'confessi' ancestry with him to the East against the violent opposition of Gonçalves and his colleagues. The report which contains his recommendation was that to Mercurian, written at Malacca in December 1577. The apparent contradiction is there for all to see in Schutte's detailed study of Valignano's missionary thinking, but Schutte makes no attempt to explain it.

C. R. Boxer, in his classic study *The Christian Century in Japan*, notes that the recommendation from Malacca became a few years later a rule of the Society.[10] He sees it as a clear sign of anti-semitism on Valignano's part, and further, Boxer contrasts this attitude with that of Ignatius Loyola and of the Society in general in its first years. After all Lainez, the second General of the Society, was of Jewish ancestry. However, he makes no reference to, and appears to have no knowledge of Valignano's struggle to take so many 'New Christians' with him as missionaries, neither do Elison, Jennes or Fujita appear to have knowlege of this either.[11]

What are we to make of this contradiction? Did the Jesuits he brought out with him so disappoint the Visitor that he decided that as a group 'New Christians' were not suitable to be Jesuits? There is no record of this anywhere nor is it suggested by any of the authorities; but other than Schutte none appear to have noted his clash with Serrao, Henriques and Gonçalves over the majority of his Spanish volunteers being 'confessi'.

To find a solution to the problem it is necessary to look at precisely what Valignano said and in what context he said it. His recommendation that 'confessi' should not be recruited into the Society of Jesus came in the report from Malacca called *Summario Indico*.[12] In this major report Valignano was attempting to give the General a thorough picture of the situation so as to enable him to make informed judgements about the situation in India when they were presented to him in letters from the East.

The first thing the Visitor wanted to make clear was the desperate need for a steady supply of fresh volunteers from Europe, the lack of whom was a continuing major handicap upon the effectiveness of the Society in India. This was so because, in the first place, the death-rate of members of the Society was so great as to be a major problem in itself. In the period 1571–4, fifty-eight members of the Society had died while serving in the Indian Province. There then followed Valignano's main point that recruitment from within the Province itself could not even begin to make up for these losses. He then reviewed the possible sources of recruits within the Province so as to make his point clear. He insisted that it would be wrong to recruit 'confessi' who already lived in the East because of the deep antagonism of the Portuguese in the East towards them. In addition none of the indigenous peoples, except the Japanese, were of any use for recruitment into the Society. Other than the Japanese none were capable of reaching the required intellectual and spiritual levels. The rest of what he said on this point is summarised by Schutte thus:

> The mestizos also, that is children of a Portuguese father and a native mother (and vice versa though there were few of this second type), were not to be admitted. Castizos, that is sons of a Portuguese father and a Mestizo mother, and vice versa, could gain admission in very exceptional cases, where vocation and talent compensated for the drawback in their native character. Even in the case of children born in India to parents both of whom were of Portuguese origin, special care had to be exercised because their rearing in the Indian climate and their education usually made them less useful.[13]

This whole discussion took place in chapter 23 of the *Summario* which has to do with the problem of who, in the East, the Society could recruit as new members. Further, its purpose was to show that the potential pool of recruits was so small as to make it essential that the General continued to send a steady stream of new recruits from Europe. This whole discussion by Valignano had nothing to do with who was recruited into the Society in Europe as Boxer and others have misunderstood him to mean. Their assumption of anti-semitism on Valignano's part is also understandable since, as we have seen, they do not appear to have noted that a majority of his Spanish recruits had been 'confessi' on whose behalf he had had to fight a battle in Lisbon before they proceeded to the East. At least that would seem to be the only explanation of why Boxer and Elison should make no attempt to explain how the anti-semitism of which they accuse Valignano can be squared with his insistence on taking so many Spanish Jesuits of Jewish ancestry with him in the 'Great Mission' of 1574.

The Society of Jesus, soon after this, did ban the entry of men of Jewish ancestry from membership of the Society but this would seem to have resulted from the constant pressure from the royal courts of Spain and Portugal and the treatment of such Jesuits within their dominions and within the Portuguese Province of the Society itself.

It is quite clear that Valignano shared the current Iberian lack of respect for the moral and intellectual qualities of Africans, Indians and the Malay peoples of Indonesia and Malaysia. His attitude towards Indians does change somewhat later as he comes to have more knowledge of Indian higher culture, of which he appears to have been unaware in his first years. However that may be, it is only with the Japanese and then the Chinese that, as early as this report of 1577, he had hopes of better things. He referred in this report and continued to do so for the rest of his life, to the Chinese and Japanese as 'gente bianca'.

It seems clear that Valignano was very pessimistic about any rapid development of Christianity among the peoples of Africa, the Indian sub-Continent and south-east Asia. He did not plan nor in any way foresee the possibility of any kind of acculturation of Christianity in those areas. Indeed from what he wrote it would appear that he would have been horrified at the suggestion of any such thing. He did not plan the mission of Rudolph Acquaviva to the Great Moghul nor did he have anything to do with the mission of de Nobili in Madura, though there is no doubt that it was the missionary principles which he formed in the missions to Japan and China that inspired the approach of de Nobili in his extraordinary experiment.

In Japan and China, among the 'gente bianca' whose sophisticated societies appeared to him to be on a cultural level with Europe's and which were external to the Padroado and the Patronato, the Jesuit Visitor shaped and oversaw the outworking of a new missionary approach. This broke with the conquistador tradition of the Iberian missions and at a deeper theological and philosophical level broke with the very concept of Christendom and with a Eurocentric understanding of religion, culture and history. Not only was his approach finally condemned as mistaken in the eighteenth century by the Papacy but it was also in effect rejected by the Protestant missionary movement when it developed after 1790. It also runs contrary to the Eurocentrism of much secular European thought of the nineteenth and the twentieth centuries which so often presumes the western European experience, and its extension in North America, to be definitive for all humanity. Just as the conquistador assumed Latin Christianity to be the only true culture so modern western man so often presumes his post-Christian secularism to be equally so.

That Valignano had a central role in the Jesuit missions in Japan and China has been recognised in some form or another by most recent scholars with one startling exception. The English scholar, J. C. H. Aveling in his book *The Jesuits* (1982), sets up a picture of Valignano which is something of a straw man and then proceeds to demolish it.

> He, it has been held, recruited and trained Ricci, Acquaviva, de Nobili and de Goes. He placed them like chessmen, in the most crucial and inaccessible parts of the East, in the Moghul Empire, along the Silk Road . . . in central India, in Korea, and in the heart of the Chinese Empire in Beijing. Once there, under Valignano's inspired direction, they implemented his bold and unorthodox plan of accommodating western Catholicism to the great cultures of the East.[14]

Aveling goes on to call this the traditional view of Valignano, though this assertion is not borne out by any consideration of the serious books on the Jesuit mission published in this century. As we have seen, Valignano had nothing to do with Acquaviva's or de Nobili's work. De Nobili only went to Madura the same year that Valignano died in Macao, and when Valignano had for a number of years been Visitor to China and Japan only.

Aveling says that in fact Valignano never got rid of his deep European racial and cultural prejudices and the radical departures in mission strategy were carried out by individuals despite Valignano. It has to be granted that Valignano never did get rid of his belief in the inferiority of the peoples of Africa, India and south-east Asia to the Europeans, but he did see the Japanese and the Chinese in quite a different light. As we shall see in the later chapters dealing with Japan and China, it is quite clear that Valignano wanted the Jesuits to become Japanese to win the Japanese and Chinese to win the Chinese. His famous *Il Ceremoniale per i Missionari del Giappone* and his *Resoluciones* for Japan of 1582, as well as his instructions to Michele Ruggieri on the initiation of the Chinese mission and his consistent backing of Matteo Ricci in that mission as it developed, all make clear a definite and unambiguous policy of attempting to build in Japan a Christian Church that was Japanese and in China a Church that was Christian but also Chinese, in stark contrast with the missionary policies of the previous five hundred years of western Christian history. As we have already noted, this approach to mission of this extraordinary group of Italian Jesuits is also in contrast with the dominant style of Protestant missionary activity in the nineteenth and early twentieth centuries.

It is true that Valignano never himself mastered Chinese or Japanese and so did not get 'inside' either of these cultures. However, he trusted those who did, and built a policy upon this belief that Japanese and Chinese cultures each contained elements that could be a foundation for the upbuilding of an indigenous Christian Church and a new Christian culture. As we shall see, every new intiative that Ricci made was done with the full agreement and co-operation of Valignano, not despite him. Certainly Valignano was never able to translate this approach to the peoples of Africa or southern Asia, but who has ever claimed he did?

Aveling also goes on to make a number of specific criticisms of actions of Valignano which are simply factually inaccurate. An example is his complaint that Valignano backed Hideyoshi's invasion of Korea and tried to get the Portuguese to aid him. As we shall see this was exactly what poor Fr Coelho did, which was specifically and fiercely condemned by Valignano! However, there is no need to pursue criticism of this eccentric view of Valignano any further.

The key period of Valignano's life when he directed the Jesuit missions in Japan and China will be considered in detail in subsequent chapters. Before summarising the rest of his career, one more preliminary point needs to be made. Valignano's struggle to prevent other Orders coming to work in Japan or China, and in particular his insistence that no missionaries should come from the Spanish dominions, has usually been interpreted as Jesuit exclusivism. However, it is not usually noted by historians that not even fellow Jesuits were to be allowed to come from the Spanish dominions; it was the 'conquistador' mentality that he feared and wanted excluded from Japan and China. These fears were only too fully confirmed by the behaviour of the Manila-based Jesuit, Alonso Sanchez, who was an irrepressible advocate of military conquest as a tool of Christian mission.[15]

It is as well to outline now, in anticipation of later chapters, the rest of Valignano's career from when he first set off for Japan until he died in Macao in 1606. In September of 1577 he left Goa and made a formal inspection of the Jesuit house and mission at Malacca from October until August 1578. He then left for Macao where he stayed for about ten months before proceeding onwards to Japan where he arrived on 25 July 1579. In February of 1582 he set sail from Nagasaki with four young Japanese noblemen who constituted the famous Japanese 'Embassy' to the Pope and the Catholic Kings of Europe. Valignano had intended to accompany these youths to Rome, but when they arrived in Goa en route for Europe, he found letters from the General which removed him from the office of Visitor and made him Provincial for India. Undeterred, he sent the young 'ambassadors' on their way accompanied, in his place, by Fr Nuno Rodrigues, the Rector of the Jesuit College in Goa.

Valignano was re-appointed Visitor for the whole of the East in 1585 but had to remain in India, despite his enthusiasm to return to Macao directly to oversee the work of the Society in Japan and China. Part of the reason for this was the difficulty he had in finding a suitable replacement as Provincial in India.

In September 1587 the Japanese 'ambassadors' arrived in Goa on their way back to Japan. Valignano felt it was essential that he return to Japan with them, and so arranged for the appointment of Fr Martins as Provincial for India. So in July 1587 the young Japanese arrived back in Japan accompanied by the man who had first conceived and then put into motion their momentous trip. The situation in Japan was a critical one politically for the Society and for the Christian community, and Valignano stayed there to deal with it until October 1592. He then sailed to Macao to supervise the opening of the China mission of the Society of Jesus. The Jesuit house in Macao was not 'a China mission' since Macao was not Chinese but a tiny Portuguese enclave within which all Europeans were normally confined. Indeed the Portuguese there were so firmly under Chinese control that it was more like a prison than the foothold it has sometimes been described as.

In 1595, when Valignano returned to what was formally his headquarters, Goa, there was confusion as to his status caused primarily by the enormous delay in correspondence to and from Rome and because correspondence was so often lost. As a result, for a time, he relinquished his office as Visitor. However, new and clear instructions arrived from the General which cleared the matter up. Valignano was made Jesuit Visitor again but this time to the Jesuit missions in Japan and China alone. This was entirely to Valignano's taste and he set up his new headquarters in Macao in July 1597. There was yet another political crisis in Japan, one which threatened the continued existence of the mission and the lives of the Christians. Valignano went there and stayed for four difficult but very important years. He returned to Macao in February 1603, greatly excited by the progress of the work of Matteo Ricci in China. He began preparing for a visit to China, in particular to be with Matteo Ricci and gain greater insight into what he was doing. However, he died in Macao on 20 January 1606, still talking of China and his projected trip there.

NOTES

1. Schutte, *Valignano's Mission Principles for Japan*. vol. 1, p. 31, n. 100.
2. The scientific liveliness of the Roman College is well brought out in D'Elia, *Galileo in China*.
3. Jesuit recruits were divided into those who would become, after ten years work and training, temporal coadjutors, whose training always included academic work, and those who would become priests and spiritual coadjutors after years of rigorous academic training and service which always included periods as teachers. Only spiritual coadjutors would be invited to take the final step of becoming 'solemnly professed of the fourth vow' usually when they were well tried veterans.
4. Even the most recent study of Valignano, J. F. Moran's splendid *The Japanese and the Jesuits*, published in 1993, attempts no explanation.

5. Schutte, op. cit., vol. I., pp. 46–7.
6. Ibid., p. 53.
7. Ibid., pp. 70–1.
8. Ibid., p. 74.
9. Elison, *Deus Destroyed*, p. 79. But in these two sentences Elison unfortunately displays something less than fairness. The Jesuits in Japan did not 'masquerade as Zen choro'. After the initial confusion as to what Xavier was, they never hid their opposition to Buddhism, which was often so overzealous as to be a handicap to the advancement of their cause. 'Sibilates' alliterates well with 'suave' in English which, though undoubtedly linguistically linked in the past to the Italian *soave*, carries a different meaning and a profoundly different nuance from that of the Italian word.
10. Boxer, *The Christian Century*, p. 81.
11. Elison, *Deus Destroyed*; Jennes, *A History of the Catholic Church in Japan*; Fujita, *Japan's Encounter with Christianity*.
12. The Report is discussed fully in Schutte, op. cit., vol. I, pp. 122–4 and 378–81.
13. Ibid., p. 137.
14. Aveling, *The Jesuits*, pp. 170–200.
15. Moran, op. cit., pp. 47–9.

CHAPTER FOUR

The Christian Century in Japan, 1549–1650

To the Death of Toyotomi Hideyoshi, 1598

The two Jesuits left by Xavier, Fr Cosme de Torres and Brother Juan Fernandez, were soon reinforced by the arrival of Fr Balthazar Gago and two lay Brothers and the work of the Society went ahead under the protection of the daimyo of Bungo, Otomo Yoshishige. The Jesuits firmly believed that there was an astonishing opportunity for the reception of Christianity in Japan, but if the opportunity was to be seized there had to be a rapid expansion of the mission staff. They therefore sent one of the newly arrived lay Brothers back to India to appeal for reinforcements, and to have the appeal transmitted onwards to Portugal and Rome. While waiting for a ship at Hirado this lay Brother improved the hour by visiting the daimyo Matsuura Takunobu, who received him courteously. This opening was followed up by Fr Gago who was able to convert many at the daimyo's court including Koteda Saemon whose family were to be staunch pillars of the Church for four generations. The daimyo gave a letter to the young Brother for the Viceroy asking that priests be sent to his dominions, which strengthened the Brother's case.

The development of the mission was always dependent upon the patronage of the local lord which at times led to what amounted to a compulsory mass conversion, as happened in Yokoseura in 1562. The local daimyo, Omura Sumitada was converted by Brother Luis d'Almeida and baptised by Fr Torres. He then embarked on a spree of burning Buddhist temples and destroying statues of the Buddha, enough to provoke a rebellion which threatened his authority for a time. Similarly when the converted Koteda Saemon took Fr Vilela to preach on his island fiefdom of Takushima and Ikitsuki, a good response was almost overturned by the burning of temples and the destruction of statues. Certainly the important leaders of the mission later, Francisco Cabral and Alessandro Valignano both condemned the kind of anti-Buddhist violence carried out at Yokoseura and at many other places, but it is not clear now who was primarily to blame for these episodes which, unfortunately for the Jesuits, were to be long remembered and bitterly resented.

The over-enthusiastic support of a genuine convert was only one side of the story; the other is of daimyo who encouraged their people to listen to the missionaries only to insist that they give up the faith if the Christian success did not lead to a share in the profits of the Portuguese trade which was of such economic importance, given the poverty of Japan as a result of the long period of almost continuous warfare of the Sengoku Jidai.

Before the Society in India or Europe could reply to the appeals of the Jesuits in Japan they received a very important addition to their number. Luis d'Almeida, a wealthy businessman already in the East, an experienced and skilful surgeon, sought out Fr Gago in 1555 and asked for guidance about his future. He entered the Society of Jesus bringing his skill and his fortune to the aid of the mission.

So it was in Bungo, in the lands of Otomo Yoshishige, that perhaps the firmest Christian foundations were laid in all of the island of Kyushu. It was there in the town of Funai that the new Jesuit, Br Luis d'Almeida, founded a hospital and a home for orphans, both endowed by his 'dowry'. There he trained Japanese assistants in surgery which was not practised in Japan, and began a service to the poor and the outcast, in particular caring for foundling children, whose alternative at that period in Japanese history was death. These two charitable institutions were the focus of a slow but steady entry of Japanese to the Christian Church. These new Christians were not being pressured into membership by their lord, neither were they aristocrats nor samurai, but peasants, artisans and merchants.

It was also in this period that Christianity penetrated the Gokinai, the 'Home Counties' of Japan around the capital Kyoto. After a number of fruitless attempts, Fr Gaspar Vilela and the ballad-singing Japanese evangelist Lourenço, eventually obtained an interview with the Shogun, Ashikaga Yositeru, who gave them a formal permit to live and preach in the Gokinai. Vilela baptised a number of enthusiastic converts, some of whom were bonzes and others samurai. He was not able to stay in the capital at all times, however, despite the permit; things were often made too difficult for him and at those times he removed to nearby Sakai. There a powerful merchant family, members of which had been attracted to Christianity by Xavier during his brief visit, protected him. Vilela's difficulties came to a climax when one of the Shogun's ministers, a devout Buddhist, decided formally to investigate the teachings of the foreign priests. If they were found to be dangerous to the State then the Shogun's permit would be revoked.

One of the minister's vassals, Takayama Hida-no-kami, was to supervise the inquisition which was to be carried out by two anti-Christian scholars, Yuki Yamashiro and Kiyohara Geki. Vilela and Lourenço were ordered to Nara to be examined. Vilela believed his presence would not help their case and so Lourenço went alone. Astonishingly, the answers of this almost blind traditional story-teller were so effective that the two judges asked for Christian instruction as did the lord Takayama. Vilela immediately proceeded to Nara where the three, together with their families, were first instructed and then baptised. As a result of this extraordinary event in 1563, the Church spread to other samurai and aristocratic groups in the Gokinai. Perhaps most noteworthy of all among Takayama's relations who were baptised was his son, Takayama Ukon, who was to be an outstanding Christian leader and soldier.

In the years up to 1570 there was a slow increase in the mission staff, both through the arrival of new members of the Society from Europe and also by the recruitment of Japanese into the Society and by the addition to the staff of a significant number of Japanese lay assistants.[1] These were of two kinds. The first, known as dojuku, were almost apprentice clergy but they were not clergy according to canon law; the others were clearly and unambiguously lay, known by the Japanese word kambo. This second category, kambo, were the local leaders of the Christian communities that grew up as a result of the mission. In the early period, given the shortage of mission staff, these men were vital during the long intervals between the visits of a priest, a Brother or even a dojuku. When the numbers of Jesuits expanded in the last quarter of the sixteenth century the Church expanded even more, and so the role of the kambo remained vital. In the period of intense persecution in the seventeenth century the role of the kambo became more important than ever as they held the local Christian communities together. In many ways the most apt comparison to be made of their role is with that of the local elders whose work has been fundamentally important in the astonishingly rapid growth of many Protestant Churches in sub-saharan Africa in the twentieth century.

The dojuku are more difficult to describe. Perhaps they have been best portrayed by the Jesuit Visitor, Alessandro Valignano, who said:

> In Japan we call these men dojuku who, whether young or old, shave their head, renounce the world and promise to devote themselves to the service of the Church. Some are studying to become religious or priests, some others in order to render various household services, which cannot be performed in Japan save by men who have shaved their heads, such as the office of sacristan, door-keeper, server of chanoyu, messenger, helper at Mass, funerals, Baptisms and other services of the Church, and in travelling with the Padres. Those among them who are qualified, also help by catechising, with preaching and with instructing the Christians. These dojuku are respected in Japan and are considered clerics. They wear a cassock but it is different from that of the Padres and Irmaos.[2]

It was also these men who taught the new European recruits Japanese and interpreted for them on their itineration. They played a vital role, too, in evangelisation of the people, as we have just seen in the case of Lourenço at Nara. In the early days, when Gago and Fernandez were struggling on alone, it was dojuku who helped them prepare hand-written sermons and a hand-written catechism for the instruction of catechumens. They were also to play a very important role once the mission established a printing press and began book and pamphlet production. Without their language skills it would appear unlikely that the Society could have produced the effective works in Japanese that it later did.

In 1570 a major change in the personnel of the Society in Japan took place. Two important newcomers arrived, Fr Francisco Cabral who came as the new mission superior and Fr Organtino Gnecci-Soldi, whose difficult to pronounce surname means he was and is usually referred to as Organtino. The new Superior, Cabral, was a Portuguese fidalgo who had come to the Indies as a soldier and only then joined the Society. He was devout, disciplined and full of life. As he got to know the situation in Japan he became convinced of the need for a number of major reforms necessary to restore proper Jesuit discipline and spirituality. In one matter of Jesuit life he had no choice but to make a change. After Xavier's famous visit to Yamaguchi in the finest clothing he had available, the members of the Society had come to dress in Japanese silk kimonos as appropriate to their status and necessary if they were to be received by Japanese of samurai rank and above. In Japanese culture formal dress and formal etiquette were of supreme importance. Both in Rome and India the authorities of the Society were astonished at this form of dress and Cabral arrived with strict instructions from the Jesuit Visitor for Asia, Fr Alvarez, to enforce the wearing of simple black cotton habits by all Jesuits. However there was much more needing to be done in Cabral's view, much of it stemming from the fact that such a small number of Jesuits were attempting to deal with such a vast area so that members of the Society sometimes lived alone for years on end. Cabral summoned all members of the Society to a special thirty-day retreat on the island of Amakusa. There he got to know them and proceeded to explain his new policies. In addition there was a deliberate policy of renewing their spiritual zeal through having some undergo again the Spiritual Exercises, and all were to attend regular meditations led by him. He arranged that in future missionaries should live together in small communities rather than singly, so that each could encourage and support the others in their personal spiritual life as well as in their missionary duties. He also decided that the Superior must constantly itinerate around the missions, which policy he pursued vigorously as soon as the missionaries returned to their stations.

In all matters, other than the cotton–silk issue where the majority of the missionaries believed the change was an error of judgement, Cabral gained their enthusiastic support. As d'Almeida wrote in October 1572,

> This portion of Christendom is making great advances. This is due in no small measure to the work of Fr Francisco Cabral. By his visitations he stimulates and helps us to such an extent that with the examples of such a shepherd – who, I pray God, will remain with us for many a year – we cannot but devote ourselves continuously to work in the vineyard. He is

beginning now to understand the country and to know how to deal with its
problems effectively.[3]

Francisco Cabral brought a new rigour and vigour to the Society and his years
as Superior saw a massive growth in the Church in Japan. His restructuring
and enlivening of the Society undoubtedly helped this process but it must be
remembered that the cutting edge of the work, the effective preaching and
teaching that led to conversions, was being done by the Japanese irmaos (young
scholastics) and dojuku. In addition changes were taking place in Japanese society that aided the work of the Jesuit mission and made its work more acceptable
to many Japanese.

Throughout the late 1550s and '60s, a daimyo on Honshu who was a brilliant soldier, Oda Nobunaga, had begun – at first apparently in the normal
way of the Sengoku Jidai – to expand his authority over neighbouring lords
and their lands. After the murder of the Shogun Ashikaga Yositeru, which
in some ways marks the worst moment of disorder in the period of baronial
conflict, Nobunaga was persuaded to intervene by Dario Takayama, who, as
we have seen, was a Christian. In 1568 Nobunaga marched triumphantly into
the Gokinai and made Yositeru's younger brother, Yoshiaki, Shogun. He also
repaired the palace of the Emperor and by generous gifts restored some dignity to the lifestyle of the descendant of the Sun Goddess, Amaterasu. More
importantly, these were the first steps in the reunification of the nation and the
beginning of the end of the Sengoku Jidai.

It became increasingly clear to all the daimyo, militant Buddhist abbots and
the Jesuit missionaries, that though the Shogun and the Emperor were honoured by Nobunaga, it was he who was the most powerful leader in Japan. By
1580, as a result of his military and diplomatic campaigns, more of Japan was
united under one leader than had been the case for a century. His authority
was only directly effective in central and southern Honshu, but the daimyo on
Kyushu were well aware of his power.

Nobunaga's rise to prominence was important to the mission of the Jesuits
because he was bitterly anti-Buddhist, and a number of his leading officers and
close allies were either Christians like Dario Takayama or sympathetic to the
Jesuits like the powerful lord Wada Koremasa. Indeed it was Wada Koremasa
who introduced Fr Frois to Nobunaga in 1568 in Kyoto. Frois and the dojuku
of the Society had had to leave Kyoto and hide in Sakai after the murder of the
Shogun Ashikaga Yositeru. Now Nobunaga gave formal permission for them
to return, and this gave the Jesuits a security they had never had before.

Nobunaga was not anti-Buddhist in any religious or philosophical sense. The
great Buddhist houses with their monk armies were significant contributors to
the division of Japan and the consequent constant warfare of the Sengoku Jidai
period. If Japan was to be united and at peace then those powerful abbots would
have to be brought down just like other recalcitrant daimyo.

Oda Nobunaga's campaigns against the militant monks began soon after his restoration of the Ashikaga Shogunate and his assistance to the Emperor. In 1571 he completely destroyed the great and beautiful complex of monasteries and temples of the Tendai sect at Hieizan, Xavier's 'Buddhist University'. Nobunaga was utterly ruthless and many thousands of monks were slaughtered, not only at Mount Hieizan but in his subsequent eight-year campaign against the sect of the Ikko who had many strongholds on Honshu. He destroyed many temples in Osaka, Sakai and Himeji and used stones from them in his new castle building programme, the most outstanding of which was his own great new fortress at Azuchi on the shores of Lake Biwa. This castle became the model for many new fortresses built in the next fifty years because it was designed with firearms in mind, the new element in these last savage campaigns that marked the end of the Sengoku Jidai.

Since, by 1570, Buddhist monks were usually bitter enemies of the Jesuits, his anti-Buddhist fervour helped the Society gain some sort of standing in Nobunaga's eyes. When first Fr Frois and then, after 1570, his new colleague in the Gokinai, Fr Organtino, each proved to be good speakers of Japanese and extremely scrupulous with regard to matters of Japanese etiquette, they were able to gain permanent access to the dictator. What is more, Organtino became his friend.

In the eleven years between Nobunaga's march on Kyoto and the arrival of Fr Valignano in Japan the Christian Church went through a period of massive growth both on Honshu and on Kyushu. On Honshu the growth of Christianity was among the followers of lords who were prominent leaders among the supporters of Nobunaga. Typical of this movement was the growth of the Church among the followers of Takayama Hida-no-Kami and his son Takayama Ukon. These men inspired passionate loyalty among their samurai and they were both deeply devout. They encouraged their followers to listen to Christian instruction and many were baptised. Hida-no-Kami built, at his headquarters at Takatsuki in Settsu just south of Kyoto, a beautiful church and house for the Society surrounded by an attractive garden and fish pond. This was done according to an entirely Japanese pattern conforming to Japanese aesthetics. Apart, that is, from a large cross erected in the garden, hopefully to become part of Japanese aesthetics. By 1579 there were about 8,000 baptised Christians at Takatsuka, of whom samurai and their families constituted the majority. This pattern was repeated in a number of other lordships in the Gokinai and Fr Valignano was to be deeply impressed by the quality of Christian life they showed when he visited them in 1580.

The weakness of these Churches was that when the lord moved to another fief, which often happened in this period, most of the congregation went with him, since it was the samurai and their families and those of other retainers that were the majority of the Christians. This movement was not one where the lord's followers were compelled to enter the Church. They were encouraged and the missionaries were given every opportunity to instruct them, but a loyal samurai who wished to remain Buddhist was still retained for his loyalty.

It was different on Kyushu. There, under the direct leadership and encouragement of Cabral, mass movements into the Church took place in a number of provinces where daimyo were converted and then compelled their people, including the Buddhist monks, to come into the Church. In the 1570s in the lordships of Omura, Amakusa, Arima and Bungo there were mass movements into the Church which meant that by the end of the decade there were approximately 130,000 Christians on Kyushu. Buddhist temples and shrines were often destroyed by these lords as they had been in Omura in 1563, and it has to be noted that if Fr Coelho and his assistants did not encourage this they certainly did nothing to stop it. The Buddhist monks in these lordships had to marry and accept Christian instruction or leave the lordship, those who chose to stay were, however, allowed to keep whatever income they were already receiving. The weakness of the Churches thus formed on Kyushu was that there were so few priests and dojuku to teach the new converts, and their motivation to receive instruction was so far from being primarily religious, that mass apostasy could happen as easily as this kind of mass conversion.

This was exposed very clearly, as Laures in his *History* records, in the Arima lordship. There more than half those baptised under the authority of lord Yoshida apostasised when his successor lord Harunobu urged them to, and then most sought reconciliation with the Church when Harunobu allowed his younger brother to be baptised and permitted Coelho to continue the work of reconciliation and conversion.[4] The outstanding example of this development was that in Omura. In 1563 the daimyo Omura Sumitada had had to survive a rebellion because of his enthusiastic destruction of Buddhist shrines and statues after his baptism. He had then cooled his ardour and the Church there remained in existence but without much growth. Then in 1574 he was faced with another rebellion of some of his subjects in alliance with external enemies, a rebellion in which a number of prominent Buddhist monks were involved. When, against the odds, he had triumphed over his enemies, he determined to stamp out Buddhism in his lands and carried out the kind of enforced instruction of his people we have already discussed; and by 1577 all the people in his fief had received instruction and been baptised.

Cabral with his accustomed energy and drive kept up a punishing round of visits to all the Christian communities and felt that he was coming to a much deeper understanding of Japanese society and culture and of the needs of the Society if it was to be effective in its missionary task in Japan. He came to believe that four things were necessary if the Society was to be able to develop and consolidate the spiritual state of those already converted, let alone expand the work.

First, that many more Jesuits be sent to help the work, some of them to be experienced priests of the Society who could form the staff of the 'College', which he had already insisted was necessary. Most of them however should be young scholastics (irmao) who could devote all their attention to learning the language thoroughly.

Second, it was essential that Japanese be recruited into the Society if the mission was to succeed. The recruits were to be young well-educated men, well versed in the doctrines of Buddhism and the traditions of their land. At this time he makes no reference to educating them in Philosophy or the Humanities, nor for that matter did he seem to be making any provision for European scholastics to receive such education either.

Third, it was essential that the head of the mission in Japan should have the ecclesiastical authority to grant various dispensations from canon law if the Church was to grow in the context of Japanese society. The most obvious instance he cited was the power to grant dispensation so that a Christian might marry a non-Christian. This was vital in a society where marrying outside one's class was impossible and so for Christians the choice was often impossibly restrictive. Also in practice the Christian partner many times won over the other to the Christian faith.

Fourth, it was essential that the mission in Japan be allowed to continue to raise funds by participation in the silk trade. This was because of the great difficulty in financing the mission in any other way, since the demands upon resources were great and Japan, after a century of continuous warfare, was a poor country. The mission had to maintain the members of the Society plus the dojuku and their dwellings; it had to contribute to the building of new churches, it had to support the almshouses and hospital at Bungo. Certainly some few prosperous Christians did contribute freely – for example the beautiful Japanese-style church in the capital Kyoto, the Church of the Assumption (in Japanese history Namban-ji, Temple of the Southern Barbarians) was built in 1576 primarily with the gifts of Japanese Christians. However, even the daimyo were not rich and were under constant pressure first from Nobunaga and then his successor Hideyoshi to contribute massively to their building programmes. Another serious drain on mission resources was the necessity of taking valuable presents whenever one visited anyone of importance. In the feudal society of Japan these visits were frequent and necessary and expensive.[5]

There were various grants made to the mission by the Portuguese crown, by Popes Gregory XIII and Sixtus V and by the Society itself from its resources in India. However these were never paid regularly and often were years in arrears; typical was a Portuguese royal grant from the crown treasury at Malacca, a supposedly readier source than Lisbon, that had not been paid for five years when Valignano arrived in Japan in 1579.

Cabral, with his insistence on rigorous commitment to the rules of the Society, had been deeply shocked at the involvement in the silk trade by the Fathers in Japan when he first arrived. The involvement had originated with the gift to the Society of all his possessions by d'Almeida. Some of the fortune founded the almshouse and hospital at Bungo, but the rest d'Almeida invested in the silk trade between China and Japan so as to contribute to general mission funds with maximum effect, and investment in the annual silk ship had continued since. However, as Cabral explained in a letter to the new Visitor in the East, Alessandro Valignano, although he deplored it and saw it as a source of much that he held to be wrong with the style of the Jesuits in Japan, its continuance was unfortunately essential until alternative sources of regular income could be found.

It is important to note that Cabral was most insistent on the admission of large numbers of Japanese to the Society if it was successfully to carry out its mission, and also his acceptance of the necessity of involvement in the silk trade which he referred to rather quaintly as 'the China-ship alms'.[6] Later in life, in Macao and in India, he would bitterly attack the admission of Japanese to the Society and condemn unreservedly the involvement of the Society in the silk trade.

Soon after the dispatch of Cabral's report to the Visitor in India, Valignano met his demands for more help by sending thirteen Jesuits in 1577 and then eight more the next year, and in addition four Europeans and four Japanese were admitted to the Society in Japan in 1578. At last there was more than a skeleton staff of Jesuits in Japan; no longer would a priest, sometimes even an irmao, be left for months on his own. However it also meant that the problem of finding an income adequate to the needs of the Society's activities became even more acute, so that Cabral felt forced to ask Valignano to send no more Jesuits to Japan for the time being.

THE FIRST VISIT OF VALIGNANO TO JAPAN

It was in July 1579 that Valignano arrived in Japan for the first time and began his inspection of the work of the Society there. He stayed until 1582, returning in 1590 and staying for two years on that occasion; and he then made his final visit in 1598 when he stayed until 1603.

Valignano's first months on Kyushu led to a period of deep disappointment and disillusion on the part of the Visitor. So upset was he by what he discovered about the Christian community there and the style of Fr Cabral's leadership of the Society – and in effect of the Church, since the Society was directly responsible for the Church, there being no secular clergy – that he was bewildered as to what must be done. Fortunately for the Church and his Society he did not rush into action, though he did write some letters expressing opinions which he would later change.

Much of the shock can be explained by the contrast between the reality he found on Kyushu and what he had been reading in the letters from Japan while still in Europe and later in India. Indeed while he was at Macao, on his way to Japan, he was full of the certainty that a glorious Christian Church was rapidly coming into being there, lacking only Japanese clergy and a bishop of its own.

The problem of the lack of an indigenous clergy would soon be solved, he felt certain, because of the vast number of suitable candidates he assumed to be eagerly awaiting training in Japan. So excited was he by the prospect of this imminent triumph that at Macao he arranged an elaborate procession followed by a High Mass to celebrate the success of the mission in Japan.

This discrepancy between what had been written in the letters to Europe from Japan and the reality was something that he could deal with immediately. As Visitor he initiated a set of new rules about how the Annual Letters to Rome were to be prepared and transmitted. However, the weakness of the Church and the unhappy state of the Society in Japan were much more serious problems and initially he did not know what to do. He decided that for a year he would travel round all the stations and listen and observe. Only then would he begin to plan his strategy.

Hitherto the Annual Letters had been simply a collection of all the letters sent in by members of the Society without any attempt to check and edit. 'Whole kingdoms' had been reported converted when, as we have seen, it was the compulsory conversion of the people of a local daimyo. Genuine stories of piety and acts of love by Japanese Christians were taken to represent the general condition of these 'converts' on Kyushu, while other letters were clearly attempts to elicit support and interest on the part of European readers rather than report what was actally going on – the dark side of support from the daimyo, the problems as well as the successes. This was something he could correct immediately and so Valignano set out new regulations for the Annual Letters. Every Jesuit was encouraged to write directly to his Superior without any limit on how often, informing him of all that he was doing, was puzzled about, was happy about or could not understand in the situation in which he found himself. However, the Annual Report was to be drawn up by the Mission Superior in two parts, the first part was to be a general survey of the situation in Japan in terms of the mission's work and the political situation and part two was to be a series of specific reports on each mission station. Valignano insisted that only 'la pura verità del cose' should appear in those letters. Part two of these reports were normally to be collections of letters from the senior missionaries in the various areas of Japan but now, under the new instructions, their letters were to be thoroughly checked before they left Japan. Even so Valignano was concerned that the world of Japanese culture was so different from anything people in Europe had experienced that he suggested to the General that these Annual Letters should not be printed and published until a general history of the Church in Japan had been compiled and published, which would provide a background into which the Annual Letters could then fit sensibly.

The other problems were much more serious; indeed they were fundamental as to whether, humanly speaking, there was any future for the Society in Japan at all. So worried was Valignano that Schutte calls this period of some months in 1579 and 1580 a period of 'Agonising Indecision',[7] a very unusual situation for the usually confident and certain young Italian Visitor to be in. In his letters to the General in 1579 and 1580 we can see Valignano struggling to recognise the fact that while Cabral had been Mission Superior the Christian Church in Japan had grown, and to give him credit for this, and yet to explain why he believed that under Cabral's leadership the future of the Society and of the Church was gloomy indeed because of the style of Cabral's government. We have seen how Valignano, while still in India, had ensured a significant reinforcement of Jesuit strength in Japan and had strongly recommended that the new recruits immediately begin language study. When he arrived the Visitor found these men complaining that Cabral had made no arrangements at all for them to study Japanese language seriously, despite Valignano's insistence on this as a necessary preliminary to their being of service. Much more serious was the fact that these men were already being influenced by the division within the Society between the European and the Japanese members. Whether Cabral was to blame for the poor estimate of Japanese people held by many of the Jesuits or not, it is quite clear that he held such a poor opinion himself and did nothing to hide it.

In a letter to the General dated 27 October 1580, Valignano summarised the situation under five heads. The first dealt in detail with the fact that Cabral did not follow the Constitution of the Society in his administration which was too dependent on his personal will. The second dealt with the problems of the members of the Society being overstretched to cope with all the work, having to live alone for far too long periods and having little time for their personal spiritual refreshment. Under the other three heads Valignano deals with the bad relations between European and Japanese members of the Society.

The Japanese irmao are treated in a harsh and humiliating manner quite differently from European irmao. They also had to conform to European manners of etiquette, diet and general living conditions which they found dirty and repulsive. Valignano goes on, 'nothing could be expected from such a condition of affairs but only certain ruin. We live in their territory and without them the Society can neither function nor continue to exist.' After all, the Visitor points out, these irmao along with the dojuku are the people who do the preaching and teaching and convert the pagans, yet there was no novitiate for them and no planning for them to undergo higher academic education as is appropriate to members of the Society in training. Cabral had made it clear that he believed this would be dangerous. The Japanese were a proud and arrogant people and this training would mean that Japanese Jesuits would rapidly come to think themselves as good as, if not better than, their European associates. Cabral the Portuguese ex-conquistador clearly did not think there was much need for academic development of any member of the Society in the Japanese situation since, as Valignano complained, he had made no provision for further study to be undertaken even by the European irmao.

On the issue of good academic and spiritual formation in the Society, the Visitor took rapid action. That same month, October 1580, a seminary was opened in Arima. The daimyo, Harunobu, had donated an old Buddhist temple for the purpose. Valignano had seen to the modification of the building personally and twenty-two students, Japanese and European, began their studies there. He also laid down the pattern of life for the student body and the curriculum of the institution. It would also appear that it was in connection with the training of these students, and those in the institute at Azuchi and any others that might be developed, that he composed a Catechism at Funai while staying there towards the end of 1580 and in the first few months of 1581. This was clearly not a catechism in the usual sense of a book of instructions for the ordinary person preparing for baptism. It was an elementary textbook of theology for students. An almost complete Japanese version of it in the form of student notes was recovered in 1960 by a Japanese researcher.[8] Its chapters were divided into topics under one of two heads, that is either dogmatic theology, or what used to be called in Scotland Apologetics. In this case the sections under the latter head were predominantly highly polemical discussion of Buddhist thought and a censorious discussion of Buddhist ethics. Various catechisms for those preparing for baptism already existed in Japan and it was not until the formal Consultation held by the Society in 1592 at Nagasaki that one was fixed on as 'the' catechism for the mission in Japan – that known as the Dochirina Kirishitan.

The other main problem facing the Society in Japan, as it appeared to him, was the very poor level of spiritual life in the congregations of the Church which he had seen so far. Valignano's 'agonising indecision' continued as he went about his task of visiting all the members of the Society and all the Christian communities in Japan. In addition he also felt challenged by the question of whether the Society should continue to attempt to expand the Church in Japan, when its resources were so limited and were scarcely capable of giving minimum pastoral care to the present number of Christians.

It was the influence of four men that changed his viewpoint, ended his indecision and restored his enthusiasm for the work in Japan. These were the daimyo Arima Harunobu and Omura Sumitada, and two Jesuits, one a senior Italian priest, Fr Organtino, the other an unusual Japanese irmao, the eighty-year old scholar and physician Paulo Yohoken, with whom Valignano was so impressed that he made him his personal assistant.

Initially his assistant and the two daimyo helped him to understand how grave the problems he faced were. They helped him realise how superficial many of the conversions on Kyushu were, and they also brought home to him how deeply aggrieved the Japanese irmao and dojuku were over their treatment within the Society and how many of the Christians were deeply upset by the behaviour of some of the European missionaries. Their wisdom and their virtues helped to establish in him greater affection and trust in Japanese people and these men put him in touch directly with the Japanese irmao and the ordinary Christians. When Valignano eventually reached the churches of the Gokinai – the 'samurai' churches that had grown under Fr Vilela and Frois and were now under the leadership of Organtino – he found churches of the quality which, in his initial mood of disillusion, he had believed were only the product of the rather imaginative 'public relations' Annual Letters. The influence of these four men, and the manifest piety and devotion of the churches in the Gokinai as well as those gathered round d'Almeida's charitable foundations in Bungo, helped the Visitor to decide on a policy for the future of the Church and of the Society in Japan.

What had immediately struck Valignano in the Gokinai was that, in dramatic contrast to the litany of complaints he had been receiving in so many parts of Kyushu, here Fr Organtino was the beloved 'Bateren Organ'. In obvious and deliberate contrast with the views of Cabral, Organtino had tried at all times to live a life that was as Japanese as possible. Although he was deeply disturbed about some aspects of Japanese culture, primarily its sexual mores, Organtino's experience of ten years had confirmed his enthusiasm for the qualities of the Japanese character and the many worthwhile values in Japanese culture. As the weeks passed in the second year of his stay in Japan, he began to put together in his mind a policy for the Society and the Church in Japan that was based on a renewed confidence in the abilities of the Japanese people and the value of Japanese culture. This time, however, this assurance was based on personal experience and tried judgement.

We can see how Valignano's mind was working by two documents he issued as formal instructions, the first in June 1580, *Regimento para el Superior de Japon* (Rules for the Japanese Superior) and the other which he sent off to Rome a few days later on 28 June 1580, *Regimento que se ha de guardar nos semynarios* (Rules for the care of our seminaries). He also tested and tried out his ideas as they were taking shape in a series of consultations with all the other members of the Society. Here he was acting according to the Constitution of the Society and not in the personally imperious and autocratic style that Cabral had been using. These consultations, whose 'acta', probably best translated as 'full minutes', were scrupulously reported to the General in Rome, discussed the issues that were fundamental to the future of the mission in Japan and around which Valignano eventually worked out the mission policy for Japan. This policy was one of adaptation or acculturation and was the foundation for the even more radical development of that policy in China. The key issues discussed were, should other Orders be invited in to help with the work, should a bishop for Japan be appointed, should seminaries be founded that would not only prepare men for the priesthood but also young laymen to become educated Christian leaders, how should the Society be organised in Japan and how far should its members adapt to Japanese culture, how were the dojuku to be fitted into the structure of the Society, and how were the Society and the Church to be financed?

One of the striking developments that began to emerge as he reported on these consultations was that Valignano was already, as early as his report on the first Bungo Consultation of 1580, looking forward to a genuinely Japanese Church in Japan under a Japanese bishop. This is revealed in his reporting of the discussion of difficulties foreseen over the appointment of such a bishop. At various times previously Valignano had changed his mind about what he held to be the best course. However he now makes a firm recommendation which is explicitly meant to lead to a truly Japanese Church. He had already recommended that as well as recruiting Japanese into the Society there should be a deliberate attempt to create a Japanese secular clergy. He went on to say that

> It was seen how unacceptable it would be to expose Portuguese and Japanese candidates for Holy Orders to a dangerous sea voyage which involved, besides, months of absence from Japan. Valignano suggested that His Holiness might perhaps grant an auxiliary bishop the authority of a Papal legate or nuncio. In this case he would have authority over the native secular clergy and be in a position to prescribe for them a rule of life, and when one of the native priests attained the requisite standard of virtue and learning the delegate could raise him to the episcopate.[9]

It is also important to note that in that same report Valignano points out that the Portuguese crown is impatient for the appointment of a bishop for Japan, but one appointed under the rules of the Padroado. Valignano insists that such an appointment under the Padroado would be quite wrong. The situation in Japan was not understood clearly in Goa or Lisbon, and given the nature of Japanese society and their fierce independence there was no way that a Portuguese colonial bishop should be appointed; and what he, the Visitor, was now suggesting was the only way ahead.

Before going on to consider further the development of Valignano's thinking on the missionary strategy to be pursued by the Jesuits in Japan, the granting of suzerainty over a Japanese city to the Society of Jesus has to be discussed. On 9 June 1580 the lord Omura Sumitada and his son Omura Yoshiaki granted the suzerainty over the port of Nagasaki and nearby Moji to the Fathers of the Society of Jesus in Japan. Before discussing why a Japanese lord should have done such a thing and the Society of Jesus go along with it, we need to consider the conflict among writers as to exactly what happened? C. R. Boxer gives a very long quotation from the Visitor's 'Summario' to the General of August, 1580.[10] It leaves the impression, though Boxer never says so explicitly, that Valignano had requested that the Society obtain control of Nagasaki and Moji. J. F. Schutte in discussing the case and basing his understanding on that same 'Summario' indicates that in it Valignano informed the General that as soon as he first met Omura in 1579, the daimyo had raised the possibility of granting the city to the Jesuits.[11] Since then Valignano had discussed it with the Fathers in the area and in Bungo, and the quotation given by Boxer is part of an explanation for the General in Rome of why he thought it was a good thing for the Society to accept the gift. This does give a very different picture of what happened to that suggested by Boxer.

Why did Omura make the offer? It was not primarily out of some sort of religious devotion but shrewd political judgement. He was under threat from a more powerful neighbour, Ryusoji Takunobu. If the port belonged to the Church then it could be a refuge for him even if defeated by his rival. He arranged that he should still receive the customs dues; and these would be great, for if the port belonged to the Church it was almost certain that the Portuguese 'Great Ship' from Macao would always come there. In fact, for technical reasons it was the best harbour for a Portuguese carrack and the captain would always prefer to go there anyway. In effect Omura had made a good deal for himself, especially since, although the document said the gift was in perpetuity, in Japanese law a donor could at any time take back such a gift.

Why did Valignano and the Fathers accept this gift? Probably the most important motive among those listed by Valignano was that it guaranteed them a base to which they could send people from other provinces displaced because of their faith, something that was happening regularly due to changes of rulers or the changing minds of rulers on Kyushu. The place could also be a refuge for the Fathers themselves in a time of massive unrest. In addition, since the daimyo was to continue to keep up the defences of the place and they were to receive the harbour dues, they were guaranteed an increase in income, a matter of vital importance to a mission whose expenditure always outran its resources – some of which, as we have seen, it never received or received only very intermittently. It must also be noted that the Fathers did not adminster or 'rule' the two towns, but appointed officers (yaku-nin) who ruled the two ports as if for the daimyo, though with some modification of the legal procedures and punishments inflicted in criminal cases which were suggested by the Society.

It was when Valignano had returned to Bungo from his visitation of the churches and mission in the Miyako that he laid down clearly and unambiguously the approach he believed necessary for the effective carrying out of the mission in Japan. The visit to the mission in the Gokinai under the direct leadership of Fr Organtino was, as we have seen, a tremendous boost to Valignano's spirit. Here was an area of dynamic Church growth where there had been neither compulsion on the part of daimyo for people to become Christians nor were the lords sympathetic to the mission in order to get a share of the Portuguese trade since no Portuguese ships came to Honshu. The Jesuit leaders, first Vilela and then Organtino and Frois, were sympathetic to Japanese culture and were enthusiastic and optimistic about the possibilities of a Japanese Church. This had clearly affected the whole atmosphere surrounding the mission and its work. Indeed Organtino was explicit about holding to two principles, that the mission be free of any identification with the Portuguese colonial state, and that Japanese culture and character were, with some correction and modification, a healthy foundation on which the mission could build the Church. He insisted that if only a hundred new Jesuits could be sent to Japan, and they all Italian, then all of Japan could become Christian.[12] His insistence on their being Italian is not irrelevant; whatever else they might be, Italians were never 'conquistadores'.

Organtino arranged that Valignano should meet Oda Nobunaga who appeared to be greatly taken with the startlingly tall and dignified Italian. Indeed, at the end of his six month stay when the Visitor wanted to take leave of Nobunaga, the dictator insisted he stay another ten days so that Valignano might be Nobunaga's guest of honour at a massive festival he was preparing. At that very public event Nobunaga went out of his way to show his special favour towards the Society of Jesus. The virtual ruler of Honshu had for some time been very sympathetic to the mission, though not in the least open to conversion as far as anyone could judge. He had granted Organtino a fine site for a new seminary at Azuchi near his new castle. There Organtino had had a handsome building erected and Nobunaga had visited it on occasion and more important, had granted a subsidy of rice for its upkeep. Each week an irmao or a padre would visit the castle from the college with a small gift of fruit or something similar for the lord, and Nobunaga's sons often returned these visits.

Valignano was deeply impressed by the spirit of the Christians in the many churches of the area and by the devotion of many leading men like Takayama Ukon. Here was a different world from that which had so depressed him during his first few weeks on Kyushu. So far from pessimism was the atmosphere in this mission area that Organtino was convinced Japan might soon be united again for the first time in over a hundred years, if Nobunaga was spared, and what an opportunity therefore lay before the Church. Whether Valignano was quite so optimistic as that is not clear, but certainly after his visit to the Gokinai his 'agonising indecision' was over and decisive action followed.

On his return to Bungo, Valignano drew up one of the most decisive documents of his career in which he laid down the cornerstone of his policy of accommodation. There is no English translation of this document so there is no accepted English name for it. Fr Jennes has called it *The Code of Behaviour*.[13] The original document is entitled *Advertimentos e Avisos acerca dos Costumes a Catangues de Jappao*, and it is readily accessible only in the Italian translation, edited with critical notes by J. F. Schutte, *Il Ceremoniale per i missionari del Giappone*.

In Japanese society there were two social hierarchies, a lay and a religious. Everyone knew where they were in one or the other, and how one behaved towards anyone else was determined by one's own and the other's position. In a sense there was also a hierarchy within the Society of Jesus, but it did not relate to Japanese society and in any case under the influence of Cabral racial distinction had distorted it. In any case, how did members of the Society and the dojuku relate to other Japanese, whether Christians or pagans, who all fitted into various Japanese categories which hitherto most missionaries had ignored, though a few, Organtino and Frois, had tried to understand and relate to this difficulty? Until then the mission had done nothing to cope with these problems, primarily because the problem had not been recognised as such. This could be seen very clearly in the pattern of life in the houses of the Society under Cabral's leadership. The problem was not only one of etiquette but life style in general. For example the keeping of animals to be slaughtered and eaten offended the Japanese, as did the general dirtiness of the European houses and of the Europeans. Again extreme shows of anger or high spirits were unacceptable forms of behaviour and were very distressing to Japanese people, since a civilised person always behaved with quiet dignity. The result was, as one Christian daimyo told Valignano, that many missionaries behaved in ways which in Japanese eyes made them appear ignorant louts. As Valignano put it in a letter a few years later,

> As a result of our not adapting ourselves to their customs, two serious evils followed, as indeed I realised from experience. They were the chief source of many others: First, we forfeited the respect and esteem of the Japanese, and second, we remained strangers, so to speak, to the Christians.[14]

The Advertimentos shows such knowledge of the detail of Japanese culture and etiquette that there must have been one or more sophisticated Japanese advisers to the Visitor. There was no way that Valignano, who had very little Japanese, could have absorbed all this knowledge in the months of his stay so taken up with business and travel.

The work was divided into seven chapters:

1: How authority is won and is preserved in dealings with Japanese.
2: How the confidence of the Christians is to be gained.
3: Of the forms of politeness which the Fathers and the irmaos have to observe with externs (non-Jesuits).
4: The manner to be adopted in presenting and receiving sakazuki and sakama (rice wine and dessert).
5: The manner to be adopted by the Fathers and the irmaos in dealing with each other and with other members of the household.
6: The manner of receiving ambassadors and other persons of distinction. Invitations to be sent and presents to be made.
7: How our houses and churches in Japan are to be built.[15]

In this work every possible detail of the life-style of the missionaries from the Provincial to the most newly recruited dojuku was laid down. The dojuku and the Japanese irmao no longer had to put up with so much that had upset them heretofore. Houses were to be built in the Japanese style, with special rooms for the tea-ceremony which was an obsession with the Japanese at that time, as well as other appropriately designed rooms for greeting important guests and women visitors. Japanese diet and Japanese standards of cleanliness, especially in toilets and kitchens, were to be scrupulously followed. Correct forms of address were always to be used in both written and spoken Japanese. All were to maintain calm dignity with no loss of temper nor extremes of laughter. All associated with the mission were now to be apportioned a grade, these grades were drawn from those of the monks and dojuku of the Zen-shu Buddhist order, perhaps the most highly regarded in Japan at the time. In this way members of the mission would be able to fit into the elaborate forms of courtesy and politeness which were fundamental to Japanese life. Only in the matter of dress did Valignano hold back; members of the Order were to wear black cotton cassocks and not the silk kimono.

This document has been summarised by a number of authors, but only by reading some at least of the text can the nature of Japanese culture be glimpsed and the seriousness of what Valignano ordered be appreciated. There is not scope in a study of this length for detailed reproduction of much of the text of the *Advertimentos*, but the following paragraph may suffice to give the reader an insight into the radical departure from any kind of European cultural imperialism which was demanded by the Visitor:

> If a Father fell in with mounted persons of the first, second and third rank, he had to dismount if they did the same; if they were on foot he was not to remain in the saddle. If he encountered a group of pagan samurai of the fourth class who, on meeting him, sprang to the ground, he, too, was to dismount. The Japanese Superior, however, could remain in the saddle, but he had to remove his hat, draw his foot from the stirrup on the side where they met him, and laying both hands on the front saddle-bow make a reverence to them. When one or two Christians, even though they were samurai, crossed the street, a Father did not need to dismount but, after performing the above ceremonial, could ride on. The irmaos, however, were to dismount and in special circumstances even anticipate them and tender them a special greeting. In pagan localities such ceremonial was a safe course for even a Father to adopt when a lord with a large retinue encountered him on foot.[16]

This development delighted Organtino and Frois, but the Japanese Superior, Fr Cabral, had already become increasingly unhappy with where he saw Valignano leading the Society. Before Valignano had set out on his visitation of the Gokinai, Cabral wrote to the General Everard Mercurian requesting that he be relieved of his post. He wrote at the same time, August 1580, to the Portuguese Secretary of the Society, Fr Fonseca, asking for the latter's support for his request. One important note in both letters is his advice that the General should not confirm any suggestions made by the Visitor about the future work of the Society in Japan.

When Valignano returned to Bungo he agreed to let Fr Cabral go, sending him to work in Macao and replacing him in Japan by Fr Coelho. C. R. Boxer and a number of other authorities declare that Valignano dismissed Cabral from his position. Although clearly Valignano's policies were distasteful to Cabral, and so contrary to the line which he had been pursuing that they could be deemed to have 'forced' him to go, Valignano did not dismiss him. Cabral formally applied to leave his post and Valignano allowed it only after an initial refusal which had provoked Cabral's appeal to the General.

When he had completed his visitation of all the Society's work in Japan Valignano held a final consultation with his Jesuits in Nagasaki, the Resolutions of which cover the same ground as the two previous Consultations he had had with the members of the Society in Bungo and in the Gokinai, and confirmed, with a few very minor modifications, the rulings of the *Advertimentos* on the accommodation of Japanese culture.

The Visitor left Japan for Macao and there composed a document summing up the situation in Japan for the authorities in both Rome and Lisbon – the '*Japanese Summary*' of 1583. He insisted that Japan was the most important missionary situation facing the Catholic Church. In this nation the Jesuits now had one college, one novitiate, two seminaries and ten residences, some with only two Jesuits but some with collegial communites of seven or eight. There were 200 churches with about 150,000 Christians served by mission personnel of about 500; he included in this number the lay leaders or kambo, and the dojuku. Of the Jesuits proper, thirty-two were priests all of whom were Europeans, fifty-three were irmaos, twenty of whom were Japanese. In this summary he pressed hard on the point that there was tremendous opportunity here, but that the work was desperately in need of funds and more had to be done on that front as well as in supplying new and well-prepared Jesuit recruits for the mission. These latter were necessary if the institutions for the preparation of a native clergy were to be effective. Because of the deep gulf between the cultures of Japan and Europe as well as the difficulty of the Japanese language, the creation of a Japanese clergy as soon as possible was essential for the future good of the Church.

It is important to note that despite all these difficulties and needs which he is urging on his readers, Valignano is equally firm in his insistence that other Orders should not be brought in to help. This is because the very many sectarian splits among the Buddhist Orders had brought them disrepute and it would an unhappy parallel if other Orders came and did not follow the same 'way' as that now being followed by the Jesuits. He is very firm on this issue and although he makes no reference in this report to Spain or the Spanish conquistador mentality his readers in Lisbon and Rome could not but link this with his letter of 28 August 1580 in which he complained of the dangers of welcoming to Macao the Franciscans who had been refused entry to China. He had pointed out very explicitly their close relations to the conquistadores of the Philippines who were apparently planning the conquest of China. Although he knew that there were some Spanish Jesuits in Manila and Mexico who supported this idea, he had pointed out how wrong he thought it was from the point of view of the Church to have anything to do with such a plan and, shrewdly, also how it must appear to the Portuguese let alone the Japanese or Chinese![17]

The main burden of the *Summary* was the matter of finance, just as it had been the one consistent worry throughout his three years in Japan. It had not gone away or been resolved as so many of the other problems with which the Visitor had started. These had lightened as he came to understand Japan and witness the real success the mission was achieving, and had come to appreciate the deep faith of many of the Japanese Christians. The problem of financial support was indeed becoming particularly acute since, as the Church expanded and he attempted to create the necessary educational institutions to provide an indigenous clergy and an educated Christian lay leadership, the gap between income and expenditure became worse. At this time, with the wars of the Sengoku Jidai not yet over in Kyushu, and barely suppressed on Honshu by Nobunaga, Japan was a poor country. Certainly some powerful lords were Christian but their resources were strained, particularly those on Kyushu, because fighting still went on there and the Christian daimyo were all on the defensive in what appeared might be a losing struggle. As a result Valignano insisted that the Jesuit investment in the silk trade between China and Japan should carry on by means of the Portuguese carracks – an involvement which was a constant embarrassment to the General in Rome – as it was absolutely essential to the survival of the mission. He pointed out that, like all their other sources of income, even it was not reliable because ships could be lost as they had been in two of the previous eight years.

The work of the mission and Church was expanding as he had explained, but there was another essential development that he believed should take place which he had not yet initiated for lack of funds. This was a plan to replicate in the other two main centres the work that had been begun by d'Almeida of a hospital and home for foundlings. Indeed he planned that there should be one agency organised by the Society which would provide, as well as a hospital and foundling home, a 'pawnshop' where people in need could get help at minimal interest and keep themselves out of the hands of moneylenders who, at that time in Japan, were charging between seventy and eighty per cent. This development was an essential part of the proclamation of the Christian message to the people of Japan but, as we shall see later, when the same procedure was followed in China, it led to the Society being condemned as money-lenders by their European Christian critics.[18]

Massive new sources of support would have to come from Europe until Japan was united, at peace, and under Christian rulers or rulers at least sympathetic to the Church. The Visitor asked the General to explain the situation to the Pope, if he Valignano did not come to Europe to do it himself, and point out that what was needed were:

10,000 ducats as annual income and 30,000–40,000 as capital. If, in addition to defraying the building costs of the German College and the Roman College, the Holy Father was in a position to make available an annual subsidy of 10,000 ducats to each of these institutions, and erected so many seminaries in different places as well, he would also be anxious to help Japan, where there was question not of a single house but a whole province with more than twenty houses and where the poorest Christian community in the whole wide world lived. It would assuredly be a noble crown for him in heaven to have put this new Christian Church on a satisfactory financial basis; for, if the necessary funds were made available, Japan could in the course of less than thirty years be wholly or at least in great part Christian.[19]

It was primarily to deal with this terrible problem of finance that Valignano decided to return to Europe. Indeed, struggling with the problem of whether to stay or go in the last few weeks before the Portuguese carrack for the year would leave, he hit on the plan for his famous Japanese Embassy to Catholic Europe. He decided to take with him to Europe four young Christian men of aristocratic stock, related to the Christian daimyo of Kyushu, as 'ambassadors' to lay before the Pope and the Catholic monarchs and princes of Europe the needs of the Japanese Church. He decided on this only at the last minute and only two of the young men chosen were related to the daimyo and then only distantly, Mancio Ito and Miguel Chijiwa. The other two, Julian Nakaura and Martinho Hara, travelled as assistants to the others. Technically the two young 'ambassadors' were meant to represent Otomo Yoshishige, Omura Sumitada and Arima Harunobu. They were in fact chosen from among the seminarians by Valignano who got the latter two daimyo formally to agree to their recognition, but had no time to discuss it with Otomo Yoshishige, who agreed to it, somewhat bemusedly, after their departure. When Valignano and the young ambassadors reached Goa, Valignano found instructions from Rome for him to remain in India, and so he sent the young men on the rest of their way to Rome escorted by other Jesuits. Their visit to Europe was an extraordinary event. It created a great deal of interest in Japan in Portugal, Spain and particularly in Italy, where the 'ambassadors' attended the Papal coronation of Sixtus V and were received very cordially by him. Among some of the other high-points of their visit was their being made senators of Rome and in Venice having their portraits painted by Tintoretto. The four young men were deeply impressed by Catholic Europe, at that time in the full ferment of Catholic reform. By the time they were preparing for their return journey, they had become very dedicated Christian ambassadors to their own people. They were, however, returning to a Japan that had changed dramatically since their departure.

THE REGENCY OF TOYOTOMI HIDEYOSHI

Toyotomi Hideyoshi was, like the future Shogun Tokugawa Ieyasu, a brilliant general in the service of Oda Nobunaga, and like his leader and friend committed to the idea of re-uniting Japan. When Nobunaga was obliged by the samurai tradition to commit suicide rather than fall into the hands of his enemies when he was attacked unexpectedly on 20 June 1582 by one of his own generals, Hideyoshi took over the task of his dead leader. In fact he far surpassed what Nobunaga had achieved, and by 1590 he had united virtually all of Japan in a way not seen for over a hundred years. During Nobunaga's period of authority military conflict had never ceased, but under Hideyoshi order was made truly effective over most of Japan. He issued edicts which became laws, laws by which he felt bound himself. Some of these outlined a pattern of society that remained throughout the succeeding two centuries of the Tokugawa Shogunate. Hideyoshi could not be made Shogun by the Emperor, as he would have liked, because of his lowly birth, and so he was granted the title Kampaku (Regent), which changed to Taiko (retired Regent) when he nominally gave power to his nephew, though he was always the de facto ruler of Japan while he lived. He died in 1598, desperately seeking to ensure that his young son Hideyori would continue to rule Japan. This son was born late in Hideyoshi's life, and in 1596 he transferred the title Kampaku to the young boy from his unhappy nephew, Hidetsugu, who was then executed.

Some of the key elements in his legislation with long term effects were the obligatory handing in of all weapons by farmers, the annual survey of all arable land for tax purposes, and legislation which held people to the class in which they were and prevented the kind of social mobility which had allowed someone like himself to become Kampaku. Indeed the rigid class distinctions with the privileged role of the samurai so characteristic of the Tokugawa age was prefigured by Hideyoshi's legislation.

Perhaps the other most important undertaking of Hideyoshi was the invasion of Korea in 1592 with the aim of achieving suzerainty, not only over Korea but also over China. After initial success against the Korean forces, a Chinese army forced the Japanese on to the defensive, but Hideyoshi did not give up and the last Japanese forces were not withdrawn till after his death.

Initially the Christian community and the Jesuits were happy at the coming to power of Hideyoshi, and he continued to put down vigorously the armed militant Buddhist groups such as the Ikko. There were many devout Christians in his entourage. Takayama Ukon became commander of his guards regiments; Konishi Yukanaga commanded one of the two armies the Kampaku sent into Korea; Gamo Ujisato was a senior officer in his bodyguard and Manase Dosan was a court physician. Things looked very well early in 1583 when the indefatigable Organtino not only got a grant of land from Hideyoshi on which to build a new church and Jesuit Residence near the Kampaku's new castle in Osaka, but Hideyoshi paid Organtino the public honour of accompanying him to choose and then lay out the site.

While Hideyoshi was planning his move to bring Kyushu into the new united state he was creating, in 1587 the Christian daimyo of the island called him to help them. The Shimazu clan of Satsuma had begun a campaign to dominate all of Kyushu and were succeeding. The venerable Christian leader Otomo Yoshishige came out of retirement to lead the opposition, but soon saw the situation as hopeless and appealed to Hideyoshi. The Kampaku led a force of 250,000 to Kyushu and brought the island fully under his control and redistributed the fiefs among the daymo. In this redistribution the Christian daimyo did well. When resting after the campaign at Hakata, a seaport on the north coast, Fr Coelho, the Jesuit vice-Provincial arrived on a well armed Portuguese ship in order to congratulate him on the success of the campaign. He had been invited by Hideyoshi to rendez-vous with him there. Their meeting was cordial and Coelho's request for land at Hakata for the building of a church was readily agreed to by Hideyoshi.

That night the Regent sat late drinking with Seyakuin Zenzo, an enemy of the Jesuits and a man with a particularly bitter hatred of Takayama Ukon, Hideyoshi's guards commander. Ironically they were both getting drunk on Portuguese wine which Coelho had brought as a gift to Hideyoshi. Hideyoshi suddenly summoned Ukon and demanded that he renounce his Christian allegiance as a proof of his loyalty. Ukon refused and was sent into exile. After this Hideyoshi, still in the middle of the night, sent to the astonished Coelho a dramatic four point letter and demanded an immediate reply:

Why do you missionaries so anxiously, even forcefully, try to make converts?
Why do you destroy Shinto shrines and Buddhist temples and persecute monks instead of being conciliatory to them?
Why do you do such unreasonable things as eat useful animals like horses and cows that serve people?
Why do the Portuguese buy many Japanese and take them to their country as slaves?

Coelho managed to produce a formal written reply there and then. He pointed out that the missionaries did not force anyone to convert – they had no power to do so – and the destruction of Shinto and Buddhist buildings had been done by Japanese Christians whom the Society did not control. He also pointed out that the missionaries had never eaten horsemeat, and nowadays rarely ate meat except a little veal occasionally which they would stop completely. He also pointed out forcefully that the selling of Japanese as slaves was being done by Japanese, the Society had condemned the trade and had threatened the Portuguese involved with excommunication: it was the Kampaku who could stop it by issuing an ordinance forbidding it. This irenic reply appeared to make no difference, and the next morning Hideyoshi raged publicly that the padres were threatening his authority and were seeking power just as the militant Buddhists had done. So now he was issuing an order for the expulsion of all the padres from Japan.

The edict of expulsion took two forms, one form circulated to all officials in Japan and a shorter one was sent to the missionaries. What is significant about the longer edict is that it still allows freedom of religion to all except lords with estates above a certain minimum size. They could only become Christians with the express permission of the Regent. If lesser people wanted to be Christian that was their personal choice. No lord was permitted to force conversion on his people and much of the rest of the document insists that the padres have been as bad as the dangerous Ikko monks whom Nobunaga as well as Hideyoshi had had to fight. The shorter edict sent to the padres is rather different. It insists that Japan is the land of gods, and the evil doctrine of foreigners should not be allowed. The padres were condemned for breaking the law and destroying Buddhist temples, and they must leave the country within twenty days. However, Portuguese traders could still come and go for trade.

When he was formally served with the edict of expulsion, Coelho pointed out that there would not be another Portuguese vessel available for several months. This was recognised by Hideyoshi and the twenty-day ruling was set aside. All the members of the Society, whether European or Japanese, were called to assemble at Hirado on Kyushu. Those who left the Gokinai did so without the irrepressible Fr Organtino and the most famous Japanese irmao, Lourenço, who remained there in hiding.

In the end only three members of the Society left Japan when the Portuguese vessel arrived and they were irmaos who were going to Macao in order to be ordained. This was because, although a large number of principal churches and all the educational institutions in important centres like Osaka were destroyed, the Society continued some education of the students elsewhere surreptitiously, and it soon became clear that Hideyoshi was not going to enforce the edict any further. It remained in existence, as a permanent threat however, and perhaps that was all that it was meant to be. We will consider the reasons for the edict of expulsion later for it relates closely to the the crucifixions of 1597.

The Jesuits gradually dispersed out among their people again, now no longer wearing the black cassock but the kimono which Organtino had always wanted and had seen as consistent with the rest of Valignano's instructions in any case. Their work had now to be done without fuss or public show in many areas, worship was in private houses or in Jesuit residences in chapels which had no door coming in from the street. However, in many parts of Kyushu priests, irmao and dojuku could work freely and the church buildings were still in operation.

When the four young Japanese 'ambassadors' arrived at Goa on their return journey, Valignano, who was again appointed Visitor to the East, decided to accompany them back to Japan. They arrived at Macao in July 1588 and there Valignano heard the news of the new attitude of Hideyoshi. He sent a message to Hideyoshi asking whether he would be welcome to accompany the young men to Osaka to visit the Regent but in his capacity as ambassador of the Governor General of the Portuguese Indies and not as a missionary. Valignano did not want to appear to be publicly flouting Hideyoshi's edicts. Hideyoshi indicated his agreement and Valignano arrived at Nagasaki in July 1590. He was held up there for months, and then when he had begun his journey he was held up again in Morutsu. He entered Kyoto with an Ambassador's train in solemn procession on 3 March 1591.

At the dinner which followed the formal reception of the ambassador, Hideyoshi was as friendly as he had ever been, showing a great interest in the four young men, who told him of Europe and both sang and played musical instruments to entertain him. Hideyoshi then kept the young Portuguese irmao, Joao Rodriguez, talking most of the night. He had used Rodriguez in the past as an interpreter and now he wanted him again to be available to serve him. This was the Joao Rodriguez, often referred to as Tcuzzu (the Interpreter) who wrote the first true Japanese Grammar and an important *History of the Church of Japan*.[20] Valignano was then allowed to make a public visitation of all the Christian communities on Honshu as well as on Kyushu. He also took the opportunity to hold two meetings with the missionaries and instructed them carefully about their future conduct. In particular he ferociously condemned Coelho for his planning to fortify Nagasaki and try to hold it against Hideyoshi. He insisted they were to be circumspect at all times. He also formally accepted the four young 'ambassadors' into the Society of Jesus at a ceremony in July 1591. The Visitor returned to Macao in October 1592.

The young 'ambassadors' had brought with them to Japan the printing press with moveable metal type which Valignano had requested. This was now put into operation and produced a number of important publications. First of all a series of theological and spiritual texts in Japanese but printed in the Roman script. These were for irmao and dojuku within the Society who were the only Japanese who could read this script. The press also produced a body of classic spiritual texts translated into Japanese, some printed in Chinese ideograms for the elite who read the Chinese script, and for the more general reading public which was not inconsiderable in Japan others were printed in the kana syllabary. Indeed many of the women in daimyo and samurai families were both brought to the faith and had their faith grow through the medium of these books. It was also on this press that Fabian Fukan's apologetic *Myotei Mondo* was printed. Of the Jesuit press, George Elison, that rigorous but fundamentally unsympathetic scholar says,

> Valignano is the spiritual Father of *Kirishitan bungaku* and he also made substantial material contribution to the culture of the host country. The introduction of the moveable type printing press into Japan may be dated 1590, the occasion being Valignano's second visit . . . The literature eventually produced by the mission press included not only devotional tracts and the rather quaint intrusion of Aesop into Japan but also works of monumental importance for the study of contemporary Japanese linguistics, such as the VOCABULARIO DA LINGOA DE IAPAM (Nagasaki 1603–1604) and the exhaustive ARTE DA LINGOA DE IAPAM of Padre Joao Rodrigues Tcuzzu (Nagasaki 1604–1608). The translations of European works such as the *Imitatio Christi*

can only be called superb, and prove that language at least formed no barrier
to spiritual transmission.[21]

The great difficulty of working under the apparently arbitrary and at times
contradictory rule of Hideyoshi became more confusing than ever soon after
the Visitor's departure. First Hideyoshi transferred his headquarters to Kyushu
because of his invasion of Korea, which seemed threatening. However, of the
two main divisions of the invading army the first was commanded by Konishi
Yukinaga, a Christian, and was made up of contingents which were almost
entirely Christian. The soldiers in these regiments wore crosses and other Christian symbols on their shields and armour. At least two Jesuits were allowed
to operate with them in Korea as chaplains. They preached regularly to the
soldiers and also to the many Korean prisoners taken, some of whom came to
swell the number of Christians in Japan.

The other astonishing development was the coming to Japan of the Franciscans as missionaries at the invitation of Hideyoshi. The firm belief propounded
by Valignano in his *Japanese Summary* of 1583 had gained the approval
of the authorities in Rome and Pope Gregory XIII had issued the Brief *Ex
pastoralis officio* on 28 January 1585. This ruled that all Orders other than the
Society of Jesus were prohibited from beginning missionary work in Japan on
pain of excommunication. The Spanish friars in the Philippines, Franciscans,
Dominicans and Augustinians, all felt strongly that the Pope had been misled
by the Jesuits. It was however precisely their presence that Valignano feared.
Without using the words Spaniard or conquistador, he had made in point 7
of the 1583 *Summario* a plea for the Jesuit monopoly in Japan. He had insisted
that an increase in the missionary Orders in Japan would increase the suspicion
many feudal lords already felt about the political role of the missionaries. He
had gone on to say also,

> Japan is not a place which can be controlled by foreigners, for the Japanese
> are neither so weak nor so stupid a race as to permit this, and the King
> of Spain neither has nor ever could have any power or jurisdiction here.
> Therefore there is no alternative to relying on training the natives in the
> way they should go and subsequently leaving them to manage the churches
> themselves. For this a single religious order will suffice.[22]

He went on to emphasise how difficult it had been for the Jesuits to adjust to
Japanese ways, which was the only possible way ahead, and how new Orders
with the experience of Mexico and the Philippines behind them might not be
able or willing to make these adjustments.

In fact in 1584 a Franciscan and two Augustinians had stayed in Hirado on
Kyushu and the daimyo had welcomed them and suggested they encourage the
authorities in Manila to open up trade with Japan and also send missionaries.
Their arrival in Manila further whetted the zeal of the Mendicant Orders there

and made the Pope's ruling, when news of it reached them, appear all the more mistaken. There was a good deal of criticism of the Jesuits in reports written to the headquarters of the Orders in Rome, criticising their life-style, their involvement in the silk-trade and their apparent timidity in failing to stand up for Christian standards.

Meanwhile a Japanese Christian trader who had visited the Philippines used his contacts at the court of Hideyoshi to encourage the opening up of trade with the Spaniards. The contacts which then followed between Japan and Manila encouraged senior members of all three Mendicant Orders to hold a conference on the issue of the ban on their entry to Japan. They were able to convince themselves that Gregory XIII's Brief no longer applied, largely because of a subsequent Brief of Sixtus V giving the Franciscans the duty to plant houses of the Order 'in Indiis occidentalibus et in regnis Sinarum' which was deemed to include Japan. Whether they were right or wrong in canon law is not an issue there is room to discuss. In any case, as we have seen, the Church of the Spanish patronato was always the King's rather than the Pope's Church. In practice they felt free to go to Japan and were therefore very willing to act as ambassadors for the Governor in Manila when he decided to send an embassy to further sound out the possibilities of trade with Japan.

On 30 May 1593 Fr Pedro Bautista Blasquez, with three other Franciscans, left Manila for Japan as Spanish Ambassadors to Hideyoshi who received them at Nagoya. An agreement about the safe-custody of Spanish vessels, crews and merchants coming to Japan was reached and the details were sent back to the Governor by the captain of the vessel which had brought the embassy. The embassy now sought and gained permission from Hideyoshi to become a mission. The four Franciscans were granted a plot of land in Kyoto on which to build and begin their work. This in an area where the Jesuit churches had been destroyed and Fr Organtino and his fellow Jesuits had to lead worship in private houses only. Fr Blasquez built an entirely Spanish-style monastery and chapel and later added a small hospital. In September 1594 three more Franciscans arrived with fresh messages for Hideyoshi from Manila, and they also were allowed by the Kampaku to change their status from ambassador to missionary. They helped build another hospital in Kyoto. Support for these institutions whose Japanese staff were all Christians who had been baptised by the Jesuits, came from, of all people, Hideyoshi himself and his nephew Hidetsugu. Most support came from the Jesuit-created Christian communities of the Gokinai who were delighted to be able to help this very public Christian presence.

Blasquez now felt able to expand the work and went to Nagasaki. There he was allowed to open up for services for Japanese Christians a Jesuit church that had been closed with all the others in Nagasaki by order of Hideyoshi. The one Jesuit church left open was for the use of Portuguese and other foreign Christians only. The very large Christian population still worshipped in private houses or other discreet places with their Jesuit Fathers. Clearly this situation created deep distrust and tension between the two groups of missionaries and left an enormous amount of room for misunderstanding.

To the Jesuits, the Franciscans appeared to be recklessly flouting the conventions of Japanese culture as well as the edicts of Hideyoshi. They were thereby endangering not only themselves but the Jesuits and all the Japanese Christians. What impertinence to ask Fr Organtino to help build their new church when he had had his churches destroyed and had to work in private houses only. In any case these friars had flouted Papal authority in coming to Japan at all. To the Franciscans, already prejudiced, as we have seen, against the Jesuit missionaries in Japan, the Jesuits now appeared timid; why did they operate in this secretive manner, wearing kimonos, and on Honshu and even some parts of Kyushu no longer using church buildings? With so much to do why did they not want help in Japan? Why did Organtino so brusquely refuse to help fellow missionaries?

As C. R. Boxer has pointed out the Franciscans had some excuse for thinking the Jesuits were making a fuss about nothing. After all had not Hideyoshi received Valignano and the new Jesuit bishop, Pedro Martins? The printing press that Valignano had brought was being allowed to operate and a mass conversion to the Church under Jesuit auspices had happened in Higo province on Kyushu without any action by the Kampaku. Surely Hideyoshi no longer threatened the Church and the missions? The Jesuits, and more important those Japanese Christians who were also senior officials, thought they knew better and warned the Franciscans to beware, but to no avail.

In the background was the tension between the Portuguese authorities in Goa and Macao who bitterly resented this apparent Spanish encroachment into their area by the Spaniards in Manila. Although Spain and Portugal were ruled by the same King – from 1580 until 1640 – the two empires were still administered as separate and self-contained Spanish and Portuguese entities. However, at this time the conflict between the imperial authorities had little or no influence on this clash between the two missionary Orders and their mutual incomprehension one of another.

The whole issue then exploded into tragedy in connection with what is referred to as the San Felipe incident. A Spanish galleon sailing from Manila to Mexico was blown badly off-course and ran aground on Shikoku. The local daimyo took charge of the ship, detaining courteously enough the crew and the vessel. He suggested that the captain appeal to Hideyoshi for his decision as to what was to happen to them. Meanwhile the daimyo wrote to Masuda Nagamori, Hideyoshi's officer who dealt with such matters, informing him that the ship was heavily armed, had many padres on board and had a very rich cargo which he suggested should be confiscated. Nagamori came down to visit and talked with the officers who were deeply upset at the prospect of their cargo being confiscated. Although there is a great deal of controversy as to what exactly happened, it does seem clear that one or more officers in an attempt to impress Nagamori showed him a world map and the vast extent of the Spanish empire. On being questioned they appear to have insisted on the important role in those conquests played by the missionary priests. Despite the attempts by Cummins and others to ignore it, the image of the conquistador, the Christian soldier with sword in one hand and Breviary in the other, the missionary friar at his side, was a popular Spanish image at that time and it seems to have been vividly communicated to the Japanese officials.

On receiving reports of these interviews Hideyoshi again acted with ferocious speed, as on the famous night with Fr Coelho in 1587. The cargo was ordered confiscated and the crew and passengers including all the padres were to be returned to Manila. All the Franciscans in Japan were to be executed. Immediately troops in Kyoto and Osaka arrested Fr Blasquez and all the Franciscans and a number of Japanese helpers to the number of about 160. The officer in charge was Mitsunari Ishida, not a Christian himself but a close friend of Takayama Ukon. He cut the number to forty-seven and then to twenty-four, apparently out of compassion for the many innocent Japanese Christians caught up in this willy-nilly. These twenty-four were to be marched to Nagasaki for execution, being ignominiously displayed in the various towns and villages on the way. The condemned included six European Franciscans, Fathers Blasquez, de la Ascencion and Blanco, and Brothers de la Parilla, Garcia and de Jesus, and ten Japanese Franciscan dojuku, Paulo Suzuki, Gabriel, Tome Ise, Tome Kozaki, Joachim Sakakibara, Ventura, Leon Karasumaru, Mathias, Antonio and Luis. Three Japanese Jesuits who happened to be in Kyoto at the time were included, an irmao, Paul Miki and two dojuku, Joao Goto and Diego Kisai. The latter two took their vows so as to become irmaos of the Society of Jesus before they reached Nagasaki. There were also five Japanese lay persons who were perhaps helpers at the hospitals. In prison in Kyoto they had part of an ear cut off, a ritual of humiliation, and then they were paraded through the city in a ritual that was followed in a number of centres on their month-long journey to Nagasaki. On the journey and during their ritual processions, they sang hymns and both Blasquez and Paul Miki took turns in preaching to the crowds who gathered to watch them, crowds which often included many Christians who joined in their singing.

In Nagasaki the Jesuits were not allowed to attend to the prisoners, though at the last, on the execution ground, Joao Rodriguez, Hideyoshi's favourite interpreter and a Portuguese layman were allowed to talk to the martyrs. On 5 February 1597 the twenty-six − for two Japanese laymen had been added to the number en route − were crucified on wooden crosses, tied by ropes, not pierced by nails. On a given signal two soldiers went to each cross and thrust a long lance into the side of the victim. There followed extraordinary scenes as hundreds ran forward to dip pieces of cloth in the blood and take these rags away as relics, as well as pieces of the martyrs' clothing or pieces cut off the crosses.

The persecution however did not end there. In March Hideyoshi ordered all Jesuits to leave the country except for Joao Rodriguez and two or three Fathers needed in Nagasaki to care for the Portuguese commercial community. Some of the remaining Jesuit church buildings in areas of Kyushu where they had been safe hitherto were now destroyed. However, the Governor of Nagasaki and other daimyo stalled on obeying the instructions. In March the Jesuit bishop Martins left with the four Franciscans who had been missed in the original sweep. In October, eleven more Jesuits left while many still stayed on and hoped for the best. Throughout 1598 everything was at a standstill and no one seemed to know what was to happen, and then in September Hideyoshi died.

Why did Hideyoshi behave in the way he did, first with the edict of banishment of 1587 and then the crucifixions and intermittent persecution of the last year of his life? At the time the Jesuits tended to opt for either one of two explanations of the 1587 edict. One was that the whole episode was a result of a drunken fit of rage which he then could not go back on, but in fact did not then subsequently enforce. Others saw it as part of a long-term plan to eradicate Christianity, but thought that Hideyoshi was held back from it by his need for Portuguese trade for which, he believed, the co-operation of the Jesuits was still necessary. A modern Japanese historian, Neil Fujita, upholds the second alternative and points out that in 1587 and then at the time of the crucifixions Hideyoshi in his edicts talks of Japan as 'land of the gods' and sees here the beginnings of the Shinkoku ideology, devotion to which logically had to lead to the eradication of Christianity. This was clearly what happened later under the Tokugawas.

Mary Elizabeth Berry in her 1982 *Hideyoshi*, a detailed study of the life of the dictator, argues convincingly for a simpler explanation.[23] As Valignano warned, Hideyoshi was aware that many thought the padres were the forerunners of a European invasion and this thought was always at the back of his mind. More immediately, in 1586 at a very happy dinner and reception in Osaka, to the horror of Organtino, Ukon and the Christian officers around him, Fr Coelho had not only offered to get Portuguese help for Hideyoshi's projected invasion of Korea, but had gone on to pledge the support of the Christian daimyo as if this was his to give. Hideyoshi did not forget and when in Kyushu he found how strong the Church was there, and the honour in which the Fathers were held, he saw in the Society of Jesus a possible menace just like the militant Buddhists had been. Hideyoshi did make that comparison at the time and Coelho, after all, had talked at Osaka as if he were such a Buddhist abbot. The exile of Ukon may have been an accident of drunken anger that night, but the edict was meant as a fierce warning to the Jesuits. It was never really intended to be rigorously imposed; it was to be a warning and a sword held over their heads, and as such it clearly worked.

With regard to the crucifixions Professor Berry points out that Hideyoshi felt himself in a crisis situation. He had been happy to see the succession fall to his nephew, a successful administrator and soldier. Then, late in life he had a son, Hideyori, and his attitude changed dramatically. He became desperate to secure the guaranteed succession to power of his son. There was added to his actions a pattern of almost mad ruthlessness. This had led him not only to the killing of his nephew but, more remarkably, all of his nephew's family including his concubines. He also chose to remind everyone of his authority by executing, for reasons no one has yet satisfactorily explained, one of his oldest and closest advisers, Sen no Rikyu, the master of the tea-ceremony. Equally Berry believes that Hideyoshi felt he could make an example of the Franciscans as a warning to the Spaniards, whose aggressive intentions had been laid bare by one or more of the San Felipe officers. In a letter to the Governor of Manila, a reply to the latter's request for the return of the confiscated cargo, he was explicit on this point. He said the executions were carried out 'Because I learned that the promulgation of this religion was a part of the scheme of your country to conquer other nations'.[24] She believes that even at this date, although referring to Christianity being alien to the way of Japan, Hideyoshi was not an ideologue. It was the Tokugawas who were to create what has been called the Shinkoku ideology.

NOTES

1. Irmao was the name for a Brother in the Society of Jesus in Japan at this time. It referred particularly to the majority who had a status which did not really exist in the Jesuit Constitutions. They were not definitely temporal coadjutors but neither were they definitely in formal training for the priesthood and on the way to becoming spiritual coadjutors. The door was left open to this possibility when, according to the strict letter of the law, they should have been definitely classed as one or the other.
2. Valignano, *Il Ceremoniale*, p. 24, n. 2.
3. Schutte, *Valignano's Mission Principles*, part 1, p. 217, n. 127.
4. Ibid., p. 203.
5. Valignano, op. cit., pp. 256–8.
6. Schutte, op. cit., part 1, pp. 236–7.
7. Ibid., part 1, p. 271.
8. Fujita, *Japan's Encounter with Christianity*, pp. 83–4.
9. Schutte, op. cit., part 2, pp. 55–6.
10. Boxer, *The Christian Century in Japan*, pp. 100–2.
11. Schutte, op. cit., part 1, pp. 327–34.
12. Ibid., part 2, p. 117, quoting a letter from Organtino to a priest in Rome.
13. Jennes, *A History of the Catholic Church in Japan*, p. 48.
14. Schutte, op. cit., part 2, p. 163, quoting a letter to all Jesuit superiors in Japan.
15. Ibid., part 2, p. 164–5.
16. Ibid., part 2, pp. 177–8.
17. Moran, *The Japanese and the Jesuits*, p. 48.

18. By the Papal Legate, de Tournon, see Chapter 9.
19. Schutte, op. cit., part 2, pp. 309–10. A translation of part of Chapter 29 of the Japanese *'Summario'* of 1583.
20. See Cooper, *Rodriguez, the Interpreter.*
21. Elison, *Deus Destroyed*, p. 20.
22. Moran, 'Letters from a Visitor to Japan'.
23. Berry, *Hideyoshi*, pp. 225–8.
24. Quoted in Fujita, op. cit., p. 138.

Matteo Ricci (top left); Adam Schall (top right); Xu Guangqi (Dr Paul), Chief
Minister of the Empire (bottom left); and Candida Xu, Dr Paul's granddaughter,
generous supporter of the Society and leader in the Church (bottom right).
From R. P. du Halde's *Description Geographique, Historique, Chronologique,
Politique et Physique de l'Empire de la Chine*, 1735,
courtesy of the Trustees of the National Library of Scotland.

Alessandro Valignano, courtesy of Edizione di Storia e Letteratura.

Maria Kannon, courtesy of the National Museum, Tokyo.
These figures of a female Bodhisattva were popular among Japanese
Buddhists, but were placed in prominent positions in the homes of
the 'hidden' Christians as well, who treated them as statues of Mary
while still publicly conforming to the Shogun's orders.

A Japanese crucifixion, from the Album of Mark Dinely.

CHAPTER FIVE

The Christian Century in Japan, 1549–1650

To the Coming of the 'Closed Land'

Hideyoshi's last years were profoundly shaped by his determination that his son Hideyori should succeed him. He looked to his old comrade in arms from the days of Nobunaga, Tokugawa Ieyasu, to guarantee his wishes. When the deterioration of his health made it clear he had not long to live, he organised a system of government to cover the period until Hideyori was old enough to accede to power. In addition to his five bugyo (ministers) through whom he had administered the country since 1585, he added a group of the most powerful daimyo with Tokugawa as their head to be tairo (regents). He also appointed a group of three churo (intermediaries) to liase between the two groups in any conflict. Before he died, Hideyoshi had them assemble at court so that together they swore an oath of loyalty to the house of Toyotomi. Whether this governmental structure would have worked is debateable, but it was never allowed to.

From the beginning Ieyasu began undermining it by creating a whole series of marriage alliances between other important houses and his own – a large number of granddaughters were a considerable diplomatic asset. Those daimyo loyal to Hideyori became very uneasy and the bugyo formally accused Tokugawa of breaking the vows taken before Hideyoshi. The country rapidly became divided into pro- and anti-Tokugawa factions and open warfare erupted in the summer of 1600. The campaign was savage and brief. In October 1600 at the battle of Sekigahara, Ieyasu was completely victorious and Japan was his. He did not carry through a large re-distribution of fiefs at this time and only the key leaders in the fighting against him lost their lands. Many daimyo who were still, potentially at least, supporters of the Toyotomi held on to their lands and Hideyori himself still held a great fiefdom. However, Ieyasu was clearly the de facto ruler of Japan, and because of his noble ancestry he was eligible to receive the formal title of Shogun from the Emperor in 1603. Unlike the last great family to hold the Shogunate, the Ashikagas, Ieyasu set up the headquarters of his house far from the court at his great fortress at Edo, modern Tokyo. In 1605 he passed the title of Shogun to his son Hidetada, although he was still the final authority in the land until his death in 1616. Hidetada in turn retired as Shogun to become 'ogosho', retired Shogun, as his father had done, and was succeeded as Shogun by his son Iemitsu in 1623.

A measure of the authority that the house of Tokugawa had achieved was seen clearly in 1612 when Ieyasu replaced the Emperor Go-Yosei with another member of the royal house, Emperor Go-Mino-o. The new Emperor was married to a Ieyasu granddaughter. Then in 1629 the daughter born to the imperial couple became Empress in her own right, the Empress Meisho, the first woman so to rule since the eighth century. The apotheosis of the house of Tokugawa reached its climax when, at Ieyasu's grave at Nikko, a shrine was built to Ieyasu as divine, Tosho-dai-gongen, Great Shining Deity of the East.

Hideyoshi had not only encouraged Portuguese traders but also the development of Japanese initiatives in overseas trading. This was one strand of policy that Ieyasu continued and developed, encouraging Japanese mercantile activity and looking for international contacts to supplement that with the Portuguese. The first Dutch ship to reach Japan had come in 1600, and its navigator, an Englishman, Will Adams, stayed on in Japan and married a Japanese woman. He eventually replaced Fr Joao Rodriguez as interpreter and confidant of Ieyasu.

The Dutch established permanent contact in 1609 when their East India Company was allowed to set up a trading post at Hirado, and so the Shogun had a number of possible sources of international trade, the Spanish and Dutch as well as the Portuguese from Macao. In Will Adams and the Dutch he had another group who constantly warned him of Spanish power and that the Jesuits especially were not to be trusted. English merchants too made an attempt to organise regular trade with Japan in 1613, but they were not very successful and gave up again in 1623, though while they were there they added to the stream of anti-Iberian and anti-Catholic opinion being passed on to Japanese officials.

The Spanish connection was re-opened by Ieyasu in 1599, when he allowed the one Franciscan, Jeronimo de Jesus, who had survived Hideyoshi's purge, and who had returned to Japan illegally, to re-start the Franciscan mission in Japan with a new church and house at Edo. In return de Jesus acted as the Tokugawa intermediary with Manila to restore trade between Manila, New Spain and Japan. Ieyasu was particularly interested in getting the help of Spanish mining experience since he wished to develop the mineral resources of Japan.

The Macao silk trade still appeared to be the single most profitable channel of commerce but it no longer had the completely dominant role it once had. Indeed, under Hideyoshi and even more under Ieyasu, there was an increase in the use of 'red seal' ships, Japanese vessels licensed to trade abroad, some to the Philippines but most to Formosa and Indo-China. Under Ieyasu as under Hideyoshi Japan was opening out to the world and seeking a dominant role in the western Pacific. Despite the disaster of the Korean episode, among Ieyasu's advisers there was serious consideration of expansion abroad, perhaps by the conquest of Formosa or the Philippines. Japanese soldiers had already gained success abroad having been used as mercenaries by the Spanish authorities in Manila and elsewhere.[1]

In 1614 edicts were issued banning the practice of the Christian religion and exiling all Christian priests from Japan. At the same time, the 'retired Shogun' Ieyasu decided to end the Toyotomi threat against him once and for all and an attack on Hideyori's stronghold at Osaka was begun. On 4 June 1615 Osaka castle fell and Hideyori and his mother Lady Yodo died in the massacre of the garrison. Strangely, despite the edict of 1614, there were Christian samurai displaying Christian symbols on their banners and armour in the Shogun's army; but there were many many more in Hideyori's forces. There were also two Jesuit, two Franciscan, an Augustinian and two Japanese secular priests serving the garrison as chaplains. They were among the few who were allowed to escape with their lives except for one of the Japanese seculars, Fr Francesco Murayama, who was killed in the actual assault.

It was now, after the destruction of the last alternative source of authority to that of the Tokugawas that Ieyasu, although technically the retired Shogun (ogosho), reorganised the fiefdoms of Japan. This reorganisation was fundamental to the structure of Tokugawa rule, which in most other ways was an extension and development of what Hideyoshi had begun. Ieyasu's three sons were each given vast fiefdoms and only these three houses could provide a Shogun should there not be a direct heir in the future. All the other fiefdoms were then divided among the daimyo, who themselves were divided into two classes, the house daimyo, Fudai, and the outer daimyo, Tozama. In this connection it is important to note that the Shogun *qua* Shogun held a collection of fiefdoms which were the single largest holding of any daimyo. The Fudai were those who had supported Ieyasu throughout the years of his coming to power. The Tozama were the rest, when the active supporters of the Toyotomi had been weeded out. The Fudai daimyo were given the key fiefdoms in terms of military security, but they were not the richest by a long way though they and they only could hold office in the government of the Shogun. Many of the Tozama daimyo held richer fiefdoms than any of the Fudai, but they could not hold office. In addition they had to spend some time each year in Edo, and their wives and children had to live there always. The former semi-autonomy of the great commercial centres, Nagasaki, Osaka and Sakai was ended and they were governed directly by a bugyo, a governor appointed by the Shogun. The class divisions laid down by Hideyoshi were reinforced and it was reasserted that there could be no movement from one class to another and that only the samurai could possess weapons. This whole system is often referred to as the Tokugawa Bakufu.

Immediately after the issuing of the edicts against Christianity there was some sporadic persecution of Christians and numbers were executed, mainly in Arima and Bungo. This was done on the initative of the local daimyo, since Ieyasu appeared not to want the spilling of blood. However as each year passed a growing number of Christians were executed on the authority of different daimyo, sometimes by decapitation sometimes by burning, till finally in 1622 Hidetada began a massive campaign of persecution in earnest with the explicit aim of stamping out Christianity altogether in Japan. When Iemitsu became Shogun in 1623, he intensified the campaign. Christianity and the threat of foreign overthrow of the Tokugawa regime were inextricably bound together in his mind and he came to believe that all foreign connections with Japan should be cut off. He greatly intensified the movement begun by Hidetada of restricting foreign connections and made Japan a 'closed country'. This was not a logical development from the policy of Ieyasu, who had overseen an outward expansion of Japanese activity and a multiplication of Japan's international connections, it was the complete reversal of Ieyasu's policy.

This dramatic new policy of Sakoku can be seen to have begun with Hidetada's edict which restricted all foreign ships to Nagasaki and Hirado. Then in 1621 came edicts which limited the opportunites for Japanese to travel abroad and forbade the building of Japanese ships capable of trans-ocean journeys. This was a blow to what had been a steadily growing class of Japanese traders and to those in governing circles who, under Ieyasu, had thought of overseas conquest. The first edict which was referred to by the name Sakoku was that of 1633, which restricted the activity of the red seal ships as well as foreign ships, and forbade the return to Japan of any Japanese who had taken up residence abroad, of whom by that time there were several thousand. In 1635 another was issued ruling that no Japanese was allowed to travel abroad on pain of death. From late in 1637 until April 1638 the Shogun had the greatest difficulty in putting down a massive Christian and peasant rebellion, the Shimabara revolt, which appeared to make Iemitsu almost paranoid about the threat of a joint Spanish and Christian attempt to overthrow the Tokugawa regime. Consequently the next year, when peace was restored, the Macao silk trade was closed down and all contact with any Catholic land was forbidden. Although a minimum Dutch presence was allowed, it took the form of a virtual house-arrest situation on an island in Nagasaki harbour. A couple of Dutch ships a year closely supervised by the authorities became Japan's only connection to the outside world. In effect the 1639 edict turned Japan into the 'Closed Land'.

THE SOCIETY OF JESUS AND THE GROWTH OF THE CHURCH TO 1614

On 5 August 1598 Alessandro Valignano, now the Visitor for China and Japan arrived at Nagasaki from his headquarters at Macao. He brought with him the new bishop, Luis Cerqueira SJ, and eight new Jesuit recruits. On his last visit he had brought with him the printing press with metal type which he had requested the Kyushu 'Ambassadors' to bring from Europe. Now on this new visit he initiated another new development in the Japanese mission. By 1598 Fr Matteo Ricci in China had gone far in gaining a deep understanding of Confucianism and other systems of thought and religion in Chinese culture. This aspect of accommodation had been studiously ignored in Japan after the disaster of the Dainichi episode at its very outset, although in practice the Japanese irmao and dojuku must have used their own knowledge of the Buddhist tradition, in which they had grown up, in their preaching and teaching by which the Church in Japan had grown. Now however Valignano sought to initiate formal study of Buddhism and Shinto in the colleges and seminaries in a way not pursued hitherto.

There was no way, however, that anything could go ahead until it was clear if the missionaries were going to be tolerated in the country or not. As soon as he arrived in Japan, Valignano sought to make contact at least with those close to Hideyoshi, even if it was not possible to reach the Taiko himself because of the edict of 1587. Valignano sent Joao Rodriguez Tcuzzu to Fushimi castle with the Portuguese commercial envoys of that year. When they reached the castle they found Hideyoshi approaching death and feverishly organising the regency so as to guarantee the eventual succession of his young son Hideyori. The Jesuits were reasonably pleased with the men appointed to serve alongside the original five bugyo or ministers that Ieyasu had selected to administer the country in 1585. They knew all of them and some had shown sympathy and, at times, support for the Society and the Church.

Of more significance for the Society was the reception Rodriguez received at Kyoto. Hideyoshi sent out gifts to the Portuguese delegation but did not give them an audience. For months before he had been giving no audiences except to men with whom he was negotiating the regency arrangements. However, that strange and puzzling man granted Tcuzzu two lengthy private interviews on successive days.[2] Soon after this visit the great man died, although the official announcement of his death was delayed for some months in an attempt to prevent any disorder.

Once upon a time many in the Society had hailed Hideyoshi as their friend but now most were relieved at his death, though even the most critical of the Jesuits saw him as an extraordinarily able man with many admirable qualities. He certainly inspired great loyalty and affection, not only among those who knew him in the flesh but in writers and scholars since. James Murdoch, the doyen of foreign historians of Japan, said of his death, 'Thus passed away the greatest man Japan has ever seen, and the greatest statesman of his century, whether in Japan or in Europe'.[3]

Clearly if Hideyoshi's edict had been vigorously enforced Valignano and the new Jesuit recruits could not have come, nor would the rest still have been there to receive them. However, as long as the edict existed it could be invoked by any senior official in the provinces whenever it suited their purpose. Certainly this ambiguous situation gravely inhibited the ability of the Jesuits to maintain the seminaries and colleges necessary for the development of a Japanese clergy.

Valignano, Organtino and Tcuzzu appeared to be confident that their careful courting of the leading families in Japan which had led to their still having in 1600, even after the horrors of the martyrdoms, so many friends at court, would guarantee that the new government would regularise and secure the continuance of the mission. To this end Rodriguez Tcuzzu was sent off by the Visitor on a round of visits to as many influential officials and daymo as were even potentially sympathetic. He was formally to announce Valignano's presence in the country as Visitor and sound these leaders out about the possibility of having Hideyoshi's edict revoked or negated in some other way.

One of these visits was to Tokugawa Ieyasu in his capacity as the senior tairo, in whose hands Hideyoshi had left the government of Japan, and as someone whom the Jesuits suspected might become ruler in his own right in any event. Valignano had instructed Tcuzzu to ask Ieyasu for official patents permitting the Jesuits to reside in Japan. Tokugawa received Tcuzzu cordially, but pointed out it would hardly do for him publicly to flout an order of Hideyoshi's so soon after his death. He asked the Jesuits to be patient and Tcuzzu understood him to imply that all would be well in the future. A Franciscan who had returned to Japan and had then been discovered and arrested in 1599 had been given permission by Ieyasu to build a church, and the regent had used him to re-open relations with the Spanish authorities in Manila. This was annoying to the Jesuits in one sense, perhaps, but was another indicator that Tokugawa was going to tolerate the open operation of the missions and the Christian Church.

The civil war which soon broke out was decided in Ieyasu's favour at the battle of Sekigahara, 21 October 1600, and did not directly influence the position of the Church and the missionaries. Although many Christians fought on the side of the house of Toyotomi, Ieyasu did not see the opposition as a Christian opposition. As we have already noted, Ieyasu did not exact a bloody toll after his victory. The Church did lose, however, two outstanding Christian figures. One was the lady Gracia Hosakawa who accepted death at the hands of her loyal bodyguard to prevent her falling into the power of her husband's enemies during the fighting. She had been the highest ranking woman in the Church, something very important in a society so obsessed with rank as was Japan. She was also hailed subsequently in Tokugawa Japan as the model for all true Japanese wives, and her Christian faith simply eliminated from the official record, though her life and witness did become an inspiring part of Japanese Christian oral tradition.[4] The other loss was important in terms of the political realities of the day. Hideyoshi's brilliant Christian general who had commanded one division of the van of the invasion of Korea, Konishi Yokinaga, stayed loyal to the house of Toyotomi. A personally devout man and a constant and brave defender of Christianity, he was captured a few days after Sekigahara. As a Christian he refused the opportunity of seppuko and so was paraded through the streets of Osaka and Kyoto and then beheaded.

Soon after the victory of Ieyasu's forces, Valignano sent Tcuzzu to interview him again. As he had hinted would happen during their last meeting, things did turn out well for the Jesuits. Ieyasu issued official decrees permitting three major Jesuit Residences at the centre of each of the three major concentrations of Christian churches in Japan, Miyako, Osaka and Nagasaki. Valignano and Bishop Cerqueira took these decrees to mean that the Society was in fact free to operate anywhere in Japan. This optimism was further sustained when bishop Cerqueira was received by Ieyasu in 1606 at a formal reception, not as some kind of Portuguese representative but as bishop of the Christian Church in Japan, and when Fr Pasio, as vice-Provincial of the Society of Jesus, was also formally received, first by Ieyasu in his castle, and then by Hidetada, the new Shogun, in Edo in 1607. All seemed to be going as well as could be expected.

Before considering the two major developments in the work of the Society in these years we should note that Joao Rodriguez Tcuzzu was now chosen by Valignano to make his solemn profession. There were other senior Jesuits in Japan of experience who were clearly of greater educational and intellectual standing than Rodriguez, the qualities usually demanded for admission to solemn profession. Why did Valignano choose Rodriguez?

In his classic study *The Christian Century* C. R. Boxer repeatedly insists that the Jesuit mission was a Portuguese presence in Japan. Of course it was technically part of the Portuguese Padroado, everyone and everything had to go through Lisbon and we have already seen how Valignano from the beginning had trouble with this. Boxer, however, means more than that formal connection. He insists that the mission was fundamentally loyal to Portugal and that that loyalty to Portugal, partially at least, explains the clash with the friars from Spanish Manila. The clash of Jesuit and friar was Portuguese-Spanish nationalist clash in essence. In support of this position he points out that a majority of the European Jesuits in Japan over the years were Portuguese, while granting the significant presence of Spaniards and Italians. However, he fails to make clear that decisions on policy in the Society of Jesus were not achieved by simple majority votes of all members. He also does not notice that the overwhwelming majority of the professed of the Four Vows in Japan at any one time throughout the history of the mission, was made up of non-Portuguese. In the Society, where structures of authority were clearly defined and discipline strict, only the 'professed' priests could vote in those few situations where a vote was called for and, more importantly, only they could hold any senior office within the Society. Therefore to ignore the very important implications of this distinction within the grades of membership of the Society leads to a serious misunderstanding of the significance of the numbers Boxer quotes. An overall Portuguese majority of all who could claim the name Jesuit is not what matters, but the non-Portuguese majority of the 'professed' priests does matter.

Valignano's opposition to the coming of the friars has already been considered and his great fear of the Spanish conquistador mentality threatening the work of the Society in Japan was, by 1600, confirmed in his mind by the San Felipe affair and the flamboyance of Franciscan behaviour once in Japan. On the other hand Portuguese trade was one of the needs of the rulers of Japan that helped them accept the presence of the Society and the connection with Portugal was needed by the Society for financial support, even though, as we have seen, this was inadequate and very irregular. Portuguese feelings simply had to be assuaged whenever possible, and in 1600 the Society was very vulnerable to Portuguese criticism since only one of the professed priests serving in Japan at that time was a Portuguese, while there were four Italian and three Spanish members of the Society's elite. Joao Rodriguez was the most fluent speaker of Japanese in the mission, he had done sterling service as a go-between with Hideyoshi and now appeared to be acceptable to Ieyasu, and he was Portuguese. Who better then for the Visitor to choose to admit to the elite of the Society? Tcuzzu made his solemn profession on 10 June 1601.

Before he left Japan, Valignano looked round to see what other Fathers were worthy of this promotion and seven more took their vows, but only two were Portuguese. The Jesuit mission in Japan was never Portuguese in the sense of having the kind of loyalty to that state that would lead the Jesuit leadership there to give a high priority to Portuguese national ends, except perhaps in the mind of vice-Provincial Coelho in his more unfortunate moments. The opposition to the friars was largely because of their direct connection with the Spanish authorities in Manila and therefore their representing the conquistador tradition of Spanish controlled missions, and their complete lack of any sense that they ought to adjust in any way to Japanese culture.

Just as Valignano had earlier left the mission with its printing press which went on to produce a significant body of Christian literature in Japanese, so now on this third and last stay in Japan he initiated another new development in the work of the Society. This was the first serious attempt to study the principal teachings of the main Buddhist traditions and the traditions of Shinto. In Nagasaki in 1603 and at the seminary in Kyoto the next year the teacher of this course of instruction was a Japanese irmao, Fabian Fukan, who in 1605 published *Myotei Mondo* – a dialogue between two ladies, one Christian and one non-Christian – in which Christianity was expounded over against specific beliefs of Buddhism, Shinto and Confucianism.

Confucianism was not, in Japan, the official belief of the ruling classes as it was of the scholar-administrators of China. It could not therefore be the basis of an intellectual accommodation between Christianity and the indigenous culture as Fr Ricci was using it in China. In Japan it had little to do with Japanese culture in general at that time, and only a handful of intellectuals studied it.

However, one of those intellectuals who opened a private Confucian academy in Kyoto, Razan Hayashi, was very close to Ieyasu and contributed some elements of Confucian thought to the creation of what was developing into what some have called the Tokugawa ideology. Others have more awkwardly designated this ideology as that of 'Japan as Shinkoku', the land of the gods. This developing ideology, based administratively on the newly invented Buddhist parish structure, was predominantly Buddhist in thought. It put to use certain elements of Confucianism contributed by Razan and then its architects tried to show that all this was what Shinto meant anyway. The beginnings of this ideology were already clear among circles around Hideyoshi. That they were present in Hideyoshi's mind when he began the process that led to the Nagasaki martyrdoms, as is suggested by Neil Fujita, is not so clear as he suggests.[5] The most recent western expert on Hideyoshi, Mary Berry, does not think so as we have already seen. However this ideology was being actively developed by thinkers close to Hideyoshi during his time in power, though it was Ieyasu's close advisers, the Buddhist abbot Tenkai, the Zen monk Konjin Suden, and Razan Hayashi the Confucianist who were its principal architects.

The new programme of training all members of the Society in the main tenets of Buddhism, Confucianism and Shinto was appropriate and should have been done earlier. Whether such a training was of any use in helping Christians deal with this new ideological amalgam is another matter.

Before he left Japan for the last time in 1602, Valignano was able to take part in the ordination to the priesthood of the first Japanese Jesuits to make it from the ranks of the irmao, Sebastian Kimura and Luis Niabara. The former died a martyr in 1619. Valignano was able also to oversee the final months of training of the first Japanese secular priests who were ordained by Bishop Cerqueira soon after the Visitor's departure. This was the start of a rapidly growing Japanese secular clergy whom, as we have seen, he had always insisted were the key to the future. That this was too little too late we will discuss later in the chapter.

Despite the difficulties of the last years of Hideyoshi's life, the years 1590 to 1614 saw a massive growth in the number of Christians and some growth in the number of Jesuits in Japan. 1607 was the year when the Jesuits had the largest number of members of the Society active in Japan, 140. The number of Christians went on growing throughout the period. In 1614 when persecution began really seriously there were, most authorities agree, about 300,000 Christians in Japan. The overwhelming majority of these were the result of the work of the Jesuits, though the Franciscans also produced some congregations, and the few Dominicans and Augustinians who were allowed to enter the country in this period played their part also. The admirable devotion and fortitude of the friars and of those Christians associated with them, does not change the fact that the Society of Jesus had been the creative force in the growth of the Japanese Church. They had been central in its creation, but during these twenty years after 1590 the Japanese Church came into its own and developed a life of its own. This does not diminish the importance of the Jesuits but, more than anything else, is a proof of the success of the work of the Society of Jesus.

The martyrdoms in Nagasaki in 1597, which were followed by the destruction of a large number of church buildings on Kyushu as well as on Honshu, did not stop growth. In fact there was a spurt in growth which continued for two more decades. This growth was very different from the first developments on Kyushu when mass conversions organised by Christian daimyo had been the order of the day. The last of these mass movements took place, strangely enough, after the martyrdoms, in 1598 in the territories of Konishi Yokinaga. The vulnerability of this kind of movement, as was seen in so many other instances, was that when put under pressure to recant, as they were when a new daimyo took over after Yokinaga's death, about half the recent converts recanted. On the other hand it could be said that it was impressive that when put under pressure half the converts did not recant.

The constant growth that took place from the early 1590s was primarily not of this kind. People became Christians because, for whatever reason, they had chosen to do so. This growth took place among all classes in Japanese society except among the daimyo, since Hideyoshi made it plain that the conversion of daimyo was not acceptable to him. The great growth in numbers of Christians from all classes of society in congregations served by the Jesuits needs to be underlined. Historians have made much of the difference between the Jesuits and the Franciscans in their approach to Japanese society, pointing out the Jesuit emphasis on capturing the ruling groups within society in contrast to the Franciscan concentration on the poor and the outcast. This contrast fails to make clear that the vast majority of the Christians in the Jesuit congregations were not the upper class elite – though there were many samurai – but were drawn from the other classes of Japanese society, craftsmen, merchants, fishermen and peasants. In these twenty-odd years of Church growth that was particularly the case. These people were not, however, the outcasts of Japanese society, the groups called 'eta' and 'hinin' together with the very numerous lepers who were outside the normal class organisation. These the Jesuit missionaries chose not to work with directly since that would have cut them off from contact with many elements in the rest of Japanese society. That is why Valignano limited the class of patient accepted in care by the institutions begun by d'Almeida and the other charitable institutions that were developed; an order made much of by his Mendicant critics at the time and by some historians since. This prohibition did not exclude the majority of Japanese, but it did exclude 'outcasts' of whatever form. The Jesuit mission reached out to the majority of Japanese, not, as is often implied, only to the political and social elite. The Society's initial policy could be characterised as 'from the top down' but it did go down, and it was effectively cut off from the 'top', the daimyo, after 1598.

It is worth noting that not all the daimyo families that became Christian did so for reasons of convenience and then readily gave up when things were inconvenient, though clearly some did. The examples of Takayama Ukon and of Gracia Hosokawa must be remembered, and the great bravery of two daimyo widows, Kuroda Maria and Justa, widow of Arima Harunobu, who were responsible for the successful hiding of priests and irmao for many years. It is to the credit of the Franciscans that it was to the outcast groups they chose to bring their message, as well as to the poorer folk in general, but this was not to 'the vast majority of ordinary Japanese ignored by the Jesuits', which the reader is often left to assume was the case.

Many old parishes were restored and many new ones opened between 1598 and 1614. Nagasaki became in effect a Christian city, all four missionary Orders had their headquarters there, the Dominicans and Augustinians had very little presence anywhere else, and churches flourished over most of Kyushu other than in Satsuma. New parishes were now opened in western Honshu, in Hiroshima, Yamaguchi and Shimonoseki. Already in 1599 Fr Organtino was out of hiding and publicly restoring the churches in Kyoto and Osaka. In 1602 he had rebuilt the Jesuit residence near Fushimi, Ieyasu's own castle, and his irmao and dojuku were reaching out to create new Christian communities in Omi, Owari and Gifu. In all this expansion the cutting edge of the work was done by the Japanese irmao, dojuku and the local 'elders' the kambo. The catechumens gathered during this effort were fewer than in the days of the daimyo-controlled mass conversions, but they were served by a larger and increasingly better trained Japanese staff. As a result they were given a much more thorough grounding in their new faith as explained in either Valignano's Catechism or more often through the *Dochirina Kirishitan*, published in the kana syllabary in Nagasaki in 1600.

It was in these years of growth that the Japanese Christians became more and more closely bound together in organisations which they saw as their own. In areas where the parish was only occasionally visited by the clergy, the parish structure itself became a semi-autonomous unit under the kambo but the key organisation that shaped this Japanese Christian identity was the 'kumiko' or in Portuguese 'confraria'.

As early as 1583, under Jesuit auspices, a house of the Portuguese religious lay Brotherhood of the Misericordia was established in Nagasaki, with one hundred local members. How soon this association of the laity spread out into the parishes is not clear, but Valignano did lay down rules for such 'confraria' during his second visit to Japan, 1590–92. There were certainly four such organisations operating in Jesuit parishes by 1614: the Confraternities of the Blessed Virgin, of the Annunciation, of the Blessed Sacrament and of the Misericordia, which was by far the biggest. Initially these had been confraternites in the literal sense, brotherhoods of men only; but in Japan they soon admitted women and in some cases children. The Franciscans and

Dominicans encouraged this development also, the most prominent of their kumiko was probably the Dominican-sponsored Confraternity of the Rosary.

All of these associations were based on tightly-organised local groups which met regularly for prayer and Christian instruction and mutual support. A copy of the rules of the Confraria de Misericordia in Japanese has survived, called *Miserikorujia no shosa* (the practice of compassion). In this movement the members had two sets of seven commandments which they were to attempt to obey and which they recited at their meetings along with the Lord's Prayer, Ave Maria, Salve Regina and the Apostles' Creed. These commandments were:

1. Feed the hungry
2. Give water to the thirsty
3. Clothe the naked
4. Care for the sick and the imprisoned
5. Give lodging to the traveller
6. Receive the refugee
7. Bury the dead

Then there followed the 'spiritual' group of rules:

1. Give good advice to others
2. Instruct the ignorant in the way
3. Console the distressed
4. Encourage the sinner
5. Forbear shame
6. Forgive the mistakes of the neighbour
7. Pray to Deus for the living, the dead, and those who sin against you[6]

These lay associations gradually developed a hierarchy of their own. Each small association became grouped with others nearby into a unit with some local identity, then these units were related to others over a much larger geographical area to form what the Jesuits referred to as 'confraria universalis'. This widespread network of associations was the essential structure of Japanese Christianity which was able to resist the persecution when it came and sustain their clergy when the Fathers and irmao became hunted men.

We have seen how initially under the rule of Ieyasu, despite his closest intellectual advisers being bitterly anti-Christian, things had gone well for the Christian Church and all four of the religous Orders with missionaries in the country. What also was an improvement on the situation under Hideyoshi was that Rome finally made rulings which regularised the situation of the friars in Japan. After all, and not simply in Jesuit eyes, they had come to Japan in direct contradiction of an explicit Papal Brief. Initially, an Apostolic Constitution of December 1600 allowed the Orders of friars to work in Japan, provided they came to Japan via Lisbon and Goa. Any who had arrived via Manila were to return there. All friars were to be subject to their Superiors in their own Orders, but for preaching and the administration of the sacraments in parishes they were to be under the authority of the bishop, who was also made Apostolic Delegate with power to adjudicate disputes between the Orders.

It was nearly three years before the official text reached Nagasaki, by which time Franciscans, Dominicans and Augustinians had already arrived from Manila. It would have been very difficult to send them all back. Cerqueira, the bishop and a Jesuit, published the document, but the Orders stalled over complying. This could have been another grounds for bitter dispute but on the whole the Jesuits let it go. Eventually in 1608 Paul V settled the matter by saying the friars could go to Japan by any route, but the rulings about the authority of the bishop and his being an Apostolic Delegate still held. This was what mattered to the Jesuits. The question of the route was an issue for the Portuguese authorities and their insistence on the dignity of the Portuguese Padroado. The fact that the Jesuits welcomed Paul V's decision is a further confirmation that the Jesuit mission was not fundamentally interested in upholding Portuguese dignity and authority as is suggested by Boxer. The Papal decision gave the Society what it wanted in Japan though it directly contradicted the Padroado at its very heart.

In what was both an indication of support but also a source of embarrassment and potentially of serious trouble for the Society, in November 1601 Ieyasu made Tcuzzu his official agent in Nagasaki for the Chinese silk trade, the most profitable single trading activity in Japan. This appointment left the Society open to criticism from the friars that as usual they were too deeply involved in worldly matters and that they were seeking unusual privileges. It also left the Society open to being an object of dislike by important Japanese who felt they were not getting their due as a result of the status and the activities of Tcuzzu, and further it was confirmation for the Dutch and Will Adams of their obsession with Jesuit plotting, typical of Protestant circles at that time. Yet when Ieyasu 'requested' that Rodriguez perform this office for him, how could the Society refuse?

This further involvement of the Jesuits with the silk trade is perhaps a convenient time to review this association which was embarrassing at the time and has been a source of criticism ever since. It appears that Valignano had no hesitation in maintaining the Society's involvement, even when it meant rather strained, to put it mildly, interpretations of the instructions he received at times from Rome. His case was that some investment in the trade was essential otherwise the Society's work in Japan would have to be curtailed. How could this work be curtailed when right up to the edict of 1614 this was arguably the outstanding area of growth of Christianity through the agency of the Society in the whole world? Japan was poor and so the Christians could not support the Society's work alone, particularly after 1600 when Ieyasu made it clear that no more daimyo were to become Christians. The money due from royal and Papal sources often did not arrive. Indeed, so far was Jesuit involvement in the silk trade making the Jesuits in Japan rich, as Protestants and Franciscans at the time and so many since have suggested, it was not even able to prevent the Society in Japan from being always in debt. Without it the work could not have gone on as it did, but it was never enough to clear the debts. Boxer quotes a letter of Valignano to some of the Jesuits in Goa who had been chiding him about involvement in the trade. It can still stand as his defence and indeed in it he shows he is willing even to contemplate other ventures in investment.

> So long as Our Lord God gives us no other help, I do not see why the capital which is normally sent to Japan should not be invested in India, in the years when this voyage is not made, for Japan has no other resources. This is all the easier if we can find some gold or silk through some reliable friend of ours, in such wise that nobody knows of it in India; and without doubt if none of our own people will make a fuss about it, nobody else is liable to object thereto. By the Grace of God I was not born the son of a merchant, nor was I ever one, but I am glad to have done what I did for the sake of Japan, and I believe that Our Lord also regards it as well done and that he gives and will give me many rewards therefor...Wherefore I believe that he who is not here but in a place where he wants for nothing, cannot be a good judge of the difficulties which beset those who are dying of hunger in great want. And if any one of your Reverences could come here and see these provinces at close quarters with their vast expenses and their miserably small income and capital, and this latter derived from such dangerous and uncertain means, I can assure you that you would not peacefully sleep away your time, but you would do the same as did Padre Francisco Cabral when he was here, wherefore your Reverence and the Father Visitor should favour us in this matter, and not argue against us before Our Paternity.[7]

One advantage of Tcuzzu's closeness to Ieyasu and his advisers was that it gave the Jesuits plenty of warning that all was not well, despite appearances to the contrary. Perhaps the most extraordinary of the events which made it appear that all was well, was Ieyasu's gift to the Jesuits of silver equivalent to 350 cruzados when he heard, in July 1603, that the annual ship with royal and Papal subventions for the mission had been captured by a Netherlands cruiser. 'Whereat the whole court was amazed, since the Shogun did not usually give anything to anybody.'[8]

Despite these and other signs of something that appeared to go beyond mere toleration, Rodriguez was able to warn the Society of real danger. Friends whom he could trust at court assured him that Ieyasu was essentially anti-Christian. Although he appeared not to care too much about the conversion of ordinary Japanese, he had already insisted that no daymo was allowed to become a Christian. The friends of the Jesuits warned them that he could turn against the mission and the Church very easily, and at any time.

The blow came in 1614 with the issue of the edict expelling the Christian clergy from Japan. The edict is so important that its whole text, other than some supporting quotations from Buddhist and Confucian authorities, is reproduced in the translation by Fr Joseph Jennes:

Japan from the commencement was the country of the gods. The unfathomableness of the Positive and the Negative principles is called god, and who shall refuse reverence and honour to the essence of all that is holy and spiritual? Man owes his existence entirely to the workings of the Positive and the Negative...he is not independent of god for a single moment.

Japan is called the land of Buddha and not without reason...God and Buddha differ in name, but their meaning is one, just as two halves of a tally be placed together. the priests and laymen of antiquity, by divine aid, sailed over the ocean and visited the far off land of China in search of the law of Buddha, and the doctrines of the principle of benevolence; unwearied they bore hither the esoteric and the exoteric books. Since that time the doctrine has been handed down from teacher to teacher in unbroken succession, and the glory of the Buddhist law has been far greater than in other lands... But the Christian band have come to Japan, not only sending their merchant vessels to exchange commodities, but also longing to disseminate an evil law, to overthrow right doctrine, so they may change the government of the country, and obtain possession of the land. This is the germ of great disaster and must be crushed.

Japan is the country of gods and Buddha; it honours gods and reveres Buddha. The principles of benevolence and right doing are held to be of prime importance and the law of good and evil is so ascertained that if there be any offenders, they are liable according to the gravity of their crime to the five punishments... The faction of the Bateren rebel against this dispensation; they disbelieve in the way of the gods, and blaspheme the true law, violate right doing and injure the good. If they see a condemned fellow they run to him with joy, bow to him and do him reverence. This they say is the essence of their belief. If this is not an evil law, what is it? They truly are the enemies of the gods and Buddha. If this be not speedily prohibited, the safety of the State will assuredly hereafter be imperilled; and if those who are charged with ordering its affairs do not put a stop to the evil, they will expose themselves to heaven's rebuke.

These must be instantly swept out, so that not an inch of soil remains to them in Japan on which to plant their feet, and if they refuse to obey this command they shall suffer penalty. We have been blessed by the commission of heaven to be the lord in Japan, and we have wielded power over this realm for years past. Abroad we have manifested the perfection of the five cardinal virtues, while at home we have returned to the doctrine of the scriptures. Quickly cast out the evil law, and spread our true law more and more; for the way of the gods and the law of Buddha to prosper, in spite of the degeneracy of the latter days, is a mark of a good ruler. Let the heaven and the four seas hear this and obey.[9]

THE FIRST PHASE OF PERSECUTION, 1614–1623

Most modern historians who have discussed this episode in Japanese history have pointed to a number of specific events which they believe pushed Ieyasu into making this fundamental decision when he did. The arrogant behaviour of the Spanish envoy sent with Ieyasu's agreement to survey the coast of Kanto, the home fiefdoms of Ieyasu, for example. This man, Sebastian Vizcaino, wanted to be formally received in the castle at Edo escorted by Spanish infantrymen with Spanish flags flying. Throughout his visit he constantly referred in conversation to the calling of the King of Spain to spread the faith and extend his dominions, language which repeated the faux pas of the officer of the San Felipe.

Again the most prominent of the remaining Christian daimyo, Arima Harunobu, was rightly convicted of having tried to extend his dominions by falsifying legal documents, and he and his accomplices, all Christians, were executed. Will Adams, now the confidant of Ieyasu, constantly warned him of the way missionaries had played their part in the expansion of the Iberian empires. He insisted to the retired Shogun that Vizcaino's charts were not to facilitate trade but invasion, the fear that had been bandied around since Nobunaga's days. The list goes on and there is no doubt that these episodes were not irrelevant to the making of Ieyasu's decision; but perhaps it was one that he was going to make anyway.

For some years the Jesuit leaders had been expecting it, since as early as 1610 senior officers close to Ieyasu, men whose judgement they trusted, warned them that a ban on Christianity and an expulsion of the clergy could take place at any time. Indeed Ieyasu had tolerated quite savage local persecutions of Christians, notably in one of the Christian heartlands, Arima. There the daimyo who took over from Harunobu, his apostate son Naozumi, decided publicly to execute eight complete Christian families. Over twenty thousand Christians turned up, assembling in orderly ranks under their kumi banners and kumi leadership, to sing and pray throughout the whole ghastly affair. They showed no desire to resist authority, they accepted passively and obediently all that was happening, but their very presence and their disciplined display of spiritual support of those being executed was a massive act of lese-majesty towards the Bakufu. It is understandable that Ieyasu saw in this astonishing show of Christian solidarity a real threat to the Tokugawa understanding of the nature of Japanese society. If any one thing finally decided him to act it was perhaps that parade of the kumiki at Nagasaki.

One channel for this action and one of the signs for everyone to see that under the Tokugawas there was a religious policy significantly different in kind and in importance from anything under Nobunaga or Hideyoshi, was the increased prestige of Buddhism combined with its integration into the structure of the Bakufu. Each major Buddhist school was ordered to have its principal temple at or near Edo. All other houses of that particular Buddhist school had then to accept the rulings of the mother house. Every district in Japan was to be divided into parishes, this for the first time in Japanese history, and each parish was to be the responsibility of a local temple of one of the Buddhist schools. There was to be no competition over theological truth or over members among these Buddhist movements, despite a history of many bitter disputes and conflicts in the past. The whole system was to be supervised by the Minister of Shrines and Temples, Shaji-bugyo. This was Buddhism as the national religion of Japan, but a tamed and controlled Buddhism. It was this Buddhist structure that was used by the Tokugawa Bakufu in its efforts to eradicate Christianity from the nation. Indeed it would appear that the campaign against Christianity was the principal reason for this new state control of Buddhism.

The edict of 1614 ordered the expulsion of all the clergy and indeed some notable Japanese Christian lay people, but along with it there were issued fifteen Articles which entrusted the exposure of 'evil religious groups' to the Buddhist congregations. Every single Japanese person was to register in a Buddhist parish, the monks in each parish had to keep a careful record of all those registered and visit every home several times a year to check any illegal religious activity. The annual records on every family in every parish were to be returned to the officials of the Shaji-bugyo. What a contrast with only sixty years before, when different brands of Buddhism competed for the hearts of the Japanese people, and when some Buddhist churches set up civil regimes in certain provinces outside the control of any feudal lord and often very popular with the ordinary people. Pure Land Buddhism, in particular, had built up widespread popularity with the ordinary people of Japan.

Initially the only dramatic action taken was that all the priests and Brothers of all four Orders, European and Japanese, were assembled in Nagasaki preparatory to their being deported. By March all had arrived, even those from the most distant areas on Honshu, which up till then, 1614, meant only as far as Edo. They had to wait in Nagasaki for the ships to take them away either to Macao or to Manila. They had to wait for several months because of the usual problems to do with the availability of Portuguese ships, of suitable prevailing winds which only blew at certain times of the year and so on. Meanwhile in the midst of all this, Bishop Cerqueira died. A properly constituted court of the Japanese diocesan clergy, ten of them in all, elected Valentin Carvalho sj to be Vicar General and Apostolic Delegate until Rome could make another appointment. Astonishingly, some Franciscans and Dominicans decided to go against the wishes of the Japanese seculars and declared the Dominican, Francisco Morales, Vicar General; fortunately the Superiors of both Orders on the spot put a stop to this extraordinary action before there was too much embarrassment. Many authorities have criticised the Jesuits for their attitude to the Mendicant friars, and they were on occasion overly harsh in their judgements, but, sad to say, this episode was only too typical of the behaviour of some Franciscans and Dominicans who seemed to be as obsessed with trying to counter a perceived Jesuit plot as Will Adams or any Dutch Calvinist.

Along with the missionaries, the families of the ex-commander of the Guard, Takayama Ukon, and Naito Tadatoshi were also exiled, among them was the Lady Naito Julia, second only to Gracia Hosakawa in rank among Japanese Christian women.

Eventually in November enough vessels were assembled to take off all who were to be exiled and eighty-five Jesuits, four Franciscans, two Dominicans, two Augustinians, two secular priests and an unknown number of dojuku set sail.

However, some priests remained in Japan illegally, including eighteen Jesuits, seven Franciscans, seven Dominicans, one Augustinian, five seculars and an unknown number of Jesuit irmao and dojuku.

With all the clergy – officially that is – together with so many influential Japanese Christian leaders like Ukon, exiled abroad and almost all Christian buildings destroyed, Ieyasu now turned to the last threat to Tokugawa rule in Japan, the prestige of Toyotomi Hideyori and the continued loyalty to the house of Toyotomi on the part of many daimyo and samurai. So he marched against the Toyotomi and, as we have seen, in a brisk and ferocious campaign Osaka castle was captured and by the end of July 1615 the last of the Toyotomi family were killed, both those who had been in the castle and those elsewhere.

The six Christian priests who had been in the garrison and survived the siege – they should not have been in Japan let alone in Osaka castle – were allowed to go free. With our knowledge of the terrible martyrdoms that were to follow, this clemency on the part of Ieyasu seems astonishing, but it reflects his attitude at this time. He had broken the power of those he supposed his enemies, he did not need to follow up every detail, certainly he did not intend a mass programme of killing Christians who refused to recant. Apart from a ferocious burst of executions of Christians in Arima, a continuation of what had already begun in 1613 and which he tolerated but did not initiate, there was no killing of Christians for being Christian on the orders of Ieyasu. Nor was there any very strenuous effort to seek out the undercover priests and irmao on his part, though they were always in danger from zealous functionaries and the prejudices of individual daimyo.

There was then, after the capture of Osaka castle, a strange period of calm for the Christian communities all over Japan. Their buildings had been destroyed and most of their priests and other religious had been exiled but otherwise, outside Arima, no very strong action was being taken against them. A number of priests and religious still moved around discreetly among them and worship and teaching went on in people's homes. The baptism of hitherto non-believers into the faith also went on at a significant rate and the Jesuits even recruited some new dojuku to serve the Society and prepare for entrance as irmao.

The most extraordinary development that proceeded from the 1614 edict was the expansion of the Church and of the work of the Jesuits and the Franciscans into areas of Honshu east and north of Edo, areas into which Christianity had barely penetrated hitherto. The movement began in the months preceding the edict when Ieyasu had been putting intense pressure on all the Christian vassals of his personal domain to give up the faith. A number of these men had gone into voluntary exile in northern Honshu along with their samurai and servants. It was from these groups that Christianity began to spread to others in the north. Jesuit and Franciscan priests followed them and began to operate in northern and western Honshu, using these groups as their bases. There was significant Christian growth particularly in the large province of Mutsu, whose daimyo tolerated the existence of a Christian community well into the 1620s, as long as it operated discreetly. Fr de Angelis, the head of the Jesuit group in the north, even went to a group of Christians who had settled on the southern tip of Hokkaido, which, at that time, was not seen as a part of Japan proper.

Some observers have seen this period of calm simply as the lull before the storm, but whether there would have been the storm of persecution and the closing of the country had Ieyasu lived longer is an interesting question. Ieyasu and his closest advisers were still concerned with expanding Japan's influence abroad to the end of his life. However, Ieyasu did not have long to live and it was his death in July 1616 that marked the beginning of change.

With the inheritance of power by Hidetada there was a massive shift. This was not simply a matter of policy towards Christianity. Hidetada began a radical realignment of Japanese policy towards the rest of the world. He first began to inhibit then to put into reverse the long-term policy of expanding Japan's international connections through foreign traders and the substantial development of her own merchant fleet. This was a policy that both Hideyoshi and Ieyasu had pursued.

Hidetada, however, set out vigorously both to eliminate Christianity and to shift Japanese international policy away from openness to the outside world, to one of restricted and limited connection with foreign nations. Soon after his father's death he promulgated edicts which imposed the death penalty on the whole family of anyone who hid or in any way gave succour to a Christian religious of any kind, and restricted the arrival of all foreign ships to Nagasaki or Hirado only. He also ruled that all foreigners should reside only in these two towns except for one carefully supervised formal visit to the capital annually. It was apparent that Christianity and involvement with the world outside Japan were, in his mind, linked threats to Tokugawa power and the Tokugawa vision of Japan.

Under Hidetada's rule organised persecution began to take effect and the number of executions of Christians mounted. Since the Nagasaki martyrdoms of 1587, only Japanese Christians had been killed for their faith, but in 1617 two European priests, a Jesuit and a Dominican, were executed in Omura. By 1622 many European Jesuits and friars were in prison in Omura while five European priests, two Japanese Jesuit priests together with twenty Japanese irmao, most of whom had been recruited since the banning edict, had been executed. They joined the throng of Japanese Christians who bore the brunt of the pressure and who gained what Boxer refers to as 'The Palm of Christian Fortitude'. By 1622 under Hidetada's administration, 323 of them, men, women and children had died rather than recant their faith.

In many areas, daimyo still sometimes chose not to push the issue very hard, and as long as people followed the Jesuit tradition of quiet discretion the Christian community was left alone. Indeed there was a consistent, though not large, stream of converts baptised during this period. Pagés lists 800 in 1617, well over

1,000 in several subsequent years and 2,000 in 1622. That same year Hidetada
became very angry about the persistence of Christianity and the continuing
attempts of more missionaries to enter Japan. This new burst of active concern
on the part of the Shogun appears to have been triggered off by the execution
in Nagasaki of a Christian trader of Sakai called Hiroyama, with twelve of his
crew and the two Augustinians he had tried to smuggle into the country. They
had not even reached Japan when they were captured by an English warship,
whose commander handed them over to a Dutch ship going to Hirado. For
reasons at which we can only guess, the Dutch officials sought to prove the
two men were illegal missionaries before the Bugyo of Nagasaki. For months
on end that senior Japanese official, Hasegawa Gonroku, stalled, sometimes
postponing hearings, at times refusing to accept the evidence presented by the
Dutch, ruling that it was improperly drafted or not relevant. He did this even
though he had known one of the priests when the latter had lived in Japan
before the ban. Eventually the two were pressured into confessing that they
were missionaries. In this whole inquisitorial effort the Dutch had had the help
of the apostate priest Tomas Araki.[10] After that confession was made Gonroku
could do nothing to save them.

This case particularly infuriated Hidetada, perhaps because a Portuguese
Captain-General then in Nagasaki had tried to arrange for the prisoners to be
freed and because it was a Christian Japanese trader who had brought the missionaries to Japan. Whatever the reason, the infuriated Hidetada now ordered
the execution of all the priests and Brothers who were being held in prison as
well as that of all Christian families who had been associated with hiding them.
This mass execution was what Catholic tradition calls The Great Martyrdom
of Nagasaki; it took place on 10 September 1622. Fifty-five Christians died,
twenty-five were burned at the stake. These included an eighty-year old woman
who was a leader of the Misericordia and a very young woman, the niece of
the Bugyo of Nagasaki, Hasegawa Gonroku, and nine European priests. The
other thirty were beheaded.

On the occasion of this martyrdom the authorities made arrange-
ments which were of significance for the future anti-Christian policy of the government. These included elaborate efforts to try to prevent the kind of witnessing
that had, up till that time, often turned scenes of martyrdom into opportunities
for strengthening the faith. All the bodies were immediately reduced to ashes
and the ashes disposed off at sea so that there could be no gathering of relics.
Anyone attempting to pray or sing hymns at the site of the executions was to
be severely punished, the men beheaded and the women publicly humiliated
naked.

Up until the 'Great Martyrdom' the many deaths that had taken place, far
from wiping out Christianity, had not even stopped the flow of new conversions.
Martyrdom was not destroying the Christian Church, it was helping it grow.
This was what Hidetada was becoming aware of in 1622, and when in 1623

he demitted office and passed the title to Iemitsu the latter determined to do something about it. The third Tokugawa Shogun took a deep personal interest in stamping out Christianity. He brought in new legislation, and rigorously enforced both the new and old legislation in a way neither of his predecessors had done.

THE FINAL SOLUTION

Iemitsu not only brought in new approaches to the problem of extirpating Christianity, he also enforced the existing edicts in a more organised and thorough way than either of his predecessors. C. R. Boxer goes farther and asserts that Iemitsu was a sadist and took satisfaction from personally supervising the torture and interrogation of Christians.[11] Be that as it may, it would appear that the discovery, in his capital Edo, of a still thriving Christian community complete with Jesuit priests, was exceptionally provoking. It seemed to the Shogun as if the Christians were determined to flout the authority of the Bakufu just when Japan should have been a scene of complete obedience, unity and order.

In response to what he perceived as a direct challenge, the Shogun called an extraordinary meeting of all the major daimyo in Edo in November 1623. At this gathering they were informed that they had to enforce the anti-Christian edicts with the utmost rigour. To reinforce his message and for their edification, Iemitsu staged a massive slaughter of Christians. On 8 December 1623 the Jesuit leader Jerome de Angelis, with his Franciscan colleague Francesco Galvez – the two had worked together in the considerable development of Christianity in the north – were burned at the stake with forty-eight Christians, all of whom were functionaries or of samurai families. Still in the capital, Iemitsu followed this up on 29 December with the slaughter of thirty-nine more people. Significantly only twenty-five were Christians, the others were killed because they had sheltered or helped the Christians in some way. Some of the northern daimyo stalled briefly, but in 1624, all over Honshu and Kyushu, Christians were killed as the daimyo showed their loyalty to the Shogun.

Strangely, in 1625 and 1626 there was another lull, and there were only about thirty martyrdoms recorded and astonishingly in the last extant records of the Kirishitan ('Christians'), we find that Jesuits priests baptised 1,500 people in 1624, 1,100 in 1625 and 2,000 in 1626. Iemitsu's initial efforts then were still far from wiping out the Church. Things changed, however, in 1627 and from then till 1634 the most terrible and effective measures were taken which did indeed virtually wipe out the traditional formal organisation of the Kirishitan. These measures were closely associated with those which closed Japan to all outside influences for two hundred years. The Shogun Iemitsu, in startling contrast with the policy of his grandfather, closed Japan to all influences from the outside world, and this was done unambiguously as part of his struggle against Christianity. His obsession with the danger posed by Christianity to the Tokugawa Bakufu was such that in 1630 he ruled that all books imported from China were to be checked to prevent any Christian works entering Japan, although only very few Japanese could read such texts in Mandarin.

Mizuno Kawachi and Takenaka Uneme, who from 1627 held authority in Nagasaki and the surrounding area, were determined to destroy the Kirishitan in their area once and for all in obedience to the desires of the Shogun. They took the lead in developing new approaches to the problem. Martyrdom was not an effective tool of destruction. They had already recognised that, in an infuriating way, it was rather a stimulus to dynamic life in the Church. Their new tactic was by means of humiliation, degradation and torture to bring about the apostasy of key Christian leaders. They believed that this would in turn cut the nerve of courage of other Christians and many would then give up the faith as a consequence. It was a slow but steadily enforced policy. They set out to remove the wealth of the wealthy, dismiss from office any Christian who still held office, prevent craftsmen from pursuing their crafts, merchants their business and then, if that was not enough, forcing the town dwellers from their homes and from the towns to live as beggars in the countryside. The lord of Arima, in conjunction with the Nagasaki bugyo, also began a systematic and sustained campaign of torture, maiming and public humiliation in an attempt to force apostasy. He and Uneme of Nagasaki, when their new methods were still not achieving the desired results, began to experiment with using the boiling sulphur springs of Unzen as a means of torture. People were scalded badly but not to death, then they were treated by a doctor and scalded again, and so on. Many did publicly abjure the faith but still no important lay leader gave way, neither did any priests, irmao or dojuku.

In their efforts to produce recantation, Uneme and his associates produced a new and very effective form of torture in Nagasaki, which was then taken up all over the country. This was the ana-tsurishi, hanging in the pit. Boxer describes it thus,

> The victim was tightly bound around the body as high as the breast (one hand being left free to give the signal of recantation) and then hung head downwards from a gallows into a pit which usually contained excreta and other filth, the top of the pit being level with the knees. In order to give the blood some vent, the forehead was lightly slashed with a knife. Some of the stronger martyrs lived more than a week in this position, but the majority did not survive more than a day or two.[12]

This technique was used on all members of the Religious Orders who were discovered, as well as on secular priests and lay Christians. An astonishing number died through this treatment without recanting. However, in 1633 the pit did achieve a great victory, and Fr Christavao Ferreira, the acting Vice-Provincial of the Jesuits in Japan, gave in after six hours. Ferreira's apostasy was a particularly effective triumph because, not immediately but after some time, he became an active helper in the process of Christian persecution. As we shall see, he became an assistant to the head Inquisitor when the office was created in 1640. In becoming an enemy of the Christian faith and of his Society, Ferreira joined the apostate priest Tomas Araki and Fabian Fukan, the brilliant young irmao who wrote *Myotei Mondo* and then after apostasising voluntarily in 1609, wrote the virulent and by far the most effective anti-Christian book *Ha-Deusu* ('God Destroyed'), produced in the anti-Christian campaign.[13] That same year fifteen priests, Jesuit and Franciscan, twelve Japanese Jesuit irmao and seven lay persons died in the pit as martyrs. This number included Ferreira's successor as Jesuit Vice-Provincial, Sebastiao Vieira, who died in the pit in June 1634.

Between 1627 and 1634 approximately 1,200 Christians died in Japan, simply executed or under torture. Then there followed a lull when, in 1635 and 1636, there were very few arrests or deaths officially reported. This was despite well publicised bounties available to anyone who gave information that led to the arrest of a priest, irmao or dojuku. Boxer says that between 1616 and 1716 the price for a priest never fell below 200 pieces of silver, 100 for a brother and 50 for a dojuku and the prices were often much higher.[14] Then, in 1637, there was a fresh wave of arrests of hidden priests and brothers who were all brought to Nagasaki. This burst of activity resulted in Marcello Mastrilli, a Jesuit priest, four Dominicans and twenty of the leading Christian men and women who were associated with them, being put in the pit. They all died there without one recantation.

This episode however was but the preliminary skirmish to a massive head-on clash between the Tokugawa Bakufu and Japanese Christianity, the Shimabara rebellion. In December 1637, the peasantry of the Shimabara peninsula and those on Amakusa Island rose in rebellion against their daymo. Shimabara was part of the old Arima fiefdom which had long been a Christian strong-hold and Amakusa had been in the hands of the devout Yukinaga Konishi for many years. The Jesuit inspired confraria were still powerful connecting links among the Christians in those areas, whose numbers had been added to by many Christian refugees during the previous decade, including – and this is very important – many Christian ronin, that is samurai who no longer had lords. These were warriors who had served the Christian lords who had been killed or exiled, since when they had been trying to live the life of peasants and fishermen, but they were still samurai.

The great initial success of the rebels was a tremendous blow to the honour and dignity of the Tokugawas, and brought back the fears of the Sengoku Jidai in many minds. However, for Iemitsu, it only confirmed the correctness of his obsession that the Christian Japanese were constantly preparing to rebel and use their outside connections to take over Japan. No one from the outside in fact helped the rebels, though a Dutch warship aided the Shogun's forces for a time. For the Jesuits armed resistance, apart from those extraordinary aberrant episodes in the thinking of Vice-Provincial Coelho, had always been condemned. If the Society of Jesus and the Christians had really wanted to take

over Japan there had been many more appropriate moments to try than in west
Kyushu in 1637, when control of the seas was rapidly becoming the prerogative
of the Dutch and English. However, obsessions are not open to argument and,
as we have seen, the rebellion was followed by Iemitsu finally closing off Japan
completely from the outside world.

What was the Shimabara rebellion? Traditional Japanese sources simply
listed it as a rebellion provoked by the Christian beliefs of the local peasantry.
They reported that the peasants believed that a messenger from God had come
and called them to take up arms and promised that God would help them
triumph. More recent Catholic historians, Laures, Jennes and Fujita, while
admitting that once the rebellion began, Christian symbolism and belief played
their part, have emphasised that the rebellion was caused essentially by the
economic and social conditions of the area in the 1630s. Laures and Jennes
in particular, clearly want to disassociate Christian belief from rebellion altogether. These historians may well have been seeking to make clear that neither
the Jesuits nor any other priests had anything to do with fomenting the rebellion; and they are quite right, there were no priests or Brothers in Shimabara
or on Amakusa at that time, unlike the garrison of Osaka castle in 1614 with
its seven chaplains. However, in contrast with that last stand of the Toyotomi
Dynasty, so many of whose troops were Christians yet whose resistance was
nothing to do with Christianity, the Shimabara rebels were Christians, fighting
with a specifically Christian inspiration. Moreover, their inspiration was their
own, coming out of their own Christian experience, not something that was
a direct part of Jesuit instruction. Yet this Christian and messianic rebellion,
inspired independently of any direct Jesuit activity, was in effect proof of the
effectiveness of ninety years of that same Jesuit activity in west Kyushu. Christianity had become so much part of the people and of their understanding
of reality that in the furnace of their suffering they had a fund of Christian
resources from which they drew, and used them to meet their needs in their
own way. Japanese Christians did this on their own.

George Elison in his *Deus Destroyed* makes much of the inability of the Christian message, particularly as purveyed by the Jesuits, to have any real impact
on Japan. In some ways the many deaths, particularly of those who suffered
long periods of torture, like the pit, without giving up, would seem to raise
questions he does not ever answer or even seriously consider in his work. It
would also appear reasonable to suggest that the Shimabara rebellion challenges even more sharply this idea of Christianity's failure to penetrate at all
into Japanese life.

Under terrible persecution from 1627 onwards, most people in Shimabara
and Amakusa had outwardly conformed to the rules of the Tokugawa government. However, the confraria appear to have still been operating and when the
people were pushed beyond human endurance by the exorbitant tax demands
and the illegal and brutal behaviour of the tax-gatherers, the response was

not just another brief disorganised peasant riot, something that was a constant feature of Japanese history, but a messianic Christian uprising in which the overwhelming majority of the 'inspired' fought to the death. This was a phenomenon of the same class as the German Bundschuh risings of the sixteenth century, the 'saints' in Munster in that same century, or, in more recent times, the Nat Turner Rebellion in the United States in 1831; or those twentieth-century messianic risings in Africa – that led by the Reverend John Chilembwe in Malawi in 1915 for example, or that led by the prophetess Alice Lenshina in Zambia in 1964. These are examples of a 'people's religion', a product of their acceptance of Christianity and its subsequent domestication to meet the needs of the situation of the ordinary Christian in ways not laid down by the official theology of those who brought the Christian Gospel to them or of the existing Church hierarchies. This kind of development is usually embarrassing to official hierarchies whether Catholic, Lutheran or Calvinist, but such movements are a confirmation that acculturation, assimilation, indigenisation or whatever the term used to describe the reality of Christianity's integration with a new culture, has occurred.

The daimyo ruling Amakusa and Shimabara in the 1630s happened to be very bad men by any standard and their treatment of their peasants most cruel. Wives and daughters were often taken as hostages against taxes due, and were often sold into prostitution or sometimes killed, whether the taxes were eventually paid or not. Traditions vary as to what exactly triggered off the rebellion. Commonly it was said that servants of the daimyo were torturing a village girl when her father killed them and the village rose up to protect him when men were sent to arrest him; on the other hand, some say that a Christian painting was discovered in a house by officials of the daimyo who publicly burned it and were then lynched by the villagers. Whatever was the trigger, by the end of December 1637 the peasants of Shimabara and Amakusa had thrown off the authority of their daimyo. They had come to accept as leader an extraordinarily handsome young man, Masuda Shiro (Amakusa Shiro in story and legend), son of a samurai who had been close to Konishi Yukinaga. The young man fulfilled the image that appeared in a poem which had been circulating in Kyushu for some years, one among many pieces of Christian prophecy that continued to appear into the last quarter of the seventeenth century on Honshu as well as Kyushu. These prophecies were not produced by missionaries but were folk products. The poem said

> When five years shall have passed five times,
> all the dead trees shall bloom;
> crimson clouds shall shine brightly in the western sky,
> and a boy of divine power shall make his appearance.
> These things shall begin a Christian revival in Japan.

There were also other brief Christian messages being passed around at that time, about an approaching time of judgement on Japan when Deusu would

judge the nation and redeem His people. In addition, the cherry trees flowered
that year out of season in the late autumn and the peculiarities of the weather
that year had caused a lot of red evening skies.[15]

The key organisers of the actual fighting tactics of the host of the saints
were a small group of Christian ronin, war-scarred veterans. However, neither
in Shimabara nor on Amakusa were there many weapons, but the ill-armed
peasants overwhelmed the first columns of sumurai sent against them and
took their arms. The Amakusa rebels after some startling early victories were
defeated in mid-January, but very many escaped death or capture and crossed
over to add to the strength of the Shimabara forces. They, meanwhile, had
come close to capturing the powerful modern castle of Shimabara. However
they failed and then retreated, with a large supply of stores and arms, to an
old earthwork castle at Hara. As Boxer points out, it is puzzling why, after
the initial successes against the forces of the local daimyo and when there was
nothing left militarily to stop them, they did not march on Nagasaki. There
is no doubt the people of the city would have welcomed them, and then they
could have raised all Arima and who knows what then might have happened.
We can look back and say they were bound to lose, but they could not have
thought so, or why start capturing castles and organising an army? Why did
they not seek to spread the revolt in an area which had had the longest and
densest Christian presence in all Japan? We simply do not know, but these
are the kinds of questions that are asked by historians of the Nat Turner,
Chilembwe and Lenshina risings. Again this is where Shimabara conforms to
the pattern of Christian millenialist risings. Did Turner think he was going to
overturn the government of the United States? Did Chilembwe think he could
defeat the British Empire? That is not how millenialist prophetic movements
work, and so with Shimabara. To ask why did they not march on Nagasaki is
to ask the wrong question. The whole movement conforms in so many details
to these Christian uprisings, which are evidence of a far deeper penetration of
Christianity into the being of people than the ability to correctly repeat prayers
or answers from the catechism.

When the local lords were clearly unable to do much about the rebellion,
and particularly as its religious aspect became known, Iemitsu and his closest
advisers took it very seriously indeed and sent a senior government official from
Edo to coordinate the efforts of all the forces on Kyushu to crush the Christians.
Despite commanding a force of 50,000 men, including the best samurai of
Kyushu, the commissioner was constantly worsted. The Christians were even
able to emerge from their fortress and defeat government columns in the open
field. The result was that the rebel leaders were able to arm over two hundred
men with muskets, men who were able to use them effectively. Indeed so long
as their commanders could keep them supplied with powder and shot they
appeared to have given the Christian army the edge militarily against the best
samurai in Japan.

When he heard he was going to be replaced by the infuriated Shogun, the commissioner, Itakura Shigemasa, mounted one last massive assault on Hara on 14 February 1638. It was beaten back with heavy loss and 5,000 samurai were killed, including Shigemasa himself while trying to rally his fleeing men. The new commander, with massive Honshu reinforcements at his disposal, ceased these expensive assault tactics and decided to starve the Christians out. In the first few days of April, almost dying of starvation, Christian patrols made sorties to try to capture food as they had often done successfully in the past. This time they failed completely and the parlous state of the garrison was obvious to the besiegers from the state of the bodies of the slain raiders. So on 12 April 1638 the assault began, the first wave was successfully driven back, yet again, but the second assault finally broke into the castle, though it took two more whole days of bloody fighting before all the garrison were finally killed.

The government now turned with renewed determination to stamp out Christianity wherever it could be uncovered. As far as we can tell there were only five priests left in Japan at that time and they were all in Honshu north of Edo; they could hardly have been further from Shimabara and still be in Japan. They were all captured early in 1639. The two Franciscans, Francesco Barajas and Bernard Osorio, were the more fortunate and were burned at the stake, the three Jesuits were put to the pit torture to try to make them recant their faith. Fr Peter Kasui died in the pit, Fathers Giovanni Porro and Martin Shikimi recanted, but 'only from the teeth out'. They were never trusted like Ferreira, and they were kept in prison for the rest of their lives and died there.

From 1639 onwards, as we have already seen, all contact with Catholic lands was forbidden, no Japanese could travel abroad and no Japanese already abroad could return on pain of death. The Dutch, by 1641, were restricted under humiliating conditions to the tiny artifical island of Deshima. This was all part of the attempt of Iemitsu to prevent any further incursion of Christianity into Japan from the outside while he extirpated it within the country.

Just how adamant he was about this task became brutally clear in 1640, when the Macao political and commercial authorities sent an embassy to Japan. For the previous decade they had been trying to dissuade the religious authorities from sending any more missionaries to Japan and to disassociate themselves from the missionaries. Although missionaries were banned by the Shogun, the Macao merchants could not believe that trade was, and so decided on an embassy to try to restore relations between Macao and Japan. This was a disaster. Iemitsu had the whole embassy, plus all of the crew of their ship, executed and their ship destroyed with its cargo still on board. Thirteen sailors had their lives spared to be returned to Macao to tell the Portuguese authorites there the news. The Portuguese merchants had risked going to Japan because of the huge amounts of cash they owed to Japanese entrepreneurs and they couldn't conceive that this debt was going to be thrown away. The Portuguese authorities in Macao learned in this brutal fashion that as far as Iemitsu was concerned the loss by some of his subjects of these vast sums of money was of no consequence when put over against his belief in the absolute necessity of extirpating Christianity in Japan and insulating the nation from any further possible contamination by it.

Internally, the system of Buddhist supervision of the population under the commisioner for Shrines and Temples was brought under a new authority. This was the 'Kirishitan-shumon-aratame-yaku', the Christian Inquisition Office, with its commisioner, 'Kirishitan bugyo', Inouye Masashige Chikugo-no-kami. Inouye is held to have been an apostate by some recent historians but the evidence is ambiguous. We do know that he had been a senior official in the Tokugawa administration since 1627 and had already been associated with the efforts of Takenaka Uneme to extort recantations from Christian leaders, lay or clerical, rather than simply killing them. From 1640 his task was to eliminate the hidden Christians, of whom there were clearly many as Shimabara had shown, and to catch any priests, Brothers or dojuku that might still be in the country, or, despite the attempts at total closure, might still enter it.

First of all the Inquisition Office made sure that the Buddhist religious supervision of all families was put into effective action everywhere. In many areas hitherto it had only been carried out in a very perfunctory manner, many Christian families being granted their certificate by the local Buddhist monks without changing their faith or their pattern of life in any way. The scheme was henceforth enforced rigorously and was reinforced by the reward scheme for the denunciation of clergy and dojuku already referred to. To that carrot a new and very hard stick was added by the new use that the Gomin-gumi organisation was put to. Gomin-gumi had been a self-help structure of families grouped in units of five or so for mutual help and support. After 1640 all families in every province had to belong to such a group. Each group was made responsible for seeking out any crypto-Christians within its membership and denouncing them. If any crypto-Christians were found who had not been thus denounced everyone in the group of families was to be executed.

The Inquisition Office was well aware that treading on a crucifix or a pic-ture of Jesus or Mary was reckoned to be tantamount to apostasy, so they introduced a system whereby everyone in a neighbourhood was asked to do this. The E-fumi ceremony, as it came to be called, became an annual event in many communities of Kyushu and was used also, off and on, throughout all Japan. The Tokugawa government, once it was firmly in power, had tried to leave a great deal of autonomy to the various daimyo but from 1640 in the matter of the suppression of Christianity there was no lee-way allowed at all. The Kirishitan-shumon-aratame was a national ministry that was very active well into the eighteenth century and was not formally stood down until 1792. As late as 1687 the government introduced an additional aspect to the inquisi-torial system. This was the 'Kirishitan-ruizoku-aratame', the Christian Family Investigation, which laid down that all relations of Christians who had been discovered and killed or died in prison should be carefully supervised for the rest of their lives, and that the direct descendants of such Christians should live under Government control for seven generations for men, four for women. A somewhat strange decision since the record of loyalty of women to the Christian faith was outstanding in Japan, and there is no clear unambiguous record of any woman turning apostate under torture in all these terrible years. This whole elaborate system of systematic suppression of Christianity was built upon the government-created Buddhist parish system as its foundation.

Dr Jurgen Elisonas in his 'Christianity and the Daymo'[16] says 'To be sure there was no real reason for this elaborate network's existence. The fact is that there were practically no Christians left in Japan by the 1660s.' The leadership of the Tokugawa Shogunate appeared to think there was good reason, and their long maintenance of the ministry and its networks of religious control was a measure of the impact that the stubborn loyalty of Japanese Christians had made upon them. In any case, Elisonas is not quite correct even at a formal statistical level. Admittedly the largest number of arrests and executions after the closing of the country came in the 1640s and 1650s, about a thousand in all. However, after 1660 there were still many arrests and executions, five hundred in Bungo between 1660 and 1670, about three hundred in Owari in 1664. Then later in Owari several hundred Christians were reported as being removed from their homes and put into segregated and controlled villages. In Mino there were about two thousand arrests in 1668, although we do not know what happened to those arrested. There were small numbers of executions recorded in some years subsequently and then the last mass executions of which we have records took place in Owari in 1697.

From the 1630s onwards Japanese Christians had been devising ways of maintaining the faith while remaining alive through apparent acceptance of their part in the Buddhist parish system. The close-knit organisation of the confraria was a help; and sometimes later, if people were fortunate, all the families in their group in the gomin-gumi system were 'hidden' Christians. They knew that any Christian in good faith can baptise, so baptism of children went on as well as their instruction in the faith. Prayers were held before a statue of Buddha, in the back of which a crucifix had been carved, or before a statue of Kannon, a sacred Buddhist image of a woman with child, which the 'hidden Christians' treated as the Virgin Mary and the child Jesus. To the astonishment of Japanese and Europeans, when in 1865 Catholic missionaries were allowed again to enter Japan, groups of the 'Hidden Christians' came out into the open. They could still say the Apostles' Creed, the Lord's Prayer, the Hail Mary, the Hail Holy Queen, the Act of Contrition and some other prayers in Japanese. From handwritten copies of the main events of the Christian Year that have been discovered it is also clear that the liturgical year was one of the pillars upon which the underground faith had been kept alive. When they tried to repeat prayers in Latin they failed and what came out was very jumbled.

This has resulted in some authorities saying that what was preserved by the 'hidden Christians' was simply a jumble of confused memories handed down through the generations. However, it was their prayer life in Japanese which was their lifeline, and although it could not be claimed to represent a very full Christianity, it was a recognisable form of the Christian faith.

The other thrust of the Inquisitorial system was the seeking out of any missionaries who did manage to break through and get into the newly 'Closed Land'. We have seen how the authorities in Macao had been desperately trying to disassociate themselves from the mission in the hope of prolonging their silk trade with Japan. So after 1640 it was impossible to get any help from Macao to enter the country. Thus, ironically, these last Jesuit attempts to bring missionaries to Japan had to set off from Manila, the very place from which Valignano had tried to prevent any missionaries ever arriving in Japan. The Jesuits were all the more determined to try because of the apostasy of Ferreira. It is clear that the motivation of many who volunteered to go to Japan after 1640 was, in some way, to make amends for him and, if possible, to reach him and bring him back to the faith, rather than to aid the struggling Church in Japan.

The Jesuit Visitor General for the East, Fr Antonio Rubino, organised two parties of Jesuits to attempt this herculean task. The first group was made up of five Jesuit priests, Rubino himself, Francisco Marques, who had a Japanese mother, Diego de Morales, a Mexican, Antonio Capece, another Italian and Albert Meczinski, a Pole. They were accompanied by three dojuku, a Portuguese, a Korean and a Japanese. All of them were captured very soon after they had landed near Nagasaki on 11 August 1642. Under Inouye's authority they were interrogated and tortured for nearly seven months and in the end they all died, Rubino, Meczinski and the three dojuku in the pit on 21 and 24 March 1643. Morales, Marques and Capece were taken from the pit and were immediately beheaded on 25 March. Some Japanese sources say that these three Fathers apostasised, but this is very unlikely since they were beheaded and not publicly displayed as apostates which would have been the usual procedure.

The second so-called Rubino group was made up of four European Jesuit priests, Pedro Marques and Alonzo de Arroyo, both Spaniards, Francisco Cassola and Giuseppe Chiara, both Italian, a Japanese irmao, Andrew Veyra and four dojuku, two Chinese and two Japanese whose names we do not know. They landed in Japan on 27 June 1643 and were also captured within a few days of landing. The dojuku appear to have been burned at the stake in Nagasaki but the irmao and four priests were sent to Edo and were dealt with personally by the Inquisitor, Inouye, on his estate near the capital. He had a prison for Christians built in the grounds of this estate, the notorious Kirishitan Yashiki, which was where he carried out his interrogations.

The result of his ministrations in this case was a great triumph for the Tokugawa regime. All of the Jesuits apostasised. One, de Arroyo, withdrew his apostasy almost immediately, and starved himself to death in prison. There is a very dramatic description of the other four in the report of a Dutch captain and his officers who were in the Kirishitan Yashiki at that time. They were being interrogated by the Japanese authorities for being in the wrong place at the wrong time. Arnoldo Montanus wrote, based on the report of Captain Peter Cornelius Schaep, of the Netherlanders seeing the Jesuits and listening to their interrogation by Ferreira, now known as Sawano Chuan.

> ... and being carried into the Place of Audience, they were commanded to sit down on Mats by four Jesuits, who look'd exceedingly pitifully; their Eyes and Cheeks strangely fallen in; their Hands black and blew; their whole Bodies sadly misused and macerated by Torture. This Company amazed the Hollanders, who were not able to judge the Reason for their being plac'd by the four Jesuits.
>
> These though they had apostatiz'd from the Christian Faith, yet declar'd publickly to the Interpreters, Kytbyoye and Phatsyosomon, that they did not freely Apostatise, but the insufferable Torments which had been inflicted upon them, had forc'd them to it.
>
> ... therefore call'd for Syovan [Ferreira] the Apostate Priest, who was there ready for that purpose. So soon as he saw the Jesuits, he look'd very fiercely upon them ... and in a scoffing manner said, 'Now fie upon you Jesuits, that make this world in an uproar ... [17]

The reality of their apostasy was never really accepted by the Japanese authorities, for these men, unlike Ferreira who regularly assisted the Inquisitor Inouye, were kept in confinement for the rest of their lives. For one of them, Fr Cassola, that was not long for he died in November 1644. They were all recorded as having joined a Buddhist congregation and were all given 'wives'. They were all, however, kept in jail and never operated freely as did Ferreira. Indeed Chiara, although his name is appended to various publicised confessions as to the Jesuits seeking to help Spain conquer Japan, behaved at other times with independence and bravery and not at all as an apostate. For example in 1674 he was ordered to write a book refuting Christian doctrine. On account of the manuscript he prepared he was tortured again and ordered to make good his membership of a Buddhist congregation; though how he was to do this, since from then on he was held under such strict security that only his 'wife' and their servants could talk with him unsupervised, is not clear.

Be that as it may, the failure of the second Rubino group appears to have decided the General of the Jesuits as well as the Papal authorities that no more attempts should be made to enter Japan. This decision was adhered to until the extraordinary lone effort of the secular priest Giovanni Bautista Sidotti. Having travelled to Macao with the Papal Legate Charles de Tournon in 1703, Sidotti went to Manila where he studied Japanese. In 1708 he landed in Japan and was immediately captured. The Inquisitor at that time was the Confucian scholar Arai Hakuseki, who interrogated him in the Kirishitan Yashiki. However, no torture was used this time. The two men had long weeks of conversation which

so impressed Hakuseki that he included accounts of the conversations in his
book, *Sei yo Kibun*. The Confucian scholar was the first important official under
the Tokugawas to suggest that the belief that the Jesuits had been planning
to assist a European invasion of Japan was mistaken. He recommended that
Sidotti be returned to his country. However the Shogun ruled that he should be
kept in the Kirishitan Yashiki where his Jesuit predecessors and so many others
had suffered. There he was looked after by an aged couple who had been the
servants of Fr Chiara till he died in 1685, and subsequently had served a Jesuit
dojuku 'apostate' who had instructed them in the Christian faith. On learning
this Sidotti baptised them. When this was discovered, Sidotti was thrown into
a tiny underground cell from which he was never allowed to emerge for any
reason and where he died in November 1715.

LITERATURE AS A TOOL OF GOVERNMENT POLICY

The Jesuits had made great use of the printing press in their mission both as a
means of teaching and of propagation of the Christian faith. It was one of their
most effective writers, the irmao Fabian Fukan, who became the only effective
intellectual critic of Christianity in print. His *Ha-Deusu* ('Refutation of Deus')
was by far the most effective literary and intellectual attack on Christianity. He
was not an apostate forced by persecution or torture but, as we have seen, left
the Society in 1609 voluntarily. From the text of *Ha-Deusu* we learn that he had
become very bitter at the slowness of promotion of Japanese to the priesthood
and the anti-Japanese attitudes of some of the Jesuits. *Ha-Deusu* was published
in 1620 but despite the increasing efforts of the Government to wipe out Christianity, there was very little else produced in the way of books and pamphlets
attempting to argue a case against the beliefs of the followers of Deusu.

There were only two other serious pieces published in the seventeenth
century. One was a work by a Kyoto Buddhist monk for the instruction of
those monks who had overseen the family investigations to discover crypto-
Christians, *Taiji Jashu-ron* ('Refutation of the evil teachings'). Even it tended to
concentrate on the argument that the spread of the Christian faith was simply
a preparation for European invasion, which Fukan had also mentioned. The
other serious piece of work published in the seventeenth century was *Kengiroku*
('Revealing of Falsehoods'). This work has been attributed to Ferreira but more
recent scholars believe it was written by a Confucianist who had, without doubt,
consulted a Jesuit priest, almost certainly Ferreira, but also had had discussions
with a Protestant. This is the only way to account for the attitude taken to the
number and nature of sacraments in Catholic Christianity.

There were other works written about Christianity by Japanese in the sixteenth century but strangely these were not published until much later. While
there were some significant anti-Christian works written in the late eighteenth
century they clearly play no part in the struggles of the seventeenth century.
The one other piece of literature of intellectual merit sometimes counted as

a piece of anti-Christian propaganda, *Daigaku Wakumon* ('Questions concern-
ing the Great Learning') by a Confucian scholar, is much more focused on
attacking Buddhism than on mounting a serious attack on Christianity.

The really effective anti-Christian writings were of a very different kind.
They were not intended to dissuade Christians from following their religion, but
to put into the minds of ordinary Japanese people a thoroughly repulsive image
of Christianity. From the middle of the seventeenth century until well into
the eighteenth there were produced and circulated in Japan, both printed and
hand-written, popular anti-Christian tales and horror stories. These were not
for the libraries of scholars and monks but for the ordinary people, and they certainly appeared to reach into the furthest corners of the land and through them
the Tokugawa Shogunate effectively built into the Japanese popular mind a
particular image of Christianity – that of a dangerous foreign religion imposed
on good innocent Japanese people by wicked magicians. Most of these stories
used as their 'data-base' two works written in the early seventeenth century,
Krishitan yurai-ki ('Historical Record of Christianity') and *Kirishitan Monogatari*
('The Christian Story'). These books were both written in Kyoto in the 1630s.
In both, and in the hundreds of tales based on them, the Fathers are wonder-
workers and miracle makers but their aim is the ultimate conquest of Japan by
the 'King of Namban' (Namban is the land of the 'Southern barbarians'). As
might be expected when the source of these stories was Kyoto, Fr Organtino
features a great deal. Under the name 'Uragan' he appears as the leading and
most powerful magician and wonder-worker, serving the King of Namban and
seeking the conquest of Japan. This is a particular irony, since it was this long-
serving devoted veteran Jesuit who was such an opponent of Cabral's Iberian
arrogance and such a firm believer in the possibility of a truly Japanese Church.
It was he who wrote to the General in 1578, 'If this nation submits to the Faith,
my opinion is that no Church in the world will surpass that of Japan.' Again
on 10 March 1589 he wrote of the Japanese Church as the 'bride of God' and
goes on,

> Any Jesuit who comes to Japan and does not foster a love for this bride
> of wondrous beauty, not caring to learn her language immediately, not
> conforming to her ways, deserves to be packed back to Europe as an inept
> and unprofitable worker in the Lord's vineyard.[18]

This popular literature was by far the most effective element in the Tokugawa
anti-Christian campaign. As we have seen, the ruthless persecution in all its
forms cut off the Christians from the ordained ministry of the Church, and
drove them underground so that only a remnant survived into the nineteenth
century, although Catholic Christianity did survive. However, this popular
literature, which was so widespread in a period when the Japanese people
were completely cut off from any contact with Christianity or the outside
world, was effective in shaping popular attitudes and popular culture in an
anti-Christian way.

CONCLUSION

Alessandro Valignano's attempt to create a truly Japanese and Catholic Christianity was handicapped in Japan in a way that his plans for China were not. This handicap was the false start made by his saintly predecessor Francis Xavier. The latter's daring translations of Christian terms into Japanese were felt to be so embarrassingly wrong that something almost the exact opposite of translating the message took place. Having got it so wrong about Dainichi, Xavier and his immediate successors put the whole process into reverse. Even modern conservative Catholic mission scholars feel that they went much further than was necessary in not translating terms but producing transliterated Portuguese or Latin words to express Biblical and theological words and concepts, Deusu for God, Artaru for altar, Ekerija for ecclesia or church and so on.[19]

Despite that serious drawback, the early Jesuit missionaries had not retreated entirely from trying, at least in some matters, to create a Japanese style for the life of the mission in Japan. When Cabral, that fidalgo y fidalgo, arrived in Japan as Superior of the mission, he was shocked by the conformity of so many of the Society to Japanese ways of behaving and dressing. He attempted to bring better discipline and direction to the Society, but with it he brought some of the worst of Iberian racial pride and arrogance to the Society in Japan.

As we have seen, Valignano tried to reshape the whole life of the Society in Japan and make it as Japanese as possible. Wherever the influence of Organtino was dominant then this was not a formality but a reality. But elsewhere there remained elements of Iberian, usually Portuguese, suspicion and distrust not only of Japanese Christians, but also of Japanese irmaos and dojuku. Despite the elaborately detailed Japanisation of all aspects of Jesuit life after 1582, this persisted and partly accounts for Fabian Fukan's renunciation of the Society and of Christianity.

Strangely, Joao Rodriguez Tcuzzu, the Jesuit most expert in Japanese, author of the first true grammar of the Japanese language, confidant of Hideyoshi and of Tokugawa Ieyasu, was an exponent of this anti-Japanese attitude. In 1598, one year after the Nagasaki martyrdom, Tcuzzu wrote a letter to the Jesuit General, Claudio Acquaviva, in which he insisted that the Society in Japan was in danger of straying from the path laid down by Ignatius by having too many Japanese members. This though none had yet been ordained priest. None should be, he insisted, because not one Japanese irmao 'has talent to govern or to penetrate deeply into things of religion, or has great zeal for souls or much disposition for Holy Orders.'[20]

Rodrigues is saying this only a year after he had witnessed the death of Br Paul Miki sj, who had preached the Christian Gospel to the crowds who had come to watch throughout his long bitter journey from Kyoto all the way onto the killing ground at Nagasaki! Michael Cooper believes that it was the same Tcuzzu who had influenced Valignano on his second visit, 1590–2, to slow down dramatically the rate of Japanese entry to the Society. It should be noted, however, that in his *Summario* of that year Valignano heavily underscored for his readers the fact that it was the Japanese irmao, dojuku and kambo who were the effective communicators of the Gospel to the Japanese people. It was because of them that there was the continuing growth of the Church that was such a joy to the Visitor.

However, as the terrible pressure on Christians increased after 1598, less and less is heard of the Rodriguez type of complaint. Rather the tone is set by the letter of Diogo de Mesquita, Rector of Nagasaki, which he wrote to the General in November 1607, complaining bitterly about the long, and in his opinion unnecessary, delay in ordaining Japanese irmao of the Society to the priesthood. As Valignano had so often pointed out, he also affirmed that it had been they, the Japanese irmao and dojuku, who had evangelised Japan. He believed that far too many European irmao had been ordained who were less worthy than some of their Japanese colleagues and that the talents of Japanese Brothers worthy of the priesthod were still going to waste.[21]

From 1614 onwards it was the Japanese leadership of the Christian Church who were called to be in charge, and how well they fulfilled their task! Because of the Dainichi disaster in Xavier's time there had been basically only a confrontational relationship with Japanese Buddhism after those early years; and Valignano did nothing about that, except to encourage, as we have seen, formal study of Buddhism and Shinto so that informed argument could be used against them. It is not clear what his attitude would have been to an attempt to relate to Japanese Buddhism along the lines that Ricci, under his authority, had adopted towards Confucianism – that is, relating Christianity to the other as in some sense its fulfilment or compliment. This only came about after long and careful study of Confucianism by Ricci.

Or again, could that Confucian dialogue not have been used in Japan? Confucianism did, after all, play a part in forming the Tokugawa religious ideology.

Although this is so, a creative dialogue with Confucianism was not a direct entry to the heart of the Japanese people. Confucianism in Japan during the 'Christian century' was the philosophy of a handful of intellectuals and certain leading political figures. Even if, with the use of Ricci's brilliant understanding of Confucianism, a large number of what Confucianists there were had been converted to Christianity nothing would have changed. It would have meant very little in numbers of converts, and it would not have altered the attitude of the Tokugawa Shoguns one bit. The Tokugawa Shogunate was creating a religious ideology that was precisely geared to support their authority over the newly united Japan, an authority they believed to be necessary for the maintenance of that unity. They were not interested in any of these three traditions

in themselves or in their integrity of thought. As Kitagawa asserts in
regard to Buddhism and Shinto, 'In other words, the Tokugawa regime was
indifferent to the religious or philosophic differences between Buddhism and
Shinto. What concerned the Shogunate was how to keep religious institutions
within the political framework.'[22] This ideology was primarily Buddhist in
form and, as we have seen, used the Buddhist 'churches' as the spiritual wing
of government authority. Confucianist elements were added to the mix and
played an important role in developing a number of moral codes, Bushido,
that of the warrior and Onna Daigaku, Great learning for Women. There
were also added, as it appeared necessary, certain elements from Shinto, the
ancient though at that time somewhat moribund traditional religion of Japan.
As the years went by both Confucian intellectuals and the traditional Shinto
priesthood began to challenge this 'faith'. Indeed it was the imposition of
the compulsory membership of Buddhist parish on all Japanese that began
the re-awakening of Shinto. The priests of the various traditional shrines
appealed to the Shogun against this regulation being applied to them. The
refusal of the authorites to listen to these pleas helped initiate a revival of
Shinto and a growing articulation of Shinto theology specifically over against
Buddhism.[23]

   What becomes the dominant religious tradition during this period was this
creation of the Tokugawa regime, shinkoku, or as some now call it Japanism.
This is a religious form difficult to define and which has no seperate liturgical,
theological or institutional structures. The modern Japanese novelist Shusaku
Endo in one of his novels makes Ferreira tell a newly captured Jesuit that
planting Christianity in Japan is like planting a young sapling in a muddy
swamp, 'the roots begin to rot, and the leaves to wither';[24] and the Japanese
sociologist Shichihei Yamamoto has written a great deal about what he calls
Japanism, which is not a religion yet is religious and demands that all religious
forms live together and in some way support the nation. Exclusivist faiths
like Christianity and several forms of Buddhism are unacceptable to it. This
may very well be an accurate understanding of the indigenous spirit of late
twentieth-century Japan. However, at the beginning of the Tokugawa Shogunate it appears that a powerful dictatorial government wanted to eliminate
all loyalties that could be an alternative to the supreme loyalty demanded by
the Bakufu. Buddhism had been so badly crushed in the preceding century
by Nobunaga and Hideyoshi that with further crushing of some independent
spirits the rest could be brought into the service of the state. This was so;
and the Buddhist churches, when thus effectively subdued, were then supported in a way never before seen in Japan. Indeed because of this distortion
of Buddhism into a spiritual police with a temple at the centre of each of
the parishes into which the whole land was divided, the number of Buddhist
temples grew in the first decades of the Tokugawa regime from under twenty
thousand to a massive figure of around four hundred thousand. Most of

these were built at the expense of the state.[25] This is state patronage with a vengeance.

The Tokugawa regime created the new ideology, it was not something natural or inherent in the Japanese culture whatever may be the case in twentieth-century Japan. To Yamamoto and Endo 'Japanism' does appear, in the late twentieth century, to be an integral part of Japanese culture. Its roots, however, do not go back to time immemorial but are firmly fixed in the deliberate policy, presaged in the rule of Hideyoshi, of total control over all Japanese society by the Tokugawas. In shaping religious structures to suit the needs of the state, Buddhism had to be tamed and Christianity virtually eliminated. Nobunaga and Hideyoshi had made a good start in destroying the independence and autonomy of the Buddhist Churches and the Tokugawas completed that process and then used the defeated Buddhists to help destroy the Christian Church.

Could the Christian Church, the Jesuits in particular, have come to some sort of modus vivendi with the Tokugawas? Theoretically it was possible. After all Matteo Ricci and his companions had already sworn allegiance to the imperial Chinese authorities and promised to be Chinese. In practice however, since almost from the beginning the Tokugawas shaped their government in ways that deliberately made things difficult for Christians, it was not possible. Hideyoshi himself had come to believe that a Spanish attack on Japan was a possibility and that the missionaries were in some sense advance agents of Spanish power. After all, as we have noted, the Spanish authorities in Manila did prepare a detailed plan for the conquest of China using Jesuits and friars as their auxiliaries, and included in that plan was the demand that the missionaries in Japan should provide a Japanese mercenary army. After the coming to power of the Tokugawas this fear was apparently authoritatively confirmed by both the Dutch and the English, who emphasised the political nature of the Jesuits in particular. They did this honestly since that was the perception of the Jesuits current at that time in both England and the Netherlands. That the Jesuits in Japan under the leadership of Valignano were embarked on a very different course and were desperately keen not to be associated with Iberian expansion was something they simply could not believe. From the very beginning of the Tokugawa regime, the missionaries, Jesuit and Mendicant, as well as Christianity itself, were seen as the enemy of the regime and there was, by that time, nothing the Jesuits could do about it.

Was then the Jesuit mission to Japan a failure? Was Christianity rejected by the Japanese as is so often stated? No, the Jesuit mission was not a failure and the Japanese people did not reject Christianity. Indeed, one can go further and say that the Jesuit mission to Japan, aided to a degree by the Franciscan mission, was one of the most successful in the history of Christianity. Where or when else have Christian missionaries in less than one hundred years produced a

Christian community of approaching half a million people in a culture already technically advanced and literate? In the pre-Constantinian Roman Empire perhaps, but nowhere else.

The very success of the Church can be measured by the fact that after 1612 it was thrown on its own resources, and what few European missionaries there were were utterly dependent on the Japanese Christians. These Christians upheld the faith and died in their thousands proclaiming it. The Shimabara rebellion which some Catholic writers seem to find somewhat embarrassing, was by its nature as a charismatic millenarian rebellion a confirmation of the success of the Jesuits in planting a seed which had grown into a plant that was flourishing independently in Japanese soil. The sheer power of the Tokugawa regime eventually reduced the Church to a small underground sect, but that does not constitute a rejection by the Japanese people. Indeed, so much part of Japanese life and so threatening to the Tokugawas was the Kirishitan, that they had to bring all Japanese people under the control of a religious police authority in order to crush it, and to achieve that same goal they felt it necessary to bring to an abrupt end a fruitful period of expansion of Japanese trade and influence in the western Pacific and make her the 'Closed Land' for over two hundred years.

NOTES

1. Boxer, *The Christian Century*, pp. 296–8.
2. Cooper, *Rodriguez, The Interpreter*, pp. 185–7.
3. Murdoch, *History of Japan*, vol. II, p. 300.
4. Laures, *Two Japanese Christian Heroes*.
5. Fujita, *Japan's Encounter with Christianity*, pp. 117–18.
6. Ibid., p. 170.
7. Boxer, op. cit., p. 365.
8. Ibid., p. 183. He gives no source for this quotation but it comes from the 1604 Annual Letter of Vice-Provincial Pasio who reports that Ieyasu also gave the Society a generous interest free loan of silver at that time.
9. Jennes, *History of the Catholic Church in Japan*, pp. 116–18.
10. Oraki is usually referred to as a Jesuit in the literature. However, according to Juan Ruiz-de-Mechina, head of the Far East Department of the Instituto Storica della Compagnie de Jesù, Oraki was a secular priest and was a member of the society at the time.
11. Boxer, op. cit., p. 362.
12. Ibid., p. 353.
13. This work is the central focus of Elison's *Deus Destroyed*.
14. Boxer, op. cit., p. 336.
15. Ibid., p. 378.
16. *Cambridge History of Japan*, vol. 4, pp. 301–72.

17. Arnoldus Montanus, *Atlas Japannensis*, pp. 328–30. Quoted in H. Cieslik, 'The case of Christovao Ferreira'.
18. Schutte, *Valignano's Mission Principles*, part 2, p. 105.
19. Jennes, *A History of the Catholic Church in Japan*, p. 87.
20. Cooper, op. cit., p. 173.
21. Ibid., p. 178.
22. Kitagawa, *Religion in Japanese History*, p. 163.
23. Ibid., pp. 170–2.
24. Quoted in Fujita, op. cit., p. 164.
25. Kitagawa, op. cit., p. 164.

CHAPTER SIX

Matteo Ricci and the Road
to Beijing

There is a man from the Far West who knows the Way,
He concerns himself more about literature and thought than we,
In the spirit of his thought there is neither Buddhism or Taoism,
His spirit is his own and yet like that of the Confucian scholar.
(Wang Tingna)

A lessandro Valignano shared with his saintly predecessor Francis Xavier the desire to have the Christian Gospel preached in China. The Visitor soon found on his first visit to Macao that the members of the Society there had given up on that aim and settled down comfortably as 'chaplains' to the Portuguese community in the tiny colony. They had also succumbed to the Iberian tradition of making what converts there were within the colony become Portuguese in dress, manners and way of life.

Faced with this, Valignano had no alternative but to bring new Jesuits to Macao who would devote themselves exclusively to preparing themselves to enter China. Michele Ruggieri was the first of these new men, and he was assigned to learn Chinese and prepare to spend the rest of his life in China. However, before he or any other Jesuit could begin the mission, the Chinese authorities had to be persuaded to allow Jesuits to reside within the empire. As we have seen, this was a time when foreigners were never granted such permission.

There had already been a number of attempts to enter China which had all ended in failure. In 1565 the Jesuit Superior in Macao, Francisco Pères, had been allowed to address the authorities in Canton and had sought permission for a Jesuit House to be established there. He had been courteously received and then sent back to Macao with the promise of being listened to if he came back again having learned Chinese in the meantime. There were also a number of unauthorised attempts at entry from Manila. One was made by a Spanish Jesuit, Ribiera, and another later by four Franciscans was made after Ruggieri had already begun his preparations for a very different approach to China.

These illegal intruders were imprisoned and so badly treated that one died. The survivors were released as a result of the diplomatic activities of the Portuguese authorities in Macao, even though these illegal attempts to enter China from Manila endangered the very existence of Macao itself. Many of the survivors of these attempts, together with the Spanish Augustinians who had accompanied the Spanish ambassador sent to Canton by the Governor of Manila, all contributed, back in Manila, to the dangerous talk of a Spanish or even a united European force being assembled to conquer China or even Japan and China.

Alessandro Valignano, as we have already seen when discussing the Jesuit mission in Japan, was only too aware of these dangerous ideas which he particularly associated with anyone coming from the 'conquistador' city of Manila. He was determined that the Society of Jesus should gain legitimate entry to the Chinese Emire and there operate only along the lines of the principles which underlay his famous Japanese *Summario* of 1582. This document was itself the outworking of the decision he made in principle in 1579 on his first visit to Macao. At that time, after a stay of over a year, he wrote to the General insisting that the work in China and Japan would have to be different from the approach used hitherto on the subject peoples of the Portuguese and Spanish empires.[1] This may very well have been a result of his seeing these two peoples as 'white' nations, but whatever the reason he was utterly committed, in Japan and China, to the general principle of the Jesuit missionaries conforming and adapting to the indigenous cultures in every way consonant with an effective proclamation of the faith.

When Michele Ruggieri began to study Chinese he was troubled by his colleagues in the Jesuit House in Macao who thought he would be better employed sharing their chaplaincy work in the colony. They insisted he would never be allowed to enter China and so learning Chinese, which was impossibly difficult, was also pointless. So persistent and unpleasant were they towards him that Ricci later referred to Ruggieri's time there as a 'little martyrdom'. Despite this very discouraging atmosphere, Ruggieri persisted and, despite his own limited linguistic abilities, doggedly stuck to his task.

He imaginatively used the regular visits made by Portuguese traders to Canton as opportunities for making contacts within the empire. He went to Canton once in 1580 and then again with the two trade embassies of 1581. Each time he paid particular attention to all the formalities of dealing with Chinese officials. By the last visit they noticed that Ruggieri knew how to behave in a way that the other Europeans did not. He was simply transferring to China the basic principles which Valignano laid out so clearly in his *Il Ceremoniale per i Missionari del Giappone*. Notably he performed the 'kou tou' when approaching a senior official which was the appropriate way to behave. At that time most Europeans saw it as something unworthy. Later in the nineteenth century, as so many Europeans thrust their way into China, they saw performing the 'kou tou' as something utterly incompatible with the dignity of the white race. This attitude of European self-importance has lasted well into the twentieth century and can be seen in Rowbotham's *Missionary and Mandarin*[2] where he complains of the Jesuits 'truckling' to senior Chinese officials when what they were doing was behaving appropriately as Chinese.

As a result of the impression he had made upon them, the senior officials in Canton gave Ruggieri permission to set up a chapel there in the quarter for foreign embassies and to say Mass there for foreign traders. Indeed, so taken with him were some of the mandarins that a number of them attended his Mass. They did not do this as worshippers but out of courtesy. A very sad sign of what was to happen later in Japan and China was that Ruggieri was criticised by Franciscans in Macao for having permitted pagans to be present at his celebration of Mass.

However that may be, next May Ruggieri was able to obtain an interview with the Viceroy of the two Provinces of Guangdong and Yuangxi in the city of Zhaoqing. Initially this visit was not an auspicious one. A group of Spaniards from the Philippines had landed in Fukien. They had been arrested, and as a result of this incident the Viceroy had insisted that the Captain-General and the Bishop of Macao come and explain to him their right to be in Macao. The arrest of the Spaniards had again raised the whole issue of any permanent foreign presence on Chinese soil. Ruggieri was used by the Portuguese delegation as interpreter for both officials. His work was a success from their point of view and, more importantly, also from his. The Viceroy and his advisers were so taken with Ruggieri that he was invited to come back and take up residence in the city.

On 27 December 1582 Ruggieri returned to Zhaoqing together with Francesco Pasio. They hoped to make this their new home, and as a symbol of the new life they were entering and as a means of identifying with Chinese life they dressed as Buddhist monks, which meant shaving their heads as well as their beards. This change was also made to indicate the religious nature of their mission. In any case it fitted the initial perception of them, as most Chinese tended to see them as a special sort of Buddhist, much as the Japanese had initially.

Unhappily this marvellous opportunity appeared to be taken away from them only too soon. The Viceroy was summoned to Beijing to answer certain accusations. This was very soon after another illegal landing had been made, this time by Spanish Franciscans from Manila. In the light of all this the Viceroy decided that the Jesuits had better go back to Macao lest they were associated in some way with the illegal landings and so made the situation worse for him. Within six months of this disappointment, Ruggieri was allowed back to Zhaoqing and his application for a piece of land on whch to build a house and a place of worship was granted. So in September 1583 Ruggieri returned to stay in Zhaoqing with a new associate, Fr Matteo Ricci.

Born in Macerata in Central Italy in 1552, the young Ricci had been sent by his father to Rome to study law. In 1571, against his father's wishes, he entered the novitiate of the Society of Jesus, where strangely enough his novice master was Alessandro Valignano. Before he was ordained priest Ricci volunteered and was accepted for service in the East. He had been a brilliant student at the Roman College, and had become very close to his professor of Mathematics, Galileo's friend and colleague Christopher Klau (Clavius),[3] creator of the Gregorian Calendar. Ricci remained Klau's friend, writing to him regularly for the rest of his life.

Arriving in Goa on 13 September 1578, Ricci spent most of his time teaching in the Jesuit College there, though he still had to complete some theological classes himself at the same time. It is important to note, however, that the foundations of his theological education had already been well laid by the then new professor at the Roman College, Robert Bellarmine. Ricci also spent a brief period doing pastoral work in Cochin where he was ordained priest in 1580.

George Dunne reports a letter Ricci wrote to the General from Goa which, he rightly insists in his *Generation of Giants*,[4] is of great significance for any attempt to understand Ricci. We have seen that Valignano was not greatly impressed by the abilities of Indian people relative to their suitability for the priesthood. In Japan, however, he had come to accept the potential of the Japanese for the priesthood. He rejected Fr Cabral's attitude towards the form of training to be adopted for Japanese candidates for ordination. Cabral's view was that 'natives' being trained for the priesthood should not be given the full training in Arts and Theology usual for Europeans, but that it should be restricted to enough Latin to say the liturgy and instruction in 'cases of conscience' so as to be able to do basic pastoral work. Valignano made sure that was not how seminary education developed in Japan, but in India in 1581 the local Superior of the Society decided that Cabral's idea was appropriate for training Indian priests. Ricci not only objected to this but was so incensed that he formally complained to the General in Rome. On 25 November 1581 he wrote,

> I do not consider the reasons which are advanced for it very strong. They say that study makes them proud and that they will not want to minister in poor parishes; and that they will hold in low esteem the many Jesuits who are frequently heard of in these parts, who make little progress in philosophy and theology. But all this, and perhaps with even better reason, could be said of those who study in our schools elsewhere than in India, even in Europe; and we don't refuse, for that reason, to teach all comers. All the more reason then, in the case of natives of this land who, however much they know, very rarely receive much credit from white men. On the other hand there is a universal custom in the whole Society to make no distinction between classes of people, and even here in India there are so many Fathers, old, holy and experienced, who open schools and are favourably disposed to all who come there. Secondly, in this way we encourage ignorance in ministers of the Church in a place where learning is so necessary. These men have

to be prepared in every way to be priests and to care for souls, and it is not a good thing if, with so many kinds of infidels, priests are so ignorant that they do not know how to answer an argument or to confirm themselves or others in our faith. We should not demand miracles where they are not necessary, and a simple casuist cannot match up to these demands. Thirdly, and this is the thing that most disturbs me, in my opinion they have none who show kindness to them except our people, and for this reason they have a special affection for us. If they come to learn that our Fathers are opposed to them and do not want to allow them to lift up their heads and obtain advantages and offices equal to others, they will come to hate us, and thus will be impeded the principal goal of the Society in India, the conversion of the infidels and their conservation in our holy faith.[5]

This is a very blunt statement indeed and it comes from someone who has already been in Goa for three years, by which time, only too often, priests had come to adopt a less than sympathetic attitude to India and Indians.

On the recommendation of Ruggieri at the end of 1582, Valignano ordered Ricci to leave Goa and join Ruggieri. In particular, Ricci was instructed by Valignano to prepare a comprehensive report on China for the Visitor. He was to describe its peoples, customs, institutions and government, all this while learning Chinese.

Ricci plunged into the task. Using a staff of Chinese interpreters he wrote up a report based on Chinese written authorities, checking what he wrote against the sympathetic judgement of Ruggieri. A lot of what he said, both complimentary and critical of China, he would correct later in other writing, but this report, which Valignano incorporated in his Life of Xavier, is the first serious and reasonably accurate report about China received in the West. Some of the writing of the Polos had not been entirely fanciful, and similarly what was still retained of the Franciscan writings of the fourteenth century was accurate enough for the China of their day. However, as yet people did not understand that Cathay was China and Khanbalic was Beijing. It was to be Ricci, whose intelligent deductions from the measurements he made to calculate the latitude and longitude of a number of Chinese cities on his later journeys to and from Beijing, who deduced that Cathay and China were one. His insight was to be confirmed by the hazardous journey of that other Jesuit hero Fr de Goes, whose overland journey was to prove conclusively the identity of China and Cathay.[6]

In Zhaoqing, Ricci buckled down to learning to speak and write Mandarin, the Chinese of the literati and of the Confucian classical literature. He had the advantage of benefiting from Ruggieri's hard-gained experience. Ruggieri was older and less able but he had worked at his task and he had understood the Chinese well enough to be singled out, as we have seen, from the ordinary run of barbarians. The task Ricci faced was still an enormous one in which there were no academic aids whatsoever. Despite the fact that there were no grammars, dictionaries or even word-lists, the two students in Zhaoqing made real progress in a task that was not simply to 'get up' enough of a spoken language to preach and create an elementary catechism. In China the task Valignano had set them was to learn to speak and to write a highly sophisticated literary language with a two thousand year old philosphic and literary history.

A young Chinese scholar was attracted to them. He decided to live with them and help them in their attempt to learn mandarin while Ricci began to instruct him in the Christian faith. He also helped them edit and prepare for publication a simple catechism composed by Ruggieri which had existed only in the form of some hand-written copies hitherto, *Tianzhu shilu, The True Account of God*.

This was in 1584. However, just as important as their literary efforts was the fact that they were now totally immersed in Chinese life and their house was the centre of interest for men from many classes of Chinese society. This constant stream of visitors was not only an important factor in speeding Ricci's progress with the language, he learned from his intercourse with them how central to Chinese society and the Chinese state were the literati.

The role of Buddhist monk which the Jesuits had adopted had been officially confirmed, as it were, by the placing of a plaque on the entrance to their house. This plaque, gifted by the magistrate Wang Pan, read 'Xian Hua Ssu' (temple of the Flower of the Saints). Ricci said this was a reference to Mary to whom the chapel in their house was dedicated. To the ordinary Chinese it appeared to indicate that this was a Buddhist temple and 'Xian' referred to those who had achieved Nirvana. This ambiguous recognition had been an advantage to the Jesuits since it enabled literati, both in and out of office, to visit them, something which otherwise would have been impossible. However, this was two-edged because all members of the literati, even the lowliest Xiucai (holders of the very first level of the first academic degree) could freely use the Jesuit house as a suitable venue for convivial as well as intellectual gatherings. In such a situation the role of the Jesuits was more akin to that of the host of a hostelry than as the hosts of honoured friends. Yet on balance Ricci held it to be to the Society's advantage. If their residence had not been held to be a 'temple' the literati could not have visited them. This was because a mandarin could not visit private residences except those of other members of the literati, but they could visit a Buddhist temple or monastery.

There is some conflict among the various authorities as to the source of the decision to adopt this role of bonze or Buddhist monk. In 1582 the whole pattern of Jesuit life in Japan was planned on the model of Zen monastic regulations about ranks and etiquette. Some have suggested that it was Valignano who, in keeping with his Japanese model, suggested this role for China. Others have said that it was the Viceroy who had insisted that this was the way Jesuits must appear if they wished to stay in the empire, yet others have suggested that Ruggieri thought of it initially and suggested it to the Viceroy who approved.

What Valignano said to Ruggieri in his initial instruction of 1579 is no longer available to us, and his instructions sent from Japan in 1582, when the Visitor was laying down his rules for the mission there, were not prescriptive as the rules for Japan were. He told Ruggieri that in addition to his language work he was to study 'the customs and all else necessary to make it possible to undertake this enterprise when it shall please Our Lord.'[7] There is nothing specific in these instructions about Buddhist dress.

Given their general aim to find a niche within Chinese society into which they were to fit, how else could the Jesuits have dressed? The dress of the literati, which they adopted later, they could not have adopted at that time because they were equipped neither in language nor in the knowledge of the Classics for such a role. The dress of any of the three ranks into which ordinary Chinese people were divided would have hidden their role, both as religious and as teachers and would have been quite wrong. It does not seem to have occurred to anyone to consider their adopting the dress of a Daoist priest, though when it was decided to give up the role of bonze the name they used intially of themselves, a name chosen by Ricci, 'daoren', was a phrase commonly used to refer to such priests.[8]

In any case, however the decision came about to adopt this role, Ruggieri had quickly appreciated that it was the only one available to them if they were to enter into Chinese society. As we have seen, at Zhaoqing it worked. Their home became a centre of gatherings of Chinese which gave the Italians contacts they would not otherwise have been able to make. In turn this gave them a knowledge of the way Chinese society operated and of the central importance of the literati in both Chinese society and the Chinese state. This stood them in good stead when the new Viceroy of the two Provinces decided he wanted the Jesuit buildings in Zhaoqing for himself. Their contacts among the scholar-administrators and their appreciation of how matters were conducted in China, enabled the Fathers to obtain a new place of residence at Shaozhou, instead of having to retreat in defeat to Macao. Indeed so skilfully did Ricci play out the negotiations that in the end a senior officer of the Viceroy accompanied the Jesuits to Shaozhou to help them gain new accomodation in August 1589. There, in the new and this time Chinese-style buildings, Ricci's household became again a focus for visits by interested literati.

Meanwhile, Ruggieri had returned to Europe on Valignano's orders. He was to put the case at the Papal court for a full scale Papal embassy to be sent to the Emperor at Beijing in order to gain his permission for the Society of Jesus to set up residences throughout the empire. Ruggieri's mission was doomed to failure for, at that time, the Papacy had much else to concern it, as had the Catholic monarchs, while the intelligentsia of Europe had not yet become obsessed with things Chinese as they were to become at the end of the seventeenth and beginning of the eighteenth centuries.[9]

At Shaozhou the most significant contact made by Ricci among the literati was with a young scholar, Qu Rukuei. This man was the son of one of the most illustrious scholar-administrators of the Ming era, Qu Jingchun. Qu Rukuei had not followed his father into the imperial service, but, though well qualified, had simply pursued the life of a gentleman scholar. Dunne calls him a dilettante which is a little unfair.[10] His scholarly qualifications were impeccable, there was nothing dilettante about his scholarship; it was his way of life, existing on family wealth and not entering the service, that was 'amateurish'.

Qu Rukuei came to have a warm affection for Ricci and Matteo for him. For the first time a Chinese scholar became interested enough in the scientific books and instruments which the Jesuits displayed in their residence to enquire seriously about western scientific knowledge. The many literati who had frequented the residence had, up till then, shown only an idle and passing curiosity about these things. The fact that Qu Rukuei's interest was aroused intitially by the hope of gaining the alchemical knowledge of turning base metals into gold did not matter, for he was soon captivated by what he learned of western science.

The one western artefact in the residence which had fascinated all the Chinese visitors was the map of the world that Ricci had drawn and put on the wall. He had annotated the map in Chinese. It always astonished and excited visitors who saw China for the first time in a global perspective. One visitor was so impressed that he had the map copied without informing Ricci or asking his permission, and then had it printed and published. The map became very popular and copies were spread far beyond Guangdong province. The extraordinarily widespread popularity of his map persuaded Ricci to work on it and make it an even more effective tool for reaching the literati. He continued to work on his Mappamondo, on and off, until he published his own final version in 1602.

Qu Rukuei became a keen student of western scientific knowledge and established a close pupil-master relationship with Ricci — or Li Madou as he had become known in Chinese. For a whole year he worked on Clavius' arithmetic and at Clavius' book on spheres, as well as on the beginning of Euclid. In addition he had Ricci teach him the more practical skills of making sundials and the elements of surveying. To Ricci's delight he did not limit his enquiries to science but sought information about the religious faith of his teacher. This was the first success of what later Jesuits would refer to as the 'scientific apostolate'. While being instructed, Qu Rukuei took careful notes and then presented Ricci with many pointed and profound questions. This period of one-to-one question and answer sessions with such a keen mind trained in the Classics, really tested Ricci and was also an excellent learning experience for the Jesuit teacher about the relation of the Christian faith to the Confucian beliefs of the literati.

Qu Rukuei also played an important role by introducing Ricci to other literati who had not chosen to visit the residence of 'the bonzes from the far west', and through his network of friends and relations he spread Ricci's fame far beyond the city and even the province. He also took Ricci to Nanxiong, where Ricci started a small Christian community among non-literati Chinese initially, but where he also became a friend of the prefect of the city, Wang Yinlin.

These friendships were of inestimable importance to the Jesuits. Through this intimacy with the literati community of the two cities, Ricci not only deepened his knowledge of the language and of the Classics, he also gained a far deeper understanding of Chinese culture in general and of the political culture of the day in particular. Qu Rukuei appears to have played an important part in directing Ricci towards changing the emphasis of the Jesuit mission. This is in part symbolised by his recommendation that they change their dress. Perhaps it would be better to say that he persuaded Ricci to change their dress to better represent what their mission already was, a mission that aimed at entering Chinese society through the intellectual world of the Confucian literati. By the end of 1592, when he had had a full year of almost daily contact with Qu Rukuei and the many scholars to whom the latter had introduced him, Ricci was clear that the clothes and role of the Buddhist monk was no longer the appropriate style to represent who the Jesuits were. Indeed some ambiguity about their role as either bonzes or, in some sense at least, 'scholars' had already arisen in 1586.

That year an imperial decree had been issued ordering the destruction of all Buddhist temples and monasteries in China. It was soon withdrawn and was never seriously enforced. However, the local magistrates at Zhaoqing had eventually decided that the edict did not apply to the Jesuits in any case because they were not truly bonzes but were, in some sense, 'scholars'.[11] They were, of course, still wearing Buddhist dress and shaving their heads and faces, but they took down the plaque from outside the residence which Wang Pan had given them which indicated that the residence was a 'temple'.

Qu Rukuei appears to have pushed Ricci hard on the inappropriateness of wearing the clothes of a bonze, but what else were Ricci and his fellow Jesuits to do? Scholar dress was what Rukuei suggested, and that certainly fitted them as they appeared in Shaozhu and it was even how some magistrates had perceived them back in Zhaoqing in 1586. However Ricci was hesitant because he knew the Jesuits would have to merit wearing that style of clothing by their knowledge of the Classics or they would appear charlatans.

Ricci was progressing fast in his knowledge of the Classics, and the process was greatly accelerated when Valignano sent him instructions to translate the *Sishu (The Four Books)* into Latin for the benefit of the Visitor who believed this was essential for the preparation of any effective catechism for China. This task, in which he was aided by a variety of his friends among the literati, was in effect Ricci's basic education in Confucianism. As he delved deeper and deeper into the Classics he began to approach the level of linguistic and literary skill that would make scholar's dress no longer inappropriate. So at the end of 1592 Ricci paid a brief visit to Macao in order to consult with Valignano about the future of the China mission.

On this visit Ricci raised with the Visitor the need to move on from Shaozhu and set up a second Jesuit residence. There needed to be additional residences otherwise the whole mission would fail if they lost possession of their one piece of property. In addition the mission, Ricci insisted, must move deeper into China to make its work more effective. Apart from all this Shaozhu was unhealthy; Ricci's first companion, Fr d'Almeida, had died there of fever in 1591. The final black mark against Shaozhu was that, despite the mission's many friends, there was still a significant number of people in the city hostile to the mission. Earlier that year a bunch of drunken rowdies had attacked the residence one night and in the resulting mêlée, while trying to summon help from the authorities, Ricci had damaged his ankle so badly that it troubled him for the rest of his life.

The other important matter he raised with Valignano was a possible change of dress for the Jesuits in China. This would certainly be a major step, but it was in keeping with the overall attitude to mission that Valignano had employed in Japan and which had shaped his instructions to Ruggieri. Indeed it was in keeping with his insistence on the need to understand *The Four Books* before a Christian Catechism could be written. Valignano's 1582 instructions to Ruggieri ordered the Jesuits to seek to do everything possible to identify with Chinese life consonant with the proclamation of the Christian faith. The problem, however, was that if they wore scholar's dress, they would be wearing the uniform of people who were clearly not what the Catholic Church could recognise as either clergy or religious. The canons of the Council of Trent might therefore be held to present some difficulties in this matter. After Ricci's departure, Valignano consulted the other Jesuits in Macao and the Bishop of Japan, whom we have already met, Luis Cerqueira about the changes. Valignano also wrote to the General in Rome and to the Pope, but this was, according to Ricci, simply to inform them that 'all this was done for the better service of God' – 'poichè tutto si faceva per magior servitio di Iddio'.[12]

How far Ricci introduced Valignano to his growing understanding of the 'original' Confucianism which he found in the Classics and the possibility of building upon it in the development of Christianity in China, is not clear in chapter nine of the *Fonte Ricciane* in which Ricci discusses this consultation. However, since it was Valignano who had asked him to translate *The Four Books* as a preparatory step necessary before Christian doctrine could be articulated in a meaningful way for Chinese Christians, it is not unreasonable to presume it did appear on the agenda of this last meeting of these two extraordinary men.

At this time Ricci had already come to believe that an essentially mono-theistic religious understanding pervaded what he called 'original' Confucianism, that is Confucian thought before the developments in the Sung era and in particular the commentaries on the Classics of the great teacher Zhuxi. The understanding of Confucianism represented in the latter's commentaries was the intellectual orthodoxy in Ming China and is usually referred to as neo-Confucianism. In disagreeing with it Ricci was by no means ploughing a lone eccentric European furrow for he had arrived in China at a time when there was a particularly rich flowering of many contrasting interpretations of

Confucius. It was this atmosphere of lively controversy which gave Ricci his
opportunity to lay the foundations for the same sort of marriage between a
philosophy, Confucianism, and the Christian faith as Thomas Aquinas had
performed with Aristotelianism. As Ricci met more and more literati, some of
them of the highest rank, on the next stage of his mission he became more
and more convinced that building on 'original' Confucianism was a worthwhile
approach.[13]

The new stage in Ricci's mission began when he was approached by a senior
official for help in restoring the man's son to health. The official was a senior
member of the War Board and had been summoned to Beijing because of the
crisis created by Hideyoshi's invasion of Korea. Ricci referred to the mandarin
as Scielou in Italian. Some authorities, for example Dunne, claim that they can
identify him but Jonathan Spence does not believe so. Scielou had heard of
Ricci as a 'scientist' and asked if he would accompany him and his family on
part of their journey to Beijing in order to get to know and help the young man
out of the deep depression into which he had fallen since failing the examination
for the Jinshi degree. It is highly probable, though Ricci, from his point of view
understandably, does not even hint at this, that Scielou saw him in Daoist terms
as something between what we would now call a scientist and a shaman.

Because of his command of mnemonic techniques Ricci was confident that
through these skills he could help the young man regain confidence so as to
tackle the examinations again in the future. The invitation was therefore a
golden opportunity to get free transport all the way to the capital. Valignano
had already made it clear that no formal embassy was going to be mounted
from Rome, but both he and Ricci at that time still believed it essential to
make contact with the Emperor and court circles in order to gain some form
of imperial permission for the work of the Society.

In answer to Ricci's request, Scielou agreed to take him all the way to the
capital. So Ricci left Fr Cattaneo with two senior Chinese irmao to man the
Shaozhu residence and set out for Beijing in April 1595. He took with him two
Chinese irmao who had been converted originally in Macao so we have only
their new Portuguese names, Juan Barradas and Domingo Fernandes. The
three missionaries with two servants joined the small fleet of river boats taking
Scielou, his family and entourage to the capital. On the journey Ricci made a
welcome visit to the small Christian community among the merchant families
of Nanxiong, a congregation he had brought into being on a visit three years
before.

A friendship between Ricci and Scielou developed during a number of
long private talks the two men had about science and religion. It was firmly
cemented, however, in a very dramatic way when the barge carrying the mandarin's wives and children struck a rock and Ricci and his little group rescued
them and took them aboard their vessel which, from courtesy, he gave up to
the ladies. This, in turn, led to a tragedy. Ricci and the young novice, Barradas,

for whom Ricci had high hopes of a distinguished career in the Society, had to transfer onto a luggage barge of the mandarin's. This overturned while traversing some notorious rapids and although the non-swimmer, Ricci, was saved by clinging to a rope, his young companion was never found again, though Scielou's servants dived many times into the river seeking his body.

These tragedies convinced the mandarin that travelling by river and canal was not auspicious and he set out to finish the journey to Beijing on horseback. Since going to the capital seemed to be no longer possible, Ricci took the opportunity to accompany some of Scielou's officers who had to go to the southern capital of the empire, Nanjing. There, in the southern capital, Ricci paid formal visits to many leading officials of his acquaintance in his new dress, that of a scholar. It had been on the long journey with Scielou that he had grown his hair and beard and put on the scholar's robes. The senior mandarin had confirmed that it was an appropriate change and this was endorsed by the many literati he visited in Nanjing.

However, the atmosphere in the city was still somewhat tense because of the war and there was a great deal of hostility to foreigners. What did not help was that it was well known that some of the best Japanese generals and troops were Christians, though luckily for Ricci and the mission, it did not appear to be known that these same troops had Jesuit chaplains with them. In any case Ricci's friends advised him not to stay in Nanjing and so, very disappointed, he began the journey south again. On the way he met and became friendly with an official travelling to Nanchang. When they arrived there at the end of June 1595 the official introduced Ricci to many of his friends. Ricci already knew that this city was renowned for its large community of scholars, in contrast with Guangdong province, so having been warmly received there he decided to make it the site of a new Jesuit residence.

Ricci's name was already known in Nanchang, in any case, because of his mappamondo and because Qu Rukuei had sung his praises to some of the literati there. His friendship with Scielou was a bonus. The Viceroy's personal physician and confidant was a close friend of Scielou's and he acted as Ricci's host at a number of dinners and receptions in the city. At one of these events, attended by most of the important officials in the city and by two princes of the imperial family, Ricci startled the guests by his knowledge of the Classics but even more by his feats of memory.[14] He repeated forwards and backwards lists of Chinese characters given to him at random and with no logical or phonetic links. Since the basic requirement for success in the Chinese examination system was accurate memory work, this feat was doubly impressive to an audience of the literati class. On other similar occasions he would recite passages from the Classics chosen by fellow guests at random. The result of all this was that his new friends prevailed upon him to write a book on mnemonic technique, which he did, and they had it published under the title *Xiguo Jifa*.

Suddenly this apparently successful entry into Nanchang society seemed threatened when Ricci was summoned to appear before the Viceroy, Luo Zhonghao. Many people felt certain this meant that Ricci would be asked to leave and a number tried to disassociate themselves from him. However, the interview went exceptionally well from Ricci's point of view. On coming before the Viceroy, Ricci punctiliously made the kou tou; the Viceroy, however, did not leave him kneeling for the rest of the interview, which would have been usual. The two men spoke for a long time about both mathematics and about Christian thought. At the end of the interview the Viceroy requested that Ricci remain in Nanchang.

'Li Madou' was now accepted widely among the literati and was soon deeply involved again in the constant round of visiting and receiving visits. He was constantly invited out to dinner where, as was the usual practice, hours were spent in serious conversations about philosophy and other intellectual matters. It was at that time that Ricci became fully aware of the intellectual ferment going on among the Confucianist scholars who belonged to the movement which originated in local associations, referred to as 'academies'. These coalesced in the first decade of the seventeenth century into an organised intellectual opposition to the combination of eunuchs and some very conservative scholars who dominated the administration of the empire under the Wanli Emperor. The scholars who were allied with the eunuchs interpreted the Confucian tradition in a narrowly neo-Confucian manner and attempted to impose it as an orthodoxy from which there could be no deviation.

The movement of intellectual and political resistance became known in the seventeenth century as the Tunglin movement. At Nanchang an outstanding scholar, Chang Huang, presided over one of the first of the 'academies' from which this movement developed. Chang was the author of *Tushu Bian* (*Encyclopedia of Geography*). He and Ricci became firm friends and each taught the other a great deal. This led to Li Madou's fame spreading even further since Chang refers to him on a number of occasions in the Encyclopedia which also included a reproduction of Ricci's mappamondo.

Thus in Nanchang the pattern of Ricci's missionary service was set for the rest of his life. He lived as a Chinese scholar among Chinese scholars as far as he could, consonant with his missionary commitment. The pattern was an exhausting one, for on top of the many visits he made and the hospitality he necessarily had to offer in return, all of which were activities central to his scholarly role, he worked at making sundials, astrolabes and other technical tools related to astronomy which were greatly admired. He engaged in theological discussion with anyone who sought it and also said Mass. All the while he still followed his study of the Classics and continued his translation work.

This punishing schedule continued to the end of his life. It is well described by Dunne who quotes a letter from Ricci to a friend, Girolama Costa.

I don't have time to eat until at least one o'clock in the afternoon. Two or three times a week I am invited to dinner and sometimes to two places on one day, and I have to go to both of them...One difficulty is that on fast days of the Church I have to fast all day inasmuch as these dinners don't start until night; but fortunately I have a good stomach.[15]

Ricci was reinforced at the new residence in the last days of December 1595 by the arrival of Fr Soeiro and the Chinese irmao Huang Mingshao, which eased his burden somewhat.

It was also at Nanchang that Ricci became so confident of his command of Mandarin that he wrote his first work directly in Chinese, *A Treatise on Friendship (Jiaoyou lun)*. He dedicated this book to one of the Ming princes whom he had come to know since arriving in the city. It was published by a Chinese friend and then republished many times, and rapidly came to be known among the literati throughout the whole empire. Without his realising it initially, this was an essential step in giving the Jesuits a firm footing in China. It was this book that finally convinced the scholar community that Ricci was someone who could be respected as a Chinese scholar, someone who had overcome his unfortunate foreign origins to become one who could be treated as if he were Chinese.

Since Ricci did not publish this book himself it did not have to go through the elaborate form of censorship exercised by the Church over books to be published by priests and members of Religious Orders. This was something for which Ricci was profoundly grateful since attempting to have a Chinese book checked by the ecclesiastical authorities in Goa, so far away both geographically and culturally, was an appallingly long and tedious process.

Although the western scientific knowledge which, first displayed by Ruggieri and then much more clearly by Ricci, was of interest to the literati, that interest, with the exception of a few individuals like Qu Rukuei, had not been much more than idle curiosity. With the publication of *Jiaoyou lun* Ricci was established as a scholar in Confucian terms, so now his scientific knowledge became something worthy of respect in the eyes of the literati. This was totally different from the picture of Ricci's missionary methods that have appeared in so many books by scholars as different as K. M. Pannikar and Nigel Cameron, who insist that western scientific knowledge was the bait played before the literati concealing the hook of Christianity.[16] In fact it was only after Matteo Ricci had been established in the eyes of leading literati as a scholar in Chinese terms that his western scientific knowledge was seen as something worth investigating.

Because Nanchang was at that time a centre of intellectual ferment and openness under the leadership of Chang Huang this set the pattern for the advance of the Jesuit mission in China. Ricci presented an intellectual and spiritual challenge in Confucian terms to the Confucian literati at a time when they were open to fresh thinking within the parameters of Confucianism. It has to be noted that of the literati who became Christians during Ricci's lifetime, and the many who did not seek baptism yet were sympathetic to the Society and whose help was often vital to the continuance of its work, all were associated with the circles that produced the Tunglin movement.

Another fundamental aspect of Ricci's missionary style also took shape in Nanchang. In 1596 he was able to buy some property which became the permanent Jesuit residence. Unlike the previous two residences, the new buildings had no public chapel. This was not to hide the fact that the Jesuits were Christians; but when they had operated public chapels they were dressed as Buddhist monks. Opening no more public chapels was part of the rejection of that role by the Society in China. It was also something which was sensible to do because in the late Ming Dynasty there was a deep suspicion of regular gatherings of people on any scale because of the fear aroused by the many religiously inspired secret revolutionary societies, like the White Lotus Society, which was very active at that time. These movements were associated with various popular forms of Buddhist piety.

The principal reasons for Ricci's decision were however two. First, he wished to end once and for all the Jesuit association with Buddhism and secondly, he was firmly convinced by then that small group discussions were the effective form of evangelism among the educated in China, not public preaching. Two letters Ricci wrote in October 1596 to friends in Italy which are printed in the *Opere Storiche* make this unambiguously clear.[17]

Jesuit missionary activity took this shape because Ricci was concentrating upon the literati. He believed that without gaining a foothold in that class and thereby winning a general toleration for the Society and its mission by that class as a whole, there was no way in which a Christian missionary presence could operate with any hope of success in China. Before the mass of commoners could be reached on any significant scale the Society had to establish itself as a part of Chinese society, and that was only possible with at least the acquiescence, if not the active support, of the literati. This was the task he believed he had been given by Valignano, and the Visitor confirmed this by supporting him in everything he did.

There is no doubt that this approach worked well in Nanchang. Not only was this a city with a large population of the scholar class, it was also an examination centre for the zhujen degree. Every three years the city was flooded with examination candidates and when this event occurred when Ricci was in the city, many of the candidates called on the famous author of *Jiaoyou lun* to pay their respects. As a result, not only was Ricci becoming widely known through his publications but many scholar-officials from all over the empire had seen him and spoken with him face to face.

Ricci's stay in Nanchang came to an end when it appeared that he had the chance to go to Beijing with sufficient contacts among the mandarins there to give him the hope of being able to establish a permanent Jesuit presence at the heart of the empire. This opportunity occurred through the good offices of an old friend from Shaozhou days.

This was Wang Honghui who had been President of the Board of Rites at the southern capital, Nanjing, but who had retired in disgust at the intrigues of the palace eunuchs. He now believed that he was going to be restored to office. He was travelling back to Nanjing and on the way stopped at Nanchang where he understood his old friend Li Madou had come to reside. He determined to take Ricci with him to Beijing where Wang had been called to attend a special celebration for the Emperor's birthday. It had occurred to him that he might suggest that Ricci be asked to help revise the Imperial Calendar which had been showing deeply disturbing inaccuracies for some time. This would be a service to the empire and would also stand Wang himself in good stead. Ricci was delighted to receive this opportunity and planned to leave Nanchang permanently. He left two priests, de Rocha and Soerio, in Nanchang to look after the growing Christian community with its many commoners and some literati. He planned to take with him to Beijing, Fr Lazzaro Cattaneo and two Chinese Jesuits, Zhong Mingren and Yu Wenhui. On 25 June 1598 they set out for Nanjing en route for Beijing.

At Nanjing, Ricci made what turned out to be a very important contact. The Viceroy of the Province had received as a gift, some years before, a copy of Ricci's 'World Map' which he treasured greatly. When he learned that the maker of the map was in Nanjing he was very insistent that Ricci spend some time with him before proceeding to Beijing. Consequently Cattaneo and the two Chinese novices went on towards Beijing while Ricci spent a week at the Viceroy's residence at Juyong. There the Viceroy, Zhao Kehuai, spent many hours discussing philosophy, science and religion with Ricci. He also brought many of his friends to banquets at his house to meet him. After a week the Viceroy allowed his new friend to leave, but not without giving him money to cover travel costs and arranging for his own boatmen to transport him to where he could catch up wth the others.

This new friendship proved very fortunate for the missionaries because their stay in Beijing, where they arrived on 7 September 1598, was brief. Wang Honghui found that his old enemies and their eunuch allies still held power and there would be no new appointment to the Board of Rites for him. The Japanese had renewed the fighting in Korea and there was again some anti-foreign excitement in the capital. Indeed so nervous did many officials become about being associated with foreigners that some old friends, and others to whom Ricci had letters of introduction, did not want to be publicly associated with him. This was one of the few times during his life in China that Ricci recorded bitter and disappointed thoughts about his own and the Society's situation there.

Ricci quickly decided there was no point in staying in the capital, so he and his fellow Jesuits withdrew and began the journey south. Ricci felt that the good contacts he had established in Nanjing were such that they could go back there and establish a new residence of the Society. They had to leave Beijing at the wrong time to travel and their barge was soon frozen in on a northern canal. Ricci left the others to guard their baggage, which contained precious gifts that had been intended for the Emperor, and made his way southwards on horseback and on foot, making for the home of his first true friend among the literati, Qu Rukuei, at Suzhou. He arrived eventually at Suzhou utterly exhausted, but at Qu Rukuei's house he was warmly received. Qu and his friends suggested that he set up a residence there and not go to Nanjing, which they felt would be dangerous for the Jesuits. Qu decided, however, that when Ricci was recovered they should both go to visit Wang Honghui in Nanjing so that he might provide letters of introduction for Ricci to present to officials in the Suzhou area.

In Nanjing, where they arrived at the beginning of February 1599, Ricci was given an overwhelmingly affectionate reception by Wang Honghui, as well as by many of the senior administrators of this southern capital, where each imperial Board of Beijing was duplicated. The commander of the imperial garrison and one of the ancient aristocracy who lived in almost imperial splendour in the city, the Duke of Wei, also made a great show of welcoming him. This was partly due to the great fame of Li Madou, partly because of the many powerful friends he now possessed and partly because everyone was exuberantly celebrating the end of the Korean war and a much vaunted Chinese victory over the Japanese rearguard.

Ricci was convinced that the security of the tiny Jesuit presence in the empire was completely dependent upon the friendships that the Jesuits had made among the literati in general and the scholar-administrators in particular. He had created a situation whereby most literati could behave towards them as if they were Chinese. However, he also knew very well that anyone in office who was opposed to them could overturn that in an instant. This was because, despite what Ruggieri thought and many writers have since repeated, they were not Chinese 'citizens'; there was no such category for those not ethnically Chinese. The Jesuits had achieved, under his leadership, a situation where they were treated as loyal subjects of the Emperor, as if they were Chinese, but it was not a permanent status in law. The ambiguity of this situation was the reason why Ricci would often not ask for written permission from an official when he wished to do something. The word of an official was taken as enough to act upon. This procedure left no written record which an ultra-conservative superior might hold against the official who had issued it. The fragility of this situation, in which they lived as if they were secure in being true Chinese while knowing it could all be denied in an instant, is clearly illustrated at this time when they were invited to set up a residence in Nanjing.

In the southern capital the most influential official was not the Viceroy nor Ricci's friend Wang Honghui, nor the Duke of Wei, but the imperial Censor,

Zu Shilu. When he joined the chorus of voices urging the Jesuits to stay their place was secure. From his position, one of the highest in the whole empire, he insisted that Ricci was no longer a foreigner and in any case who could object to his staying in Nanjing 'where there were so many Hui-hui' (Muslims).[18] Yet only two years later in Beijing, some senior officials were to insist, just as firmly, that Ricci was a foreigner and could not stay in the empire. Yet Ricci's was an astonishing achievement. He had become such a master of Chinese and the Confucian Classics that the literati as a class could treat him as if one of them-selves. This was so even when he disagreed with some of them over intellectual points. Indeed the arguments and debates he was encouraged to take part in by his literati hosts are in some ways the ultimate confirmation of his acceptance. However, all this could be overlooked and he was a 'foreigner' again if it was politically expedient for a scholar so to insist.

In Nanjing, Ricci made a very wide circle of friends among whom were some very distinguished literati indeed, and this at a time when the 'academy' move-ment was growing in strength among them. Indeed these circles in Nanjing were one of the key formative bases for the opposition Tunglin movement of the future. In Nanjing this movement was particularly anti-Buddhist, which was in Ricci's favour. His 'original' Confucianism was contrasted with the current neo-Confucianist orthodoxy which was created in the Sung era and which many held to be the product of Buddhist influences.

A small community of baptised Christians was also created in the city, drawn both from the literati and among ordinary Chinese of the other classes. As at the other Jesuit residences, Ricci was always on the look-out for those in whom real Christian faith was born so that they might be baptised and a worshipping community created. There were such congregations at Zhaoqing, Shaozhou, Nanxiong, Nanchang and now Nanjing.

However, Matteo Ricci was completely clear that his task was not primarily to build up worshipping congregations, and certainly not to attempt to initiate any kind of mass conversion movement as had been done on Kyushu. He understood his job to be to lay a firm foundation for the future. He was so to shape the Jesuit mission that it became part of Chinese society. When that happened, that is when the Jesuits and the faith they proclaimed were no longer alien but in some sense Chinese, then a truly Chinese and Christian Church could be built which could then take up the task of the conversion of the nation. Valignano had from the beginning insisted on this fundamental strategy, from which Ricci never found reason to depart. Harris quotes Valignano as warning Ricci at the very beginning of the latter's career in China against 'the great error and thoughtless zeal of immediately converting large numbers of people.'[19]

The friends Ricci made during this stay in Nanjing were of inestimable importance to the future of the work of the Society in China. Some of these literati would also later play an important role in the history of the Christian Church in China and in the history of China itself. Notably Yeh Xiangao, an official on the Board of Rites, who became a close friend of Ricci's and was deeply interested in Christianity but who, for a long time, could not come to terms with the doctrine of the Incarnation. In 1607 he joined his friend Li Madou in Beijing, but by then Yeh was Grand Secretary, the supreme civil servant of the empire. He held this post until 1625 during which time he led the Tunglin party in opposition to the power of the palace eunuchs during the reign of the Tienchi Emperor (1621–7). He had to demit office in 1625 and retired to Fujian Province where he was an ardent supporter of Fr Giulio Aleni in the latter's efforts to propagate Christianity in that province. Or again the brilliant and highly irascible scholar Li Zhi who was a Confucian scholar of the highest rank but who had a deep understanding of and sympathy for Buddhism. He became a close friend of Ricci's and distributed *Jiaoyou lun* to his own disciples in other provinces. His radical attacks on Sung neo-Confucianism made him the leading national critic of official intellectual orthodoxy. As Spence movingly describes, Ricci still fondly hoped that one day he would baptise the old scholar when, in 1603, he was deeply upset by the news that Li Zhi had committed suicide in prison after intellectual enemies had procured his arrest and the burning of some of his books by the imperial Censor.[20]

In April 1599 Ricci was able to buy cheaply a commodious group of three buildings to be the new Jesuit residence in Nanjing. He was able to do this because no one else would use them since they were supposed to be haunted. It was at that time that Fr Cattaneo and the other Jesuits arrived from the north with the baggage that had been frozen in on the canal.

Cattaneo had to go on, however, to Macao in order to try to raise some more funds. Although he had got the buildings at a bargain price, Ricci had only been able to put up half the cost of purchase. As in Japan, the mission was in constant need of funds. These were not always available in Macao as we have seen when discussing the mission in Japan; but even when they were, there was still a problem. Even more than in Japan, Valignano and Ricci wanted to disassociate the Jesuit mission in China entirely from any connection with European political authority. Despite this policy, there was no way out but to go to Macao from time to time, as Cattaneo had to in this instance of extreme financial difficulty. When he sent Cattaneo back into China, Valignano sent with him a new member of the mission, the Castilian Diego de Pantoia and several new gifts to be added to those already at Nanjing for presentation to the Emperor when Ricci should finally get to Beijing. Among these was a clavichord.[21] This gift presented something of a problem. Cattaneo was an accomplished musician, indeed Ricci had already used Cattaneo's musical knowledge and fine ear to help him work out the problems of tone in Chinese when he, Cattaneo and Zhong Mingren were attempting to create a new Chinese vocabulary with a more accurate form of romanisation of the language. However, if the opportunity came to go north to the capital, Cattaneo, it was clear, would have to stay in Nanjing in charge of the Residence since he knew the language and customs needed to carry out the necessary pastoral and evangelical duties there. The new arrival, Pantoia, would have to accompany Ricci when he set out for the north. The young Spaniard, however, did not know how to play the clavichord! Fortunately he was musical and there was time for Cattaneo to embark on a crash-course of musical instruction so that the young priest learned both to play and tune the instrument.

It was possible to undertake this extra course of instruction for the newly arrived recruit because Ricci was still seeking an appropriate opportunity to reach Beijing if it was with the possibility of gaining residence there and an audience with the Emperor. In the meanwhile he continued his apostolate in the city, visiting and receiving guests, taking part in hours of long and intense discussion both theological and philosophical, making western scientific artefacts and teaching mathematics to those who were interested.

Ricci had been amazed to find in Nanjing a very well equipped observatory and astronomical laboratory. The instruments he found in it were as good as any in Europe but they were no longer being used. Ricci believed that they were about two hundred years old and had been made by a non-Chinese who had been trained in the West. He came to this view because of the comparative backwardness of Chinese astronomy in his day, which was the reason for the deeply worrying errors in the Imperial Calendar. In fact he was wrong, as he did not know the history of Chinese astronomy. We know that the laboratory was the creation of a brilliant Chinese astronomer and mathematician Guo Shoujing (d. 1316) who was in charge during the reign of Khubilai Khan, when Arab mathematics and astronomy had been fruitfully grafted on to the Chinese system. During the years of the Ming Dynasty Chinese mathematics and astronomy had fallen back from their previous high standards, though Chinese interest in them was of necessity still intense because of the vital importance of the Imperial Calendar. Now that Ricci was recognised as a scholar in Confucian terms his mathematical and other skills could be taken seriously, and to some of the senior mandarins they appeared as a possible way of correcting the Calendar.

Ricci did not want any more false starts in the vital matter of getting to Beijing and obtaining an audience with the Emperor. He called together some of his closest friends among the literati to discuss the problem and see if they could find a new way forward. Qu Rukuei came up to Nanjing and together with Li Xinzhai they discussed the matter with Ricci. They advised him to approach the Censor, Zhu Shilu, for his advice. To the delight of the three supplicants, the Censor did not simply give advice but offered to give Ricci a passport to travel to the capital and letters of introduction to senior officials there. After this meeting several other senior officials, who all knew Ricci well, also added their letters of introduction for him to take to Beijing.

This appeared to Ricci as a break-through, for then with the Censor's aid a eunuch, who was in charge of taking a flotilla of boats carrying silk to the capital was persuaded to give passage on his ships to Ricci, Pantoia, the irmaos, Zhong Mingren and Yu Wenhui, together with their luggage which included the precious clavichord and the other presents for the Emperor. The Beijing mission set sail from Nanjing on 18 May 1600. On this journey the Jesuits were not in any way trying to merge into the background. They paraded the dignity and seriousness of their mission to present gifts to the Emperor, and as a result they were given very commodious accommodation on board ship. The eunuch in charge welcomed them aboard as important guests. At the many stops on the way, local dignitaries came on board to greet Li Madou and to inspect the precious gifts. Indeed this very public progress greatly aided the speed of their journey, the astute eunuch demanding and getting priority over the queues of ships at the very busy locks on the waterways, because of transporting 'the Emperor's precious gifts'.

All seemed to be going extraordinarily well. At Jining the party of Jesuits were warmly welcomed by Li Zhi, the scholar and poet, who introduced them to a very senior administrator indeed, Liu Dongxing, who was in charge of the transporting of rice to the capital and was also President of the Board of Censors. He paid a formal visit to the ships to inspect the presents and this gesture made a great impact on the townspeople. He then took the whole missionary party to spend the day with him and his family. He reviewed the memorial that had been prepared at Nanjing for presentation to the Emperor and, after consultation with Ricci, had another amended, and he believed more effective, memorial prepared by his family archivist. He also gave to Ricci letters of introduction to various of his friends and colleagues in the capital.

At Jining also, and much less happily, the Viceroy of Shandong came aboard with Ma Tang, the eunuch in charge of the imperial Customs service. Ma Tang, who was at that time one of the most powerful figures in the empire, had plans of his own for the Jesuits. They and all their luggage were taken into custody by the eunuch and moved to the fortress at Tianjin (Tientsin). What Ma Tang intended is not clear. His behaviour towards them was a strange mixture of the very gracious and the extremely menacing. He entertained them to an incredible banquet and a show of dancers and acrobats which Ricci reported as charming. Yet repeated searches of their luggage and his insistence on taking into his keeping some of the presents for the Emperor 'for safety's sake', caused the Jesuits to fear he would steal their belongings and they would never see Beijing. There was an even worse moment when, during yet another search of their baggage, Ma Tang came across a vividly realistic crucifix and screamed aloud that it was a magic fetish for bringing harm to the Emperor. Fortunately he calmed down and accepted the Fathers' assurance that it was no such thing.

Because Ma Tang forwarded reports to the palace that he was holding strangers with gifts for the Emperor and requesting instructions, it would appear that it was not theft that was the motive of his actions. While perhaps taking some of the gifts for himself, it would appear he hoped to get credit for introducing these bearers of exotic gifts to the imperial court. The four Jesuits did not know this and they went through agonies wondering what was to happen. They sat there in Ma Tang's custody for five long months. Then word came that they were to proceed to the capital and so, escorted by soldiers of Ma Tang's retinue, the Jesuit mission was transported by horses and porters of the imperial post and entered Beijing on 24 January 1601. Their troubles were not yet over, however. They had arrived in the capital at a time when the scholar-administrators were attempting to win a head-on confrontation with the eunuchs to whom the Wanli Emperor had given so much power. The mandarins were trying to get the Emperor to declare that his eldest son, Zhu Changlo, was the heir to the throne. The Wanli Emperor, his eunuchs and their allied mandarins favoured a younger son by a concubine. The Jesuits became a pawn in this struggle for authority.

A division of the Board of Rites was responsible for the screening of all foreigners seeking entry to the capital to present gifts to the Emperor. Ma Tang had bypassed this, clearly as yet another way of challenging mandarin authority. At first he got away with it. The eunuchs presented the Jesuit gifts to the Emperor at the end of January. The Emperor was most interested in the two chiming clocks among the many gifts with which he had been presented. Ricci and Pantoia were brought within the walls of the Forbidden City and stayed in the Bureau of Mathematics while they trained four designated eunuchs in how to look after the clocks. In addition Pantoia went to the palace itself daily for a month to teach another four eunuchs how to play the clavichord. Ricci took advantage of this opportunity to compose eight motets with lyrics which inculcated Christian moral lessons. Pantoia and the younger two of the cunuchs helped Ricci with the music, for despite his many extraordinary skills, music was not one of them. Then Pantoia taught the eunuchs to sing and play these as part of their musical education. In this way the teachings of Li Madou entered into the inner palace where only eunuchs, concubines and the Emperor's closest relations could go.

These songs were later published by friends of the Jesuits. Though long after Ricci's death, their publication added to his posthumous fame and along with *Jiaoyou lun* were greatly admired by the literati in the seventeenth and eighteenth centuries.

However, Cai Xianchen, the mandarin directly responsible for the control of foreigners in the capital, sent his police and took the Jesuits from the supervision of Ma Tang. This mandarin later became a friend of Ricci's but on this occasion he kept the Jesuit on his knees before him for an hour in public court, taking him to task for using the eunuchs to circumvent the authority of the appropriate government office. Ricci was able to explain how things had been taken out of the control of the Jesuits. He also politely insisted that since he had stayed so long in China and had behaved as a Chinese for all that time, he was not a foreigner in the ordinary sense. Cai Xianchen accepted his explanation and gave Ricci and the other Jesuits special quarters in the otherwise very primitive accommodation reserved for foreign embassies in the capital. He also invited them to dinner on a number of occasions and was delighted when Ricci made him a quadrant and a celestial sphere.

The acting head of the Board of Rites, Zhu Guozu, decided to make the Jesuits a test case in his struggle with the eunuchs. He examined the Jesuits very thoroughly, then recommended to the throne that though they had not intended any harm they should be sent to Canton and deported. When after several weeks he had received no reply to his original nor to any of his four subsequent reports, each of which had been progressively more sympathetic to the Jesuits, Zhu then allowed them to move about the city freely and visit their friends. Some of those friends of Ricci's were very important officials who knew and admired him as someone who could be treated as if he were one of them. This made it all the more unfortunate that he should be punished by a fellow mandarin as part of their struggle with the eunuchs. Eventually, when his fifth memorial to the throne had still not been answered, Zhu listened to the urgent protests of these senior mandarins, particularly the Beijing Censor, Cao Yubian, and released Ricci and his companions. He went further and granted the Jesuits permission to remain in the city.

Because the Board of Rites had sent them to the residence for foreign tribute-bringers, the Jesuits had been awarded rations from the imperial treasury which consisted of rice, meat, salt, vegetables, wine and firewood enough for five people. When Ricci and his companions were released from the custody of the Board, they were, after a time, given verbal permission from the palace to rent a house. The rations which should have ended were allowed to continue and in addition they were awarded a small imperial grant of eight ducats in silver per month. Several senior officials also helped the Jesuits. One guaranteed the money equivalent of the rations if they were not delivered, as sometimes happened, since their grants were all administered through the notoriously corrupt eunuch bureaucracy of the palace. Others gave gifts more haphazardly but they were often very generous, such as one from the Grand Secretary, Shen Yiguan, of silver and many bolts of cloth and furs.

The most important aspect of all this was that the Jesuit mission now had tacit imperial permission to stay in the capital. The vital importance of that decision can be seen in the response among the literati who knew them or knew of them to the fact that Li Madou was now resident in the capital and had been within the Forbidden City, and was visited by and visited many of the members of the Ministries, including the Grand Secretary himself. This granted the European Jesuits a status and position within Chinese society that no other foreigners had achieved. They had to an extraordinary degree shed their foreignness.

NOTES

1. Bernard-Maître, *Aux Portes de la Chine*, p. 141.
2. Rowbotham, *Missionary and Mandarin*, p. 10.
3. See D'Elia, *Galileo in China*, pp. 8-12.
4. Dunne, *Generation of Giants*, p. 25.
5. Paul Rule's translation of Tacchi Venturi, *Opere Storiche*, vol. II, pp. 20–1.
6. Benedetto de Goes walked and rode the overland journey from Agra to the Chinese border where he was met by Jesuits from Beijing, confirming, by following the old medieval route from Mongol times, that Beijing was Khanbalic and Cathay was China.
7. Quoted in Harris, 'The mission of Matteo Ricci', p. 81.
8. Dr Chan has informed me that the term 'daoren' was also sometimes used to refer to scholars, notably the famous literatus and painter Wu Chen (1280–1354) who had as his title Mei-hua daoren.
9. Ruggieri was particularly unfortunate since, following his arrival in Rome, four Popes died in an extraordinarily short space of time: Sixtus V on 27 August 1590; Urban VII on 27 September 1590; Gregory XIV on 16 October 1591; and Innocent IX on 30 December 1591. The resulting disturbance in the Papal court can be readily imagined.
10. Dunne, op. cit., pp. 33–4.
11. Harris, op. cit., pp. 87–8.
12. D'Elia, *Fonte Ricciane*, vol. 1, p. 377.
13. Original Confucianism is the phrase used by J. D. Young in *Confucianism and Christianity* to convey Ricci's concept.
14. Ricci's technical expertise as a teacher of mnemonic techniques is the theme round which Jonathan Spence has built his exciting and stimulating *The Memory Palace of Matteo Ricci*.
15. Dunne, op. cit., p. 41, quoting Tacchi Venturi, op. cit., vol. 2, p. 186.
16. Pannikar, *Asia and Western Dominance*, p. 41. Cameron, *Barbarians and Mandarins*, p. 161.
17. Dunne, op. cit., pp. 46–7.
18. Harris, op. cit., p. 69.
19. Ibid., p. 98.
20. Spence, op. cit., pp. 256–7. There is an affectionate obituary by Ricci recorded in D'Elia, op. cit., vol. 2, p. 106.
21. This is what Harris calls it. Spence calls it a harpsichord. Ricci referred to it by two different Italian words both now archaic, one of which 'gravicembalo' can mean either cymbal or harpsichord! The actual instrument would appear to have been a harpsichord played with a plectrum and not by a keyboard.

CHAPTER SEVEN

Christian Priest and
Confucian Intellectual

efore considering the last extraordinary fruitful years of his life which Ricci
B spent in Beijing, one preliminary matter ought to be cleared up. Very early
in his stay, rumour had it among the literati that Ricci had talked with the Wanli
Emperor himself. This was something which not even the Grand Secretary
had done for years since the Emperor had hidden himself away among his
concubines and eunuchs. Many historians have since repeated versions of this
belief, so widely held at the time; a belief that clearly did the Jesuits no harm.
Ricci himself was aware of the story and somewhat puzzled as to how it had
arisen since he had not, at any time, met the Wanli Emperor. Ricci suggested
that the story had come about as a result of the eunuchs in charge of the chiming
clock bringing it out of the palace to the Jesuit residence. The Emperor had
heard of this and insisted that it was not to happen again, and that Ricci should
come to the palace to repair it in the future. Perhaps this and Pantoia's going to
the palace to teach the eunuchs to play the clavichord and to sing the motets
written by Ricci were what lay at the root of the long and widely held belief in
Ricci's ready access to the inner palace and to the Wanli Emperor.

During these first months in Beijing, Ricci was finally convinced that the idea
of gaining a formal endorsement from the Emperor was not the way to obtain
permanent security for the work of the Society in China. His and Valignano's
policy that the Jesuits had to fit into a specific category or role within Chinese
society was unchanged. All European Jesuits had so to steep themselves in the
Classics and conform themselves to the culture of China that they would be
treated as if they were Chinese and literati. They had to be constantly aware,
however, that this could be reversed in an instant if it suited the political ends
of a senior official. This was where Xavier's original idea which Valignano and
Ricci had supported for a long time would have come into play, that is to avert
this danger by gaining imperial protection.

Ricci was convinced after a few months in Beijing of what he had begun
to suspect already from what he learned in Nanjing, that imperial authority

simply could not give that kind of security. To ask for a formal endorsement or permit from the Emperor would, he believed, have the opposite effect and almost certainly produce a formal denial of imperial protection. The Emperor would resent, just as Ricci already knew senior mandarins did, being put on the spot by such a formal request. In any case, even if a formal permit was issued, at this time in the reign of the Wanli Emperor it would be issued by the alternative eunuch officials whom the Wanli Emperor used in preference to the offical ministries. The permit would then become a pawn in the ongoing struggle between the reform-minded mandarins and the eunuchs and those mandarins who supported them.

Ricci became quite clear that the best policy for the Society was to accept the present tacit endorsement they had received and which, if it suited the Emperor, could be readily denied just as the acceptance of the Jesuits by the literati could. The Society had to carry on as if formal permission existed, and in practice this worked and would continue to work so long as the missionaries and their flock continued to behave in the mode so beloved of Valignano and Ricci, 'il modo soave'.

From his arrival in Beijing until his death, Father Matteo Ricci, 'Li Madou', was considered by the Confucian literati as someone worthy of their respect, indeed in most things as one of themselves. His hope was that all Jesuits who came from Europe would be of the intellectual and spiritual calibre to achieve this status also. To this end, and as ever with Valignano's full agreement, he prescribed the Confucian *Four Books* as the 'set texts' for Jesuits to work on after arriving in China. In this way they not only learned classical literary Chinese but, equally important, they also were immersed in Confucian thought.

In a long letter written near the end of his life in 1609 to his old friend Francesco Pasio, the Jesuit Vice-Provincial in Japan, Ricci laid out in detail his mature missionary strategy for China.[1] In this letter he did not describe a new theory but the practice he had followed since his arival in Beijing in 1601, a practice that was the product of the hard-earned experience of those apprentice years in Shaozhu, Nanchang and Nanjing. It was also a practice that was specifically endorsed by Alessandro Valignano as the working out in China of his general understanding of the nature of mission. With Ricci as his 'field commander', as it were, the Jesuit Visitor was able to carry out and develop his missionary approach in China in a way that he had not been able to do in Japan. In China, Valignano guided the work from the beginning. He attempted to have his missionaries penetrate deeply into Chinese culture before any decision about terminology needed to be made and so, hopefully, the kind of error made by Xavier could be avoided. It was for this purpose that he had instructed Ricci to translate the *Four Books* for him. As Ricci achieved a more and more profound knowledge of Confucian thought so he and Valignano moved towards the idea that as St Thomas Aquinas had married

Aristotelianism to the Christian faith, so something similar might be done with Confucianism.

This is what we see in this letter of Ricci's to Pasio. The letter is fundamental to understanding what Ricci was doing and how he understood Chinese society and culture as well as how he understood the Christian mission. It was not a 'theology of mission' as someone would write it today. It was, at least in part, an 'apologia pro vita sua' by Ricci and also in some ways a 'confessio', a statement of faith. His analysis of the nature of his work took the form of a list of what he called 'reasons for hope'. There were eight in the original letter, but they can be summarised rather differently when we try to understand them from a late twentieth-century perspective.

Absolutely basic was Ricci's belief, most clearly expressed under heads five and eight, that the Confucian morality, both of its ancient as well as of its contemporary practitioners, was compatible with the moral concerns of the Christian faith. Also, and this is vital, in their following of Confucian morality many of the ancients could, through the light God had given them by His grace through the natural law, have so persevered that they were now in Paradise. It is because of this agreement between Christianity and Confucian concern for virtue that Ricci says he is able to use Confucian thought in combating 'the followers of idols' as he refers to Buddhism. He sees Confucianism as an ally against Buddhism.

Secondly, 'those of the sect of the literati', as he calls them in this letter, carried on the government of China and were the highest level in the hierarchically divided Chinese society. He points out to Pasio that they were not a hereditary class; on the contrary, their position was dependent upon their learning. Concern for learning and love of books were fundamental to Chinese society. Two things flowed from this. The first was that if the Jesuits could make Christians from among the ranks of the literati, that would not only give Christianity enormous influence but also give to the Society the only security it could achieve in the China of that day. The second was that if the Society could produce books that were acceptable by Chinese standards and have them readily distributed in China, the gospel message could be spread far more widely and quickly than could be achieved even by a large staff of priests which in any case the mission did not have.

Thirdly, through showing the knowledge necessary to be a scholar in Chinese terms and then bringing to China the scientific knowledge and technical expertise of the West, the Jesuits had become accepted by the literati as worthy to be regarded both as Chinese and as intellectual equals. This, Ricci insisted, was far more important than having made ten thousand converts because this was the way, and he clearly insisted the only way, to any future conversion of the whole kingdom.

Fourthly, it was then a matter of necessity that European members of the Society had to follow the path of acquiring Confucian learning through studying the Classics. This was a major step and took the members of the Society much further down the road of what, in the second half of the twentieth century, is called 'indigenisation' than had been travelled in Japan, for it was not only in dress, way of life, manners and food that the missionaries had to follow Chinese cultural norms, they had to train their minds so as to enter into the Confucian intellectual world. Just how much further they had gone in China compared with Japan can be seen first of all in the use of Confucian terminology in Ricci's revision of the Catechism in 1587 and the use of this terminology and the citing of Confucian texts in *The True Meaning of the Lord of Heaven*, to both explain and justify Christian truth.[2]

Ricci mentioned that a particular Buddhist writer had called him a 'sycophant of the literati', an accusation which has been paralleled by some later western historians, even moderately sympathetic ones like Rowbotham. Ricci accepted that his policy could be attacked in this way, but pointed out to Pasio that his adopting the role of 'literatus' had not prevented him challenging some ideas which were held to be of fundamental importance by some of the literati. This was a reference to his perennial argument with the supporters of neo-Confucian orthodoxy about the nature of 'original' Confucian thought which we will discuss a little later.

In 1601 in Beijing, Ricci believed he was as secure as he could be in Ming China and so felt able to concentrate entirely on what he considered his primary task. This was to present Christianity as a faith that could be adopted by a Confucian scholar-administrator while he remained an official of the empire and a follower of the philosophy of Confucius. As we have seen, Ricci was already accepted as a scholar because of his Mappamondo and *Jiaoyou lun*, and he already had a network of friends and acquaintances among the literati throughout the empire. As soon as it became clear that the Jesuits were legal residents of the capital, many more distinguished scholars and administrators flocked to visit Ricci in the Jesuit residence. These included men as distinguished as Feng Qi, the Minister of Rites, Li Dai, Secretary of the Board of Personnel and even the Grand Secretary himself, Shen Yiguan. So in Beijing there began again the exhausting rounds of visits that had characterised Ricci's life in Nanjing. He was still firmly convinced that discussions among friends was the primary way of bringing about conversion among the literati.

Almost as important, however, was the use of the printed word. As we have seen, he had long ago insisted that more could be done through books than by any other means to spread ideas across the vast area of China. He decided that in Beijing he must concentrate upon this literary task which he was, at that time, uniquely qualified to fulfil. With the help of his friends among the literati, Ricci plunged into an exhausting period of writing and translating. It was the most productive period of his life. The books produced by this effort were not just on philosophy and religion but also on mathematics and astronomy, on the movement of the spheres as well as on ethics. This was not because Ricci was offering western learning as a 'come on' to Chinese intellectuals as has often been suggested,[3] but because he believed that Christianity had to appeal as a complete philosophy if it was to be presented effectively to Confucian intellectuals. The world view of Chinese intellectuals was a unified one in which science, philosophy, ethics, religion and technology formed an interrelated whole. He therefore sought to present Christianity in the same way, but not as an alternative to the Chinese system but as something that could be integrated into it because of its fundamental agreement with 'original' Confucianism. What he sought to present was what many of his literati friends referred to as 'celestial learning', Tianxue, a phrase he used himself at times.[4] In 1603 his single most important contribution to this task was published, a book of Christian apologetic, *Tianzhu shiyi*, 'On the True Meaning of the Lord of Heaven'.

This was a book that was long in preparation. It goes back to Valignano's complaint to Ricci about the inadequacy of Ruggieri's simple catechism of 1581, revised by Ricci with the help of a sympathetic graduate in 1584. Most specialist scholars seem to agree that the book, in the form it later appeared, was begun seriously about 1596. It was ready before Ricci arrived in Beijing, but in 1601 he was still waiting to have his Latin translation of his original work in Chinese given the imprimatur by the ecclesiastical authorities in Goa who knew nothing of China or of Confucianism. This procedure had to be followed despite the fact that Valignano had already, in 1597, approved the penultimate draft of the book. After the Visitor had read it, some of its linguistic forms were improved by the distinguished Confucian scholar and adminstrator, Feng Yingjing. This bold opponent of the palace eunuchs was in prison in Beijing in 1601 and while there read Ricci's book, made these stylistic improvements and wrote a complimentary preface for it. Feng also, while still in prison, organised the publishing of an important little work on morals which he had encouraged Ricci to write as a Christian parallel to the popular Chinese Buddhist work *The Sutra of Forty-two Chapters*. This was *Ershiwu yan*, 'The Twenty-five Sentences', which appeared with a preface by Feng and one by Xu Guangqi, the future Grand Secretary of the empire.

To return to *Tianzhu shiyi*, this was a book of extraordinary importance and also one which has been the source of a great deal of misunderstanding both of Ricci's work and of the essential nature of the missionary initiative of Valignano and Ricci. It is so important because of its widespread impact on all those influenced by Confucian thought, both within and without China. Perhaps most striking was its impact on a group of Korean intellectuals which led to the beginning of Catholic Christianity in Korea before the arrival of any missionaries in the country.

The criticism and misunderstanding of the *Tianzhu shiyi* go together since a great deal of the apparently most pointed and pertinent criticisms have been based on a misunderstanding of what the book was and what Ricci's purpose was in writing it. Many have understood the book to be an exposition of the

Christian message as it was presented by the Jesuits in China. The fact that it has been referred to, even by Ricci himself at times, as a catechism, has encouraged this. In one seventeenth-century meaning of 'catechism' Ricci's use of the word was not wrong since catechism originally meant simply a work in question and answer form. However, even then, and much more subsequently, the word catechism has come to mean a full exposition of the Christian faith in question and answer form prepared, usually, for those seeking baptism into the faith or for Christian young people prior to confirmation. As a result of this understanding of the word catechism many writers have taken the *Tianzhu* to be that kind of full exposition of the Christian faith. In turn this has led these critics to insist that the Jesuits in China so watered down Christianity as to render what they preached simply a form of Confucianism. These accusations have varied from the crude accusations of someone like the famous nineteenth-century Protestant missionary S. Wells Williams, to much more subtle recent questioning as to whether the leading mandarins who became Christians had believed in anything save a very superficially 'christianised' Confucianism. These criticisms would have great weight if the *Tianzhu* had been a full exposition of the Jesuit teaching of Christianity, a Christian catechism, since undoubtedly large areas of central Christian doctrine are barely touched upon and then only in the last pages of the book in what is almost a postscript.[5]

In writing the *Tianzhu* Ricci was not aiming at producing a 'catechism' of the type of the Calvinist Smaller and Greater Catechisms. He was writing a piece of Christian 'apologetic', that is an intellectual defence of the Christian faith in philosophic terms. Ricci was setting out to show that there was a belief in a transcendent God contained in what he insisted was original Confucianism, and that this transcendent Lord of Heaven and the God of the Bible were the same. What is so extraordinary was that in the eyes of a large number of the literati he succeeded in proving his point. In their eyes, including some of the most outstanding of the day, Ricci, in the words of Xu Guangqi, had produced a system which 'does away with idols and completes the law of the literati'.[6] Perhaps even more impressive was the way Feng Yingjing helped Ricci with some stylistic modifications and wrote a preface to the work, since he was still a Confucian scholar when the eunuchs and his neo-Confucian enemies contrived his death in the prison in Beijing.

As Ricci's knowledge of the Confucian Classics deepened he had come to believe that in the time of the ancient sages the Chinese had known of one Creator God; they had not been polytheists with a pantheon of deities such as had the Greeks, Romans, Teutons, and the Hinduism and Mahayana Buddhism which Ricci had encountered. This was, in his view, of the utmost importance for it would seem to indicate that the ancient culture of China still retained traces of the primal revelation of God to His creation in a form unpolluted by polytheism and idolatry. This fact, as well as the compatibility of the basic ethics of Confucianism with Christianity, combined to allow him to present

Christianity as something that completed what was ancient and true within China's own history and culture.

In any culture, if Christianity can be understood as in some way building on what is already there, the potential for growth and indigenisation is present. All over Africa south of the Sahara, Christianity in many forms has seen an astonishing growth since the mid-nineteenth century. One vital factor has often been overlooked in discussing this phenomenon; that is, that almost everywhere missionaries went, when they translated Biblical texts they used the local name for God as the name of the God of Israel and the Church. A new God was not being proclaimed but good news about the God whom the people already worshipped, even if, usually, only indirectly through the ancestors. This was what happened despite what many missionaries themselves believed or understood or consciously preached. Whenever they used the local name for God then a message of continuity not discontinuity was being proclaimed, whether they consciously intended it or not. In that situation the elements of discontinuity appeared like pruning the living plant, a very different matter from uprooting it and substituting a wholly new plant.

Ricci was very clear and certain about the message of continuity he was attempting to proclaim. His Confucian classical learning impressed him more and more with the apparent unique monotheism of 'original' Chinese culture. This he believed had been badly distorted by the the thinkers who created neo-Confucianism in Sung times as a result, he supposed, of Buddhist influence.

This understanding had a very important effect on the choice of Chinese words for the translation of essential Christian terms such as a name for God. 'Tianzhu', the earliest Chinese equivalent used by the Jesuits to translate the Biblical God in the first catechism, was a genuinely Chinese word and had its roots in both Confucian and Daoist traditions, but it was not common and had no universally accepted meaning.[7] It was therefore comparatively easy to fill it with a Christian meaning. However, once Ricci had come to a deep understanding of the Confucian classics, he insisted that the classical divinity, 'Tian' (Heaven) or 'Shangdi' (Lord-on-high) to whom sacrifices and worship had been offered in the days of Confucius, referred to the transcendent Creator God of the Bible. He was well aware that this was not how most of his contemporaries among the literati understood these terms. This was because of what had happened in the Tang and Sung dynasties. Then the leading Confucian thinkers had sought to give Confucianism a metaphysic to help defend it from the intellectual and spiritual threat presented by Buddhism. In doing so, Ricci asserted, they severely damaged Confucianism. Everyone agreed with him that Confucianism had been modified in that era from which had emerged what is referred to in English as neo-Confucianism, though this was by no means generally understood as a damaged Confucianism as Ricci asserted.

In neo-Confucianism 'Tian' and 'Shangdi' were interpreted unambiguously in an impersonal sense; more than that, they were treated as being the equivalent of 'taiji', which was the 'Supreme Ultimate', the immanent universal order of reality. Ricci emphasised that in the Classics there was no indication that 'taiji' was ever worshipped or revered so that, in what he insisted on calling 'original' Confucianism, 'taiji' – the impersonal nature of things – was not the same as the worshipped and sacrificed-to 'Tian' and 'Shangdi'. Therefore a transcendent personal Creator God was part of 'original' Confucianism. Neo-Confucianism did not accept this because it had blended the original socio-political ethical system of Confucius with an alien metaphysical system drawn from Buddhism. Ricci's assertion was that in contrast, Christianity completed Confucianism more fully in accord with its origins.

His assertions about the nature of Confucianism and his teaching in general were challenged by a number of scholars. Most of these critical texts still available to us appear to have been written sometime after Ricci's death in Fukien and were aimed at contradicting the teaching of Giulio Aleni, after Ricci perhaps the Jesuit who immersed himself most deeply in Confucian thought.[8] Professor Gernet has studied those writings carefully and used them in his *China and the Christian Impact*. Ultimately Gernet seems to believe that Ricci was attempting the impossible and that there was and is an impassable gulf between the intellectual world that produced Chinese religion and culture and that of the West, which in Gernet's thought includes India.[9]

What is important historically, however, is that although a significant section of the literati of the late Ming era disagreed with Ricci, they treated him as an intellectual equal, as if he were one of themselves. What is even more important, a significant number of the literati, including some of the most outstanding Confucian scholars of the day, agreed with Ricci's interpretation or, in the case of others, agreed that it was one that was allowable in the discussion of the meaning of the teaching of the Master. Twentieth-century scholars of Confucian thought may very well believe that these seventeenth-century literati were wrong, and the large group of leading mandarins who agreed with Ricci, and even more those who accepted baptism, were deluding themselves in some way; but that does not alter the historic truth that Ricci's interpretation of Confucius was accepted as a valid form of Confucian discourse by the literati of late Ming China. More startling is that Ricci's *Tianzhu shiyi* was included in the *Ssuku Chuanshu*, the great bibliographical compilation made in the 1780s under the auspices of the Qianlong Emperor – in English 'The complete Library of the Four Branches of Literature'. Despite Professor Gernet and others it would seem that Confucians thought that Ricci's was at least a tenable Confucian position. Admittedly by that time, of course, it was a position no longer accepted by the Christian world, Catholic or Protestant.

To return to our main theme, it is important to remember that Ricci was only beginning the process. His work was the opening of the dialogue between Christianity and Confucianism, though perhaps Ruggieri left him more to build on than is sometimes recognised.[10] It was Matteo Ricci who was the first westerner to immerse himself in the Classics and have some real understanding of them. As Paul Rule points out, he introduced Confucius to the West.[11] Although he knew he was pioneering he was sure that there was a foundation upon which a building could be erected. As he wrote

> The Literati deny that they belong to a sect and claim that their class or society is rather an academy instituted for the proper government and general good of the kingdom. One might say in truth that the teachings of this academy, save in some few instances, are so far from being contrary to Christian principles, that such an institution could derive great benefit from Christianity and might be developed and perfected by it.[12]

He began the dialogue, but it did not progress much further because of tensions and divisions in western Christianity which brought the experiment to an abrupt end.

In contrast with his attitude to Confucianism, Ricci shows clearly in his writings that he was unable to understand Buddhism. There is only one reference to him ever visiting a monastery, the normal centre of Buddhist activity, and indeed he admitted he had not studied Buddhism. The literati with whom he was closest and whose support he saw as vital for the continued existence of the Christian mission were anti-Buddhist, and saw Buddhism as the root of the distortion of Confucian thought in the Tang and Sung dynasties which produced neo-Confucianism. Buddhist monism, of which he did have some understanding, seemed to him to be irreconcilable with the Biblical perception of reality. Perhaps even more important was the fact that Ricci was the intellectual product of Italian Catholic humanism. It was therefore very easy for him to relate readily to Confucian humanism. To his very superficial understanding gleaned primarily through literati antagonistic towards it, Buddhism appeared superstitious, idolatrous and the opposite of any form of humanism. The set debates with Buddhist priests arranged by literati in Nanjing appeared to confirm Buddhism as inimical to Christianity.[13]

It is worth noting, however, that his attitude still left open the possibility of a more constructive relationship developing. After remarking on the scorn and hatred often shown towards both Daoists and Buddhists by the literati, Ricci insists that

> It is better to refute than to hate; and it is better still to use clear reasoning than to refute them merely with many words; for Taoists and Buddhists are all produced by our Great Father, the Lord of Heaven, and we are therefore

The development of further understanding of Confucianism and any attempt to begin to understand Buddhism had to be left to his successors. As he said himself on his deathbed, he had left 'an open door' to his successors, not a successfully occupied house.[15]

The eventual failure of this Jesuit initiative was directly due to problems within Europe and western Christianity. Whether the Jesuit initiative could have provided China with a Chinese Christianity, as there had developed a genuinely Chinese Buddhism which also had been bitterly criticised and opposed at various times in Chinese history, we cannot tell since it was not allowed time. In less than one hundred years it was banned by its own authorities. After only one hundred years from its introduction how far had Buddhism gone in becoming a permanent part of Chinese culture?

The intellectual problems of providing a Christian apologetic which would make Christianity acceptable to the literati was only one of the problems facing Matteo Ricci as the Superior of the Society of Jesus in China. Christian congregations were coming into being which were made up of members of the three classes into which the majority of Chinese people were divided, as well as a number of the literati elite. This meant that Ricci, always under Valignano's authority, had to decide on a large number of controversial problems over what was to be Christian practice and morality in the new Chinese Church.

Fundamental to Chinese morality was devotion and obedience towards parents, filial piety. This pre-dated Confucius but was basic to Confucian thought. The observances associated with the dead of a person's family were an integral part of this basis of the moral order of civilisation, filial piety. As Fr Harris has pointed out, as Buddhism entered China and Daoism developed as an hierarchically organised Church, Chinese people had for the first time the possibility of 'voluntary religion', choosing to belong to a particular religious faith.[16] This possibility of choice however did not free them from the obligations due to parents, which was obligatory and simply could not be avoided, and so was built into the Chinese Buddhist and Daoist religious organisations. These observances were basic to Chinese life and seen as the foundation of all morality, the stability of earth and heaven. The problem was, what part could Christians play in them?

To refuse Christians any participation in these ancestral rites and for the literati the additional Confucian rites, would mean there would be no Chinese Christianity at all. If, as was to be suggested by the friars when they arrived in China, the major part of these activities were worship and involved the worship of idols, then despite the consequences there could be no alternative but to forbid them.

After careful study and long and patient questioning of literati friends, Ricci came to the conclusion that participation in the majority of these 'rites' was permissible to Christians. He knew that among the uneducated many did understand the family ceremonies in a 'superstitious' way, expecting material blessing from the ancestors in return for their correct performance. However, with Valignano's agreement, he decided in favour of Christian participation. He ruled that no paper money was to be burned before the ancestral tablet and participants had to affirm that the dead did not need nourishment from the food, which in any case was consumed by the participants. With these modifications Christians continued to follow the family 'rites' associated with the funeral of the newly dead and with showing respect to the ancestors. Ricci hoped that in the future when the Chinese Church would reach maturity they would make their own choices as to what were the modification of these rites necessary to make them more fully Christian, but that would be up to them.

Fundamentally Ricci saw the whole complex of rites associated with the dead as a ritual reinforcement of filial piety and therefore of personal and social morality, a morality which he believed to be compatible with Christianity. As he reported in his journals,

> As they themselves say, they consider this ceremony as an honour bestowed upon their departed ancestors, just as they might honour them if they were living...Indeed, it is asserted by many that this particular rite was first instituted for the benefit of the living rather than for that of the dead. In this way it was hoped that children, and unlearned adults as well, might learn how to respect and to support their parents who were living, when they saw that parents departed were so highly honoured by those who were educated and prominent.[17]

Ricci saw no 'superstitious' accretions around the Confucian rites of the literati and so had no hesitation in endorsing the participation of Christians in all the ceremonies attached to the award of the three degrees of Confucian scholarship. However there were certain annual solemn sacrifices in honour of Master Kung (Confucius) which, although he believed they were not worship, gave such an appearance of superstition that Christian literati were not to attend. He was quite clear that he hoped that in due course a Chinese Church would modify these customs in a way that purged them from all hint of superstition, but that could be left to the future.[18]

These years were a period of enormous literary productivity on the part of Ricci, despite the pressure of miriad details he had to look after for the whole mission in China which he headed independently of Macao, from which the China mission was happily detached by Valignano in 1603.

In this literary work he was helped by two outstanding Confucian scholars, Li Zhizao and Xu Guangqi. Li was a keen geographer and a senior official in the Ministry of Public Works. He came to Ricci first because of his fascination with Ricci's Mappamondo and worked with Ricci for years at scientific and mathematical studies. Many of his family became baptised Christians, but although he had asked for baptism in 1603 it was always refused him because he simply could not give up his concubines. Because of this Pantoia, ever the ascetic Spaniard, was unhappy about the continued closeness of Li and Ricci.[19] At last, only two months before his own death, Ricci was able to welcome Li into the Church after his baptism in March 1610. The other scholar, Xu Guangqi, was one of the most brilliant of his day and became in 1607 one of the staff of the Hanlin Academy in Beijing, the pinnacle of the Confucian educational system. As well as a scholar all sources appear to agree that Xu Guangqi was also a saintly man.

With the constant co-operation of these two men, Ricci produced a series of important works of western science in Chinese. With Xu he made a Chinese version of the first six books of Euclid, with Li he wrote an introduction to Geometry, a translation of Clavius' *Practical Arithmetic*, and a work on astronomy which was reproduced in full in the great Qin Encyclopedia produced under the auspices of the Qianlong Emperor in the 1780s. Li also published at his own expense a new edition of Ricci's *Tianzhu shiyi*, and another edition of Ricci's *Jiaoyou lun* ('on Friendship'). Li and Xu together persuaded Ricci to prepare and publish a new work of Christian apologetic, *Jiren Shipian*, which is translated in many ways but most authorities now appear to agree on 'Ten Discourses by a Paradoxical Man'. This became perhaps the most widely read of Ricci's books in his own lifetime and several extra printings were made of it, not only in Beijing but in Nanjing and Nanchang also. In 1608 he produced a final annotated version of the Mappamondo for the imperial palace.

On top of all these tasks as teacher of science, Christian apologist, parish priest, Jesuit Superior, he also had the exhausting task of greeting in the elaborate and time-consuming Chinese way all important guests and of returning these visits. In 1603 and 1610, the years when Beijing was filled with candidates for the jinshi examinations, the pressure of visitors keen to speak with Li Madou was so great that there were some days when he was not free to rest or eat from dawn till late evening.

Quite suddenly on 3 May 1610 he fell ill and with great calmness he died on 11 May, though he seems to have had some premonition of his death. His body 'lay in state' and hundreds of mandarins joined the Christians in paying their respects to Li Madou.

Almost immediately after Ricci's death, Fr Pantoia and Li Zhizao drew up a petition to the Emperor for the setting aside by imperial authority of a special place to house the tomb of the 'far Westerner' who had become Chinese. The petition was presented to the Emperor on 18 June with the formal support of the Ministry of Rites and of the Grand Secretary himself, Yeh Xiangao. A villa was designated near the western gate of the city by imperial authority to hold Ricci's tomb. Li Madou was buried there in the villa transformed into a chapel on 1 November 1610, with a great deal of pomp and solemnity. Some years later the imperial Governor of the city had erected on the tomb a plaque with the famous words,

> To one who loved righteousness
> and wrote illustrious books,
> to Li Madou, Far-Westerner.
>
> Erected by Huang Jishi,
> Governor of Beijing.

As Trigault pointed out,[20] this granting of a special tomb by the Emperor was something reserved as an award only for outstanding mandarins and utterly unheard of for an ordinary Chinese let alone a foreigner.

NOTES

1. Tacchi Venturi, *Opere Storiche*, vol. 2, pp. 383–7. A full summary in Bernard, *Le Père Matthieu Ricci et la société Chinoise*, vol. 2, pp. 329–31.
2. Malatesta, *True Meaning of the Lord of Heaven*, pp. 329–33.
3. See Chapter 6, n. 13.
4. Sebes, 'A Bridge between East and West', p. 588.
5. Malatesta, op. cit., pp. 445–53.
6. Gallagher, *China in the Sixteenth Century*, p. 448.
7. It is the term still used by Roman Catholic Christians in China to-day.
8. Gernet, *China and the Christian Impact*, pp. 10–12.
9. Ibid., p. 3.
10. It should be noted that Dr Albert Chan sj has discovered fifty-three poems in Chinese by Michele Ruggieri. His study and translation of these is to be published in *Monumenta Serica* shortly, and will be an important step in enhancing our knowledge of Ruggieri who, Dr Chan points out, had already essayed a translation of the *Four Books* and had clearly gone further in his study and understanding of Chinese culture than has been recognised hereto.
11. Rule, *K'ung-tzu or Confucius*, pp. 116ff.
12. Gallagher, op. cit., p. 98.
13. Spence, *Memory Palace of Matteo Ricci*, pp. 254–5.
14. Malatesta, op. cit., p. 101.
15. Dunne, *Generation of Giants*, p. 109.
16. Harris, 'The Mission of Matteo Ricci', p. 112.
17. Gallagher, op. cit., p. 96.
18. Rule, op. cit., pp. 49–50.
19. Dunne, op. cit., p. 99.
20. Gallagher, op. cit., p. 593.

CHAPTER EIGHT

The China Mission under Schall and Verbiest

R icci had nominated the Sicilian, Nicolo Longobardo, to the General as his successor in the headship of the mission. This was an interesting appointment since Longobardo had not hidden from Ricci that he did not fully accept the whole of the latter's missionary policy. Longobardo had no difficulty over the permissibility of Christians performing the traditional ceremonies honouring the dead and Confucius, but he was not sure of Ricci's use of the concept of 'original Confucianism' to justify the use of Tian and Shangdi for God. He agreed that Ricci's interpretation was almost certainly correct, that there was a clear distinction between original Confucianism and neo-Confucianism and that original Confucianism was not atheistic as neo-Confucianism was; after all great Chinese scholars like Xu Guangqi agreed with Ricci. However Longobardo felt strongly that since a majority of scholars of their day accepted the Sung neo-Confucian interpretations of the texts as correct, then Confucian terms like Tian and Shangdi could not be used for the God of the Bible since most people would understand them in the neo-Confucian sense. Rather, something like the Deusu of the Church in Japan should be used in China in their stead.

This dispute was always internal to the Society and the leaders of the Christian community. It was the subject of very serious debate among the Jesuits and the leading Christian literati but this never resulted in public attacks on each other by members of the Society nor any kind of bitter recrimination. It ended with the members of the China mission agreeing that Ricci was correct and accepting the ruling and getting ahead with their work. Later Domingo Navarette OP, the bitter critic of the Valignano–Ricci missionary approach, obtained one of Longobardo's critical papers and used it in his attacks on the Jesuit mission in China. But this division of opinion was not the the opening of the so-called Rites Controversy, which at the beginning of the eighteenth century was to bring the Valignano experiment to a more final end in China than even the Tokugawa persecutions had done in Japan. That was still to come.

Longobardo took over the mission at a time when optimism as to the future of Christianity in China seemed justified. The friends of the Jesuits among the literati held many important posts, as did the very much smaller group of outstanding scholars who were baptised Christians. So confident were these mandarins of the successful integration of the members of the Society into Chinese life that Xu Guangqi petitioned the throne in the early months of 1611 for the Jesuit Fathers in Beijing, Pantoia and de Ursis, to be given the task of reviewing the whole system of preparing the Imperial Calendar and the work of the Astronomy Bureau. This, he insisted, was necessary after the disastrously wrong prediction of the timing of an eclipse by the officials of the Bureau in December 1610. The Emperor agreed to this rather extraordinary appointment. Perhaps not so extraordinary since it was only an extension of the situation which Ricci had created, that is that European Jesuits could be considered as truly Chinese when it suited the administration.

After a period of very serious discussion as to its appropriateness, the members of the Society in China agreed that Jesuits could accept such appointments under the Emperor because of the advantages it gave for the propagation of Christianity. After all St Ignatius had insisted, and the *Spiritual Exercises* pressed home, that any activity that was not itself immoral could be undertaken by a Jesuit if it could be performed for the greater glory of God. News of the appointments was spread rapidly throughout the empire via the network of scholar-administrators. It gave a new security to the place of the Society in China for in practice this appointment of Pantoia and de Ursis was very close to being a de facto imperial endorsement of the Society and its work in China.

Pantoia and de Ursis had only just begun their mathematical revisions when the whole project was cancelled. This was because the existing mathematicians of the Bureau caused such a fuss – and to this was added the vociferous complaints of conservative elements among the leading officials, particularly those opposed to Xu Guangqi and Li Zhizao – that the Emperor felt it necessary to take the easy way out of an embarrassing imbroglio and withdrew the appointments.

That the appointments were made at all, however, confirmed the de facto scholar status the Jesuits now enjoyed in the empire due to the work of Ricci, and it was this status which saved the Society when, in 1617, a direct attack was mounted on the continued existence of its mission in China. The instigator of this attack was a senior mandarin, Shen Que. On his appointment as Vice-President of the Nanjing Board of Rites in 1615 he had begun his campaign against what he saw as a threat to the stability of the empire posed by the work of the Society.

He and others suspicious of the Jesuits and of Christianty were given an opportunity to begin formal proceedings against the Jesuits by the conduct of Fr Vagnoni in Nanjing. Vagnoni had felt that the time for 'il modo soave' of Valignano and Ricci was past and that a much more direct and flamboyant

approach was the way ahead. In Canton he built the first public church to
be erected in China. This was opened in 1611 with much public pomp and
display, in particular with public street processions. The flourishing Christian
community of Canton was divided into three parishes each with its own lay
leadership which organised a great deal of charity work among the poor and
the ill. Unfortunately in addition to this highly commendable activity – though
much more in the public eye than any other Christian work heretofore in
China – Vagnoni added a great deal of public denigration of Buddhism and
its bad effect on true Confucianism. All this led to many in Nanjing becoming
increasingly unhappy at the Christian presence. Shen was able to turn this
growing disquiet to his advantage when a group of young scholars, holders of
the first degree (xiucai), signed a joint petition asking for the expulsion of the
Jesuits from the empire. The core of their accusations against the Jesuits was that
they were creating a subversive organisation among the people. At a time
when there was increasing unrest across the country and there was serious
organised anti-government activity led by the White Lotus Society,[1] this was
an accusation that would always be taken very seriously. Any public gatherings
of people in numbers was looked on with suspicion, so the style of Vagnoni's
parish in Canton was a provocation.

In 1616 Shen was, as a result, able to send reports to the Emperor requesting
the expulsion of the Jesuits as people causing public disturbance and threatening
the security of the empire. In response to the first of his petitions Yang Tingyun[2]
wrote to him defending the Society and its beliefs, and later Yang expanded this
letter into an essay in defence of Christianity and had it published together with
a similar essay written by Li Zhizau. Shen ignored these and because of silence
from Beijing repeated his petition. The second petition, now with the support
of the president of the Ministry of Rites, was published in an official publication
which caused Xu Guangqi to submit to the palace a long reply to Shen's petition
which not only defended Christianity but called on the Emperor to grant it the
same status as Buddhism, Daoism and Islam.

Nothing came from the palace in reply to all this literary activity and the
President of the Ministry of Rites now acted on his own. Orders were issued
by him to every province that all the European Jesuits were to be arrested
and expelled from the country. This was at the end of August 1616. Except in
Nanjing where Shen supervised the business, the order was not taken seriously.
In Nanjing, however, Fathers Vagnoni and Semedo were arrested, and then a
little later the two Chinese irmao in the residence there, Chung Mingjen and
Louis Paris[3] were also put in jail together with some Christians who happened
to be at the residence when the police arrived. Shen became increasingly angry
when, having been brought before various tribunals, the Jesuits were found
innocent of being a threat to the empire. He was also aware that nothing was
happening elsewhere in the empire in response to the edict of the President
of the Ministry of Rites, so he continued to bombard Beijing with documents

insisting on the threat that the Jesuits posed. In January 1617 he got the response he wanted and on 14 February an anti-Jesuit edict was signed by the Emperor which appeared to order the expulsion of all European Jesuits from the empire. However, only two Jesuits were actually named as having to be deported to their own lands. It is worth noting that when naming Pantoia the edict admitted that he, together with other Jesuits unnamed, had been raised to the rank of mandarin by the Emperor himself only two years before.[4]

That this did not spell the end of the Jesuit mission in China was due to the nature of the Confucian traditions of the literati civil service and the position the Jesuits had gained among the literati as a result of the Valignano–Ricci policy of accommodation. The Confucian tradition of the administrators was not one of applying all imperial edicts literally and inflexibly. Confucius and Mencius both taught that the offical was to be a mediator between the ruler and the subject and that his role was to be a 'good father and mother' to the people in his charge. Wide discretionary powers were held by all senior officials to be an essential element of the system. There certainly was an elaborate system of supervision of officials to make sure they fulfilled their duties but they were more often dismissed or censured for too great severity than for exercising their discretion in favour of the people. Despite this imperial rescript, a very large number of the most senior officials did not see the Jesuits as a threat to the stability of the empire as was the White Lotus Society. The two Jesuits specifically named to be deported were deported, that could not be avoided; but outside Nanjing senior officials exercised their traditional freedom of judgement on how to apply the imperial rescript in their provinces and they did so universally in favour of the Jesuits.

In Beijing, other than the two named Jesuits who were deported, the remaining Jesuits, Fathers Longobardo and Sambiasi and the two Brothers Ni Yicheng and Yu Wenhui, left the Jesuit residence vacant but stayed in the city though taking care not to draw attention to themselves in any way. Elsewhere it was the same, though in some places friendly mandarins had the Jesuits moved to another town with instructions to remain there as unobtrusively as possible. Others of the Society went to Hangzhou where they were under the protection of Yang Tingyun. Though Hangzhou was very close to Nanjing and Shen Que was well aware of Yang's actions, the latter's prestige was such that Shen Que made no attempt to have any action taken against him.

However, in Nanjing, where Shen was the dominant magisterial official, the imperial edict was enforced with the utmost rigour. Here Fathers Vagnoni and Semedo underwent long and rigorous interrogations and only illness prevented Semedo receiving the savage bastinado which Vagnoni received and from which it took him several months to recover. Semedo and Vagnoni were then sent off to Canton bound in chains and carried in the small bamboo cages normally reserved for those condemned to die. Mercifully they were released by the senior mandarin in the city of Nanxiong when the cavalcade reached there, though they were again treated very badly as they passed through Shaozhou.

Shortly after they arrived in Canton, having endured a gruelling month on the road, they were joined by Pantoia and de Ursis. The latters' journey from Beijing could not have been more different and again highlights the amount of freedom of action that was allowed to senior mandarins in China. One day out of Beijing, on giving their parole that they would go to Canton and hand themselves over to the authorities there, Pantoia and de Ursis were set free by their escort who returned to Beijing while the two Fathers travelled on alone to Canton.

In Canton the senior magistrate of the city put all four Jesuits in prison together. Then, after considering their case, he allowed them out of confinement and after permitting them to live for some months in the city under parole, he then had them escorted courteously to Macao.

Fourteen Jesuits were then left in China, eight Europeans who were priests and six Chinese Brothers; in addition there were in Macao the four of the China mission who had been expelled, of whom Vagnoni and Semedo would both return to serve in China. They were joined later in Macao by the new recruits brought out to serve the China mission by Fr Nicolas Trigault who had been sent on a recruiting and publicity tour to Europe. We will return to this tour later. Vagnoni used his time in exile to perfect his knowledge of literary Chinese and of the classic texts.[5] Education in literary Chinese and further training in the Classics were also the main emphases in the life of those Jesuits who had gathered under Yang Tingyun's protection in Hangzhou. Yang encouraged their study and Giulio Aleni rapidly became his favourite pupil and a close friend. In the judgement of some scholars Aleni was seen even to rival Ricci in his mastery of the classical texts and of literary Chinese.

This period was difficult for the Christian community but priests and Brothers still tried to visit the scattered congregations of Christians. Paradoxically the dispersion of the Jesuits away from their missions in practice helped to spread Christianity and led to the creation of new residences in the areas of their exile once their status was restored and they could operate publicly again. When they did operate publicly again it was in the way of Ricci and not the way Vagnoni had chosen in Nanjing; the Jesuits had learned from having their fingers burned.

In 1621 Shen Que was removed from office in Nanjing and the Chinese Church could breath more easily. A new centre of Jesuit activity was opened at Kiating. This was again done on the iniative of a prominent Christian mandarin Sun Yuanhua. Kiating rapidly became a house of study and the centre for the training of new Chinese members of the Society and of newly arrived European members of the mission. Fathers Trigault and Semedo re-entered the empire that year to be followed early in 1622 by four new recruits from Europe among whom was Adam Schall von Bell.

This was a period of great turmoil in the state which partly accounts for the troubles through which the mission was passing. In August 1620 the Wanli Emperor died. The reform-minded mandarins brilliantly outflanked the palace eunuchs and their allied mandarins and made sure that the legitimate heir came to the throne as the Tai Chang Emperor. He appeared to be ready to carry out a programme of reform and bring to an end the alternative eunuch power structure, but he died within weeks of coming to the throne, apparently poisoned. Again the reforming Tunglin mandarins ensured the legitimate heir succeeded. This however was no help towards reform of the crumbling authority of the Ming dynasty. The Tianqi Emperor handed over all power to an extraordinary eunuch who dominated the government of China till the Emperor's death in 1627. This man, Wei Zhongxian, set out to remove the members of the Tunglin movement from all positions of authority and to a large extent he succeeded. Many reformers were driven from office and some were even stripped of their status as literati.

At an early stage in his period of power the Jesuits faced what appeared to be the greatest threat to their work that had yet arisen. This was the calling of Shen Que to Beijing to take up the appointment of Grand Secretary of the Empire in 1622. At the same time a massive rebellion led by the White Lotus Society took place against the government. In Nanjing Shen's supporters among the magistracy arrested a large number of Christians and accused them of being members of the White Lotus Society. Indeed they asserted that Christianity and the White Lotus Society were one and the same. With a lack of courtesy unusual in officials, they dismissed the appeals addressed to them from Xu Guangqi and Yang Tingyun explaining that Christianity was not at all related to the White Lotus movement. The situation was extremely serious, but in the strange atmosphere of the court under the power of Wei, Shen was as suddenly dismissed from office in September 1622 as he had been summoned to it. As a result the direct pressure was now off the Jesuits and the Christian community. Wei had no active concern about Christianity, though what he did affected them indirectly in as much as the majority of the senior mandarins who were Christians or who were friends of the Jesuits were all either part of or associated with the Tunglin movement. As a result most of these mandarins were dismissed from senior office both in the capital and in the provinces during the period of his power.

During this time of turmoil an external threat to the Dynasty also appeared. This was on the northern frontiers of the empire where the Manchu tribes were being united under an able warrior leader, Nurhaci. He not only united the tribes but began the reorganisation of Manchu society so that it was administered more efficiently and better organised for concerted military action. Ominously for the Ming, Nurhaci, the leader of a sinicised people, proclaimed himself Emperor and gave himself a Chinese reign title. In attempting to make his title real he did not successfully conquer more than some fringe territories of the empire in the North, but the aim of supplanting the Ming dynasty was explicitly his policy and this ambition passed to his successors.

In 1621 the Manchu threat was great and it was at this time that Xu Guangqi and many other mandarins resigned in despair when their attempts to strengthen the empire militarily and administratively were frustrated by the policies of the the eunuch Wei Zhongxian, the de facto ruler. However, before he got rid of the majority of Tunglin mandarins, the Jesuits were restored to an official and public presence within the capital, which indirectly gave official recognition to those in other parts of the empire. Yeh Xiangao, who had first befriended Matteo Ricci in Nanjing in 1600, was still a Grand Secretary in Beijing. One of his closest friends was the distinguished literatus who had become a Jesuit, Qiu Lianghou, who was in the Beijing residence. Another of the most senior mandarins, the President of the Ministry of War, was also a friend of the Jesuits, Sun Chengzong, whose son was later to play a large role in developing the Jesuit mission in Shaanxi. These men put together what, in western eyes, appears to be a legal charade in order to regain official recognition of the presence of the Society in the empire. The two senior mandarins, Yeh and Sun, memorialised the throne to have two Jesuits established in the capital as 'military experts' needed to help with the projected establishment of Portuguese-trained artillery in the Chinese army.

Fathers Longobardo and Manoel Dias were examined by the Ministry of War, and although they answered truthfully that they had no military expertise, the Ministry recommended that the Emperor affirm their presence in the capital as necessary for the good of the state. This recommendation received the imperial assent and Ricci's old residence was again occupied by members of the Society, its physical rehabilitation paid for by the Christian mandarins. Dunne says of this episode, 'The whole affair was a gracious comedy in which Yeh Hsiang-kao, Chang Weng-ta, Sun Cheng-tsung, Li Chih-tsao and other prominent Chinese statesmen collaborated to restore the Jesuits to their position in Beijing and China.'[6] Luckily for the Jesuits they were able to act out this comedy before Wei Zhongxian had gained full control of affairs and forced out from all senior offices the Tunglin and other reform-minded mandarins.

The Jesuits were now back in the same position as they had been before the first troubles of 1617. That is, they were to be treated as Chinese if it suited the administration and their activities throughout the empire were tolerated because of the position held by the Jesuits in the capital and because of the patronage of so many of the most distinguished literati who were either Christians or were sympathetic to the Society. The Jesuits could again resume their activities, though always with caution and circumspection. The dismissal or resignation from high office of so many of their friends because of the eunuch Wei worked to the advantage of the mission because as these high officials returned to their home areas they often encouraged the Jesuits to visit them, and in some cases set up new residences so spreading the work into areas hitherto unreached. The expansion was possible because members of the Society exiled to Macao now returned along with new men recruited by Trigault on his tour, making this expansion of the number of mission centres possible.

The new recruits were a product of Trigault's visit to Europe to which we must now return. In 1613 Longobardo had sent Nicolas Trigault to Europe with instructions to carry out certain very precise tasks, the most important of which was to appeal directly to the General and through him to the Pope about certain matters in China needing his decision. In order to do so he had to circumvent the authorities in Macao. The Portuguese secular and ecclesiastical authorities there were unhappy about the clear disassocation of the China mission from the Padroado. Macao was also the Jesuit headquarters for Japan. The leadership of the Japan mission were also very unhappy with the China mission because of the 'Confucian' terms used to translate God and other key Christian concepts, and did not want a direct appeal by the China mission to the Pope to bypass them since they saw China as subordinate to the Japanese Province. Indeed the famous veteran of the Japan mission, Rodriguez (the 'Interpreter') was in Macao at this time and was very critical of this 'Italian' mission in China.[7]

Trigault did not follow the Padroado route but after reaching Goa he made his own way to Persia and from there travelled on through Asia Minor and got a ship to Rome. He then sought, with the assistance of the General, to place before the Pope a description of the mission and of China to prepare the way for the request for Papal authorisation of the translation and publication of the Bible in Literary Chinese. He further requested that various liturgies should be so translated, including that of the Mass, and that permission be granted for Mass to be celebrated in Chinese once Chinese Brothers had been elevated to the priesthood. Permission was also sought to allow, straightway, the celebrant to preside over the Mass wearing a suitable hat since it was unacceptable in Chinese culture for someone to conduct a solemn ritual with their head uncovered.

As instructed by Longobardo, Trigault also travelled to the courts of the more important Catholic rulers to raise subsidies for the mission. Further, he was to gather as many suitable recruits as possible. In particular Longobardo had insisted that he find some Jesuit scholars who were well trained in the latest developments in mathematics and astronomy, and who were to bring with them to China as many books as possible on these subjects. Longobardo hoped to have a scientific library in each Jesuit residence but most of all he wanted a good up-to-date science library in the Beijing residence.

How deeply committed Longobardo was to what later Jesuit writers would refer to as the 'scientific apostolate' has been debated, but he wrote two long letters to the General on this matter forcefully appealing for mathematicians to carry out what Ricci had wanted. This was also a policy pursued with great persistence by Xu Guangqi who had never given up hope that the Imperial

Calendar could be revised to make it accurate and that this should be done by the Jesuits.[8]

Trigault's mission was successful beyond his expectations. Permission was given by Pope Paul V for the celebrant at Mass to wear a suitable headgear in China. It was also agreed, after long discussion in which Cardinal Bellarmine played an important role in support of the requests from China, that the Bible and the most important liturgies of the Church, including that of the Mass, should be translated into literary Chinese so that, when Chinese were ordained as priests, they could celebrate Mass in the vernacular.

Trigault also translated into Latin and published Matteo Ricci's *Journals*, a hugely successful piece of publicity for the Chinese mission. His visits to various great Catholic cities and courts were also a success, indeed he inspired so many Jesuits to volunteer for the China mission that many Provincials complained to the General about his drawing away their best men. He was able to recruit and take with him on the voyage to the East, this time obediently following the approved Padroado route via Lisbon, four brilliant Jesuit scientists. Two were already well known in the scientific community, Johann Terrenz Schrek and Wenceslaus Kirwitzer who were friends and colleagues of Galileo and of Kepler. The other two were not yet distinguished scientifically but were to become so, the young Italian, Giacomo Rho and the Rhinelander, Johann Adam Schall von Bell.[9] They were able to build up a large library of scientific books to bring with them, but they were disappointed when their appeals to Galileo for help were turned down by the Pisan scholar.[10]

It was not until July 1619 that Trigault and his new recruits reached Macao and the newcomers began their training in literary Chinese and in the Classics. In 1621 the recruits were able to enter the empire, as we have seen, and take up various posts in the work of the Society as it opened up again after the ending of the ban. The key areas of long-term development were in Shaanxi, Shanxi and Fujian. In the latter area Aleni, under the patronage of Yeh Xiangao and of Candida Xu, Xu Guangqi's granddaughter, saw a very substantial growth of Christianity with the creation of over twenty new congregations. Some of these had chapels built at the expense of Candida who was not only a devout Christian but a highly educated woman of enormous authority and influence.

While temporarily in exile from the centres of power in his home village of Xujaihui near Shanghai, Xu Guangqi built a large church and Jesuit residence on his estate. From this centre the Shanghai area saw significant growth of the Christian community in the next thirty years.

However, perhaps the most exciting development of all at this time was not the opening of new residences but the finding of a stone. It was in Xian that the famous Nestorian Tablet was found in 1625. It was the Jesuits and Christian literati who first saw its importance. The stone was a large tablet on which, in both Mandarin and Syriac the story of the coming of Christianity to China through the Nestorian missionaries was told. This discovery was of enormous importance to the Chinese Church. As Li Zhizao wrote, although many had come to admire or even accept the teaching first proclaimed by Li Madou there had always been the nagging question of its newness, it was not rooted in China's past. He was therefore both excited and triumphant as he published the text of the inscriptions on the stone with a commentary.[11] It was so important that nearly a thousand years ago the Gospel had been preached in China and gained the approval of the highly esteemed Emperors of the Tang Dynasty. During the later Rites Controversy many insisted that the whole thing was a trick of the Jesuits; this was asserted by Catholic critics, Protestant scholars quoting the Catholic critics and, most scathingly, by Voltaire. In the twentieth century research in the Tang archives has once and for all made nonsense of these accusations. This work has shown that as early as 638 the great Tai Zong Emperor issued an edict making Christianity a legal religion in China and giving a subsidy for the building and maintaining of a monastery of twenty-one monks in the capital. Christianity therefore was not a new import but part of China's past.

With new confidence the Society and the leading Chinese Christians sought to make the mission secure. In Beijing events seemed to be moving towards gaining long term security for the Jesuit mission. We have seen how the Jesuit presence in the capital was publicly acknowledged and recognised by the almost ritual performance at the Ministry of War. Now in the capital there arrived two of the well trained astronomers that Longobardo had requested, Terrenz and Adam Schall.

The newcomers immediately began to make friends with scholars and to make known and available their skills and their books. Schall for example listed all the new scientific works he had brought with him and had the list sent to the court. Terrenz began to write new works on astronomy in Chinese with the help of Christian and other sympathetic literati. Schall predicted exactly a lunar eclipse which took place on 8 October 1623. This attracted a great deal of attention from the most senior mandarins in the government and Xu Guangqi again petitioned the Ministry of Rites, as he had done a decade before, for the Jesuit scholars to be recognised and to play a role in the reform of the Imperial Calendar.

This was the wrong time for this kind of advance since the eunuch Wei Zhongxian was still struggling to remove all reforming and Tunglin mandarins from positions of authority. He got rid of Yeh Xiangao in 1624 with, as we have seen, some advantage to Christianity because of his patronage of Aleni in Fujian during his period of retirement in his home province. Others continued the struggle but lost disastrously, some of them even losing their status as literati. Five were put to death and have since been remembered as heroic martyrs for true Confucian ideals of government.[12] So many of their friends were in internal exile and disgrace, the Jesuits in the capital kept a very low profile and the chance of helping the Bureau of Astronomy seemed so unlikely that Schall was transferred to the residence at Xian.

In 1627 the Tianqi Emperor died and with the coming to the throne of the Chongzhen Emperor the power of the eunuch, Wei, was over. The new Emperor restored their rank to those who had been stripped of their status in the previous reign. By 1629 the changeover was apparently going well with a large number of senior positions being given to men who had resigned or been removed from office by Wei. Among those who came to power was Xu Guangqi who became Vice-President of the Ministry of Rites. However the new Emperor, the last of the Ming dynasty, was not strong enough to sweep away completely the old 'eunuch party' who were still able to influence affairs and inhibit the attempts at radical reform that the Tunglin reformers and their allies among the literati were pushing for.

For the Jesuit mission and the growth of Christianity in China this was, despite the signs of dynastic collapse around them, a period of peaceful and successful development. The restoration to positions of authority of the prominent Christian literati and of many others friendly to the Society gave the Church security it had not had since before 1617. Now Xu Guangqi was able again to renew his attempts to get the whole of the Astronomical Bureau reformed and he believed only the Jesuit scientists could do it. Xu, as Vice-President of the Ministry of Rites arranged what was a public competition. A solar eclipse was expected and the two official boards of mathematicians, the Chinese and the Muslim, were told to forecast its exact occurrence and Terrenz was also to make the same forecast. The government mathematicians got it wrong but Terrenz got it exactly right. Xu then reported to the Emperor that the official mathematicians were not to be punished. They had followed their rule books exactly, it was their system that was wrong and needed reform. He requested that some of the Jesuits of the China mission be invited to carry out the reform process. He took some time to persuade the members of the Ministry of Rites to make this the official recommendation of the Board to the Emperor, but he did succeed. The Emperor's response was to issue an edict which allowed the Ministry to appoint Jesuits to carry out the reform of the Calendar and of the working of the Bureau.

Xu appointed two leading Chinese Christian literati and two Jesuits, Li Zhizao, Wang Zhen, Longobardo and Terrenz to carry out the task of reform. Trigault's mission had provided the Society in China with the resources with which to face this challenge, not only by recruiting scientifically trained missionaries but also by the importation of an up-to-date scientific library. This was just as well since before the first year of his service in the Bureau was up, Terrenz died on 13 May 1630. Xu now called on two young Jesuits to enter the service of the Bureau to replace Terrenz, these were Giacomo Rho and Adam Schall. The two men were brought from their provincial residences by imperial post.

The place of the Jesuits within the structure of Chinese society now appeared secure and results of this could be seen throughout these last years of the Ming Dynasty, from 1630 until 1644. In this period there was a massive growth of the numbers of Christians everywhere in the empire where the Jesuits operated. As Ricci and Valignano had planned, by achieving a secure place within Chinese society, the Jesuit missionaries were able to oversee the growth of a Chinese Christian Church. Without the leadership of the distinguished Christian literati, most of whom like Xu Guangqi were converted in Ricci's lifetime, this would not have occurred. However they had only become Christian because of Ricci's ability to present Christianity as the fulfilment of Confucianism. They were a product of the accommodation policy and reinforced its effectiveness.

The bulk of the new converts were drawn from the three classes into which the vast majority of the Chinese population fell, merchants, craftsmen and peasants. The number of Christians among the literati was, though very important, always small, and it is worth noting again that among the xiucai the number of conversions was always negligible. The Scholars who became Christian were those who had achieved security in the highly competitive examination system. Also negligible was the growth of Christianity among the outcaste groups in Chinese society. Since they conformed so well to Chinese society, the Jesuits were inhibited from working among outcaste groups as they had been with the equivalent groups in Japan. It was, then, among the ranks of the ordinary Chinese people that the Church grew.

This is important to note because it was in 1633 that missionaries of the Mendicant orders first arrived in China. From that time till now it has often been asserted that the Jesuit propagation of the faith with its 'from the top down' philosophy concentrated simply on the literati elite and ignored the ordinary people of China who had to wait for the coming of the Mendicants to get attention. One would not want to deny the devotion of the Dominican and Franciscan missionaries, nor their outstanding concern for the poor and the outcaste. However alongside that recognition it must be insisted that the great growth in the numbers of Christians in the churches served by the Jesuit missionaries was drawn from the three classes that made up the overwhelming majority of the Chinese people. The acceptance of the Jesuits by the literati was what made everything else possible, without it there could be no missionary outreach to anyone at all in China, either by Mendicant or by Jesuit. This was made very clear during these last years of the Ming Dynasty when it was the prestige of the Society's role in the Bureau of Astronomy and the prestige and authority of the mandarin Christians that allowed the rapid growth of the Church and the opportunity granted the friars of the Dominican and Franciscan Orders to be free to operate within the frontiers of the empire.

The role of Johann Adam Schall von Bell was vital to the work of the Christian mission in China for the next thirty years after his first appointment by Xu Guangqi to work in the Bureau of Astronomy. With Xu's co-operation

Schall and Rho, who were still technically advisers to the officials of the Bureau, were put in charge of a school where young Chinese were trained in western mathematics. This school was also set the task of translating appropriate basic western texts. Immediately, however, Rho and Schall had to translate some of the books central to their revision work, Xu polishing the literary style of their manuscripts. By 1635 this effort had produced a small library of mathematical and astronomical texts in literary Chinese which included Schall's own little work on the construction and uses of the telescope, which he had composed and had translated into good literary form by a Christian literatus, Li Zubai, in 1626.[13]

Nevertheless, their position seemed always to be under threat. Conservative neo-Confucians together with some elements among the eunuchs were constantly attempting to challenge their right to be in such a position of authority. Even after the death in 1633 of the Grand Secretary and leading Christian of the empire, Xu Guangqi, they still maintained their position. This was because of the accuracy of their work and the trust the Chongzhen Emperor placed in them. The last of the Mings was as cut off from any direct contact with the world outside the palace as the Wanli Emperor had been, but he kept in regular touch with the Jesuit mathematicians through intermediaries.

It was, however, the death of Giacomo Rho that marked the new status of the Jesuits in the structure of Chinese society. A large public and manifestly Christian funeral with formal procession was allowed by the Emperor, the first such ceremony since the burial of Ricci. This was followed by a large gift of silver from the Emperor to the Society of Jesus in China, a very welcome gift, since as we have so often seen the Society was in constant need of funds and wished above all that they should come from within China, or at least not through the Portuguese authorities. The Emperor now also granted a generous monthly salary which Schall used to subsidise the Beijing residence. Even more important for the work of the mission was the decision made by the Chongzen Emperor to give to the Beijing residence of the Society an imperial baiben. This was a silk banner on which there were four ideograms and the dragon symbol of royalty. The ideograms were qin, bao, tian, xue which reads 'the Emperor praises the celestial doctrine'. This could be taken to mean astronomy but the Jesuits always used this phrase to represent Christianity, and most people would read it to mean that. That this was what the Emperor intended can be seen from the fact that smaller copies of the original were ceremonially presented to every other Jesuit residence within the empire, none of which had to do with astronomy. At each residence throughout China where the baiben was displayed all the local magistracy had to pay a formal visit and perform the kou tou before it as the crowds had done in the streets of Beijing when the original was carried by heralds to the Jesuit residence.

The imperial baiben was followed by similar baiben presented to the Beijing residence first by the Grand Secretary and then another by the President of the

Ministry of Rites. Schall, as was appropriate, now presented gifts to the Emperor in return. These included a beautifully illustrated manuscript life of Christ which Trigault had brought back from Europe. Schall wrote a Chinese translation on the back of each illustration for the Emperor's benefit.

It was during this period that a number of important palace eunuchs who had become Christians in the early 1630s became the channel through which a large number of the women of the imperial household were baptised as Christians. Neither Jesuit priest nor brother could be in direct touch with the women of the palace. They were converted through reading books and through the teaching of the Christian eunuchs, notably Pang Tianshou (Achilles) and one whom we simply know as Joseph Wang. By 1642 these Christian women, some of whom were of the highest rank, numbered fifty and had formed a sort of informal Christian community with its own rules and what was, in effect, a Christian chapel inside the palace.

Throughout the empire the imperial patronage of the Society allowed the missionaries of the Society to work freely and also allowed more people to come forward for baptism without the fear of being regarded as 'un-Chinese'. As a result in these last ten years of the Ming Dynasty the baptisms of adult converts was running at around five thousand a year.

THE COMING OF THE MANCHU

The Chongzhen Emperor was not strong enough to save the Ming Dynasty, or perhaps the situation was beyond redemption when he ascended the throne; whatever the final judgement of historians, the era of Ming was coming to an end. It was internal rebellion that brought the Dynasty down rather than Manchu invasion. A powerful rebel, Li Zicheng, made Xian his capital, declared himself Emperor early in 1644 and gained more and more support as he moved on Beijing. The Emperor refused to flee but made the classic Ming error of trusting eunuchs to command his troops defending the capital. They were well equipped and had the new cannon that Schall, as commanded by the Emperor, had designed and manufactured for the Ministry of War. The majority of the eunuchs were traitors and actually turned the guns in on the city as it was captured by Li. The Emperor committed suicide. Of him Schall wrote,

> He died abandoned by all, the victim of the betrayal of his servants and officials but also of his own mismanagement. With him the Dynasty which bore the name Ta-ming, the Brilliant Realm, came to an end after 276 years, and their kindred who numbered 80,000 died out also. He did not renounce the religion of his ancestors, but he rendered great service to the Church of Jesus Christ; Catholicism had already gained a number of adherents in the time of his grandfather, but he did not merely tolerate it, he extolled and encouraged it for the greater good of his people.[14]

Schall acted as a leader of the Christian community in the subsequent chaos and managed to save the residence and the lives of many people. The imperial general on the northern frontier was so incensed at the rebels that he co-operated with the Manchu and invited them to help destroy the rebels. The Manchu armies did just that and their brilliant leader Dorgon, uncle of the child Manchu 'Emperor', was soon in command of Beijing and all of north China. Ming loyalists, among whom were many Christians and members of the Tunglin party as well as a number of Jesuits, held out in the south for some years but the Ming era was over.[15] On 19 October 1644 the new Manchu Emperor – the Shunzhi Emperor – the first of the Qing Dynasty, entered Beijing.

As with the great Yuan (Mongol) Dynasty, under the Qing the day-to-day government of China remained in the hands of the civil service produced by the Confucian examination system. There were Manchu garrisons in every province and at the highest level Manchus were brought into the system, for instance the Council of State now consisted of fourteen councillors, seven Manchus and seven of the most senior Chinese mandarins, the Grand Secretaries.

On the take-over of Beijing it was decreed that the northern half of the city should be evacuated by all Chinese and become a Manchu city. Schall petitioned that the Jesuit residence should remain where it was in the northern area because of his role in the Bureau of the Calendar. This was a bold initiative by Schall to attempt to maintain the Jesuit position under the new Dynasty. The latter, in a very Chinese way, wanted a new Calendar. The mathematicians of the old Bureau prepared one and so did Schall, and it was Schall who won the competition and was instructed to prepare the Calendar for 1645. His position was clinched when he presented an exact forecast for an eclipse of the sun for 1 September 1644, adding details of the exact timing of the eclipse for viewing in all the provincial capitals. At the Ministry of Rites Schall and his Chinese students explained the eclipse to the most senior Councillors, Chinese and Manchu. They also used the telescope to project the eclipse onto a sheet of paper so that ministers could study every phase of the event.

It was now decided that hall should be the mandarin in charge of the official Bureau of the Calendar with authority to appoint his own staff and design his own form of training. This put Schall in a quandary as a Jesuit was not allowed to accept office. Loyola had decreed this so that his best men would not be tied up in ecclesiastical appointments that restricted their freedom to go anywhere and do anything needful for the spread of the faith. Yet the founder also insisted that any activity that was in itself not immoral could be carried out by a Jesuit if it was to the glory of God. Schall refused the appointment again and again as the Emperor continued to order him to take it. Finally he was warned that both he and the mission of the Society was in danger of being the object of the Emperor's anger if this continued. Fr Furtado, as mission superior, formally instructed him to accept the office and he did so as was his duty as a member of the Society. Schall was no longer, as so many Jesuits had been before in China, someone treated as if they were a Confucian Scholar. He was now a mandarin of the fifth grade of the First Division, a position which usually only the holder of the jinshi degree could hold. He was not being treated as if he were a mandarin, he was a mandarin. There was an attempt by the President of the Ministry of Rites to have him dismissed, but this failed and indeed the whole event strengthened Schall's position since the Emperor insisted his accusers should publicly apologise to him and then had them dismissed from the imperial service.

Even more dramatic was the relationship that developed between Schall and the first Qing Emperor after he had dismissed the regents and taken power into his own hands in February 1651. The young Shunzhi Emperor was not a prisoner of palace eunuchs as the later Ming Emperors had been, but went where he liked when he liked with as little or as much pomp as he chose. What he did like to do was drop in on Fr Schall and quiz him about anything and everything under the sun. He would sometimes spend hours in the priest's room sitting at his desk or sprawled on his bed reading a book. Symbolic of the nature of the relationship that developed was that the Emperor came to address Schall by the Manchu words 'ma fa', an affectionate term used for older members of one's family.

Just as the granting of the imperial baiben by the last of the Ming Dynasty had had a profound effect throughout all the provinces on the position of the the Jesuits and the Christian Church in general, so it was now with the special position of Schall in the affections of the Emperor. By 1652 missionaries were writing to the General in Rome that their situation was now so much more secure because of Fr Schall's position in Beijing.[16]

All was not sweetness and light however. A Portuguese Jesuit Gabriel de Magalhaes spent many years attacking Schall and seeking his dismissal from the Society. Much that he wrote and said was based on rumour or misunderstanding, some of it clearly a result of sheer malice, but some of it came from a very old and deep-seated difficulty within the Society. This was the ancient difference between the style of spirituality of the Portuguese province and that style which Valignano called 'il modo soave' which we have already noted. Magalhaes was quite correct when he again and again insisted that Schall was not a good 'religious' in that his pattern of life in the Beijing residence was not strictly and formally conducted. So much of what he complained about arose because of the role that Schall had to pursue as a mandarin, but that was exactly what Loyola had anticipated in the Constitutions. Jesuits were to be so profoundly shaped by the experience of the *Exercises* that they could be free to operate 'in the world' with a freedom that no other 'religious' had. As we saw in Chapter Three the Portuguese Province seemed to want a stricter and more formally legalistic and authoritarian routine discipline than Valignano believed that Ignatius Loyola had intended. Indeed the strict pattern of a traditional 'religious' would in practice prevent Jesuits carrying out the Christian mission in the many ways they did, notably Schall's activities as a senior official of the imperial government of China.

De Magalhaes and Fr Buglio had been doing sterling work in Sichuan when the province was overrun by a bloodthirsty psychotic tyrant, popularly known as the Yellow Tiger, in 1644. He kept the two Jesuits close to him and made them serve him in many ways. They witnessed the most appalling events reminiscent to modern readers of the killing fields of Cambodia under Pol Pot. They were eventually saved from execution by the arrival of the Manchu army. At first they were to be executed by the Manchu since they had served the tyrant. They were saved from this because they were Jesuits and therefore related to Schall. On being told of their arrest Schall prepared a petition for their release. This was not presented because the two prisoners felt it would reflect on the General who took them and was now treating them with great courtesy and they felt sure would have them released on his return to Beijing. Tragically for them this General was dismissed from office because of political differences internal to the Manchu regency, and they were now treated as rebels again. Just at this time, when they were emotionally exhausted after their long series of misadventures, it was reported to them that Schall thought they had been particularly stupid in some of the decisions they had made. This perhaps makes it more understandable why de Magalhaes from then on sought every opportunity he could to attack Schall.

What did not help was that Schall had a sense of humour that was not always shared by his colleagues, and things said in a joking conversation when quoted out of context could appear very strange indeed. There were times when a number of Fathers did join de Magalhaes in appealing to Rome against Schall, but in the end de Magalhaes was left isolated in this vendetta and the Society's authorities in Rome expressed confidence in Schall and confirmed the appropriateness of his holding office as the mandarin in charge of tfhe Calendar Office. Any other result would have been extraordinary since he refused the office so often and only took it, as we have seen, when ordered to do so by his Superior Fr Furtado as an issue of solemn obedience under the rules of the Society.

One long-term problem left by this unpleasant episode which is very carefully explored in Dunne's *Generation of Giants* was the accusation of sexual sin and the fathering of a son. This story was developed and used in later Catholic anti-Jesuit writing of the eighteenth century. The story had its origins in the distress of the Shunzhi Emperor that his friend Tang Ruowang, i.e. Schall, had no descendants to carry on his name. He therefore instructed Schall to adopt a child as a grandson who could them carry his name forward. Schall chose the five-year-old son of his steward to be his adopted grandson. This child was later to feature as his illegitimate son in these stories.

Schall's position in the Emperor's trust continued until he was granted the rank of court Chamberlain, which made him a mandarin of the first grade of the first division, a rank shared with the Grand Secretaries of the various ministries and princes of the royal family. On his headress he wore the red button and on his robe the golden crane. In this situation Schall was an intimate adviser of the Emperor, and in his shadow not only the Jesuits but all the Christian missionaries were safe so long as they did not infringe the laws of the empire.

It must be insisted that Schall was by no means a 'yes man', he was unafraid to challenge the Emperor over judgements or behaviour with which he disagreed. This led, in the end, to a cooling of relations between the Shunzhi Emperor and his 'ma fa' when they clashed over a David and Bathsheba incident with the Emperor playing David. After this the young Emperor turned more towards some Buddhist monk advisers, though on his deathbed, still only twenty-five, the Emperor did talk with Schall who did him one last service. The Shunzhi Emperor favoured naming a cousin as his successor, while the Manchu princes wanted one of his sons, as did the Dowager Empress. Shunzhi asked Schall's advice and Schall recommended to the Emperor that he choose his third son. To the delight of the Dowager, Shunzhi agreed to this which meant his heir was the boy who was to grow up to be the Kangxi Emperor, one of the greatest in all China's long history.

TROUBLES DURING THE REGENCY

Initially the death of the Emperor made no difference to the situation of the Christian mission in China. The Regents were in office on behalf of a young prince who was the heir at least partly because of the influence which Fr Schall had with the Shunzhi Emperor. Indeed when, in 1663, Schall celebrated his seventy-first birthday, he received a number of formal congratulatory essays written in his honour by two of the outstanding scholar-officials of the day, Jin Zhizhun and Gong Dingzhi; and the Grand Secretary himself, Hu Shian, sent him a letter of congratulation when Schall's 'grandson' was admitted to the Imperial Academy that year.

Schall was, however, the subject of intense antagonism on the part of the Muslim astronomers, and this was only made worse when he protected them from official wrath when they challenged his official bureau over some calculations and were proved wrong. They really were not a dangerous threat until they were turned to for help by a veteran mandarin, Yang Guangxian, who was a passionately sincere neo-Confucianist and believed that all China's ills stemmed from allowing the Jesuits to propagate their ideas inside the empire. He had long been a critic of the Jesuits and the tradition of Li Madou and began a fresh assault on the Jesuits in 1660. He sent in a series of petitions to the throne but appeared to be getting nowhere. Indeed from his perspective things were getting worse when in 1663 one of the imperial Censors, Xu Zhijian, wrote a preface for a new Christian evangelistic booklet. Yang protested bitterly to the the Censor and was ignored. However, when Yang presented a petition to the Regents in the last weeks of 1664 he included an accusation that Schall had chosen an inauspicious day for the burial of the son of the Empress in 1658 which had led to her death and also the death of the Shunzhi Emperor.

It is somewhat ironic that this deeply committed neo-Confucianist was only able to gain official interest in his complaints when backed by the Muslim astronomers, and when he touched on the fear of sorcery deep in the hearts of the still shamanist Manchu warrior princes who were the Regents. In April 1665 Schall, his new assistant Ferdinand Verbiest, and the leading Chinese Christian officials of the Calendar Bureau were all arrested and a long period of interrogation and formal investigative procedures began. Almost as soon as this opened Schall was stricken with paralysis and lay on a pallet unable to speak throughout all the long weary days of formal process. His recently arrived assistant, Fr Ferdinand Verbiest had to act as spokesman. He was, through the medium of a number of challenges, able to prove the accuracy of the Jesuit astronomy; but to the Regents that was no longer the issue – the issue was sorcery. Their obsession with sorcery was what led to the death penalty being decreed by the Regents for all the Jesuits in Beijing as well as most of the Chinese staff of the Bureau. However, this same belief was what saved Schall and the other Jesuits. The day the decision to execute them was announced an earthquake shook Beijing and a fire ravaged the imperial palace a few days later. Senior Manchu leaders insisted this was a sign in favour of the innocence of the Jesuits, and the Empress Dowager pressed this home very hard in her appeals for the release of the Christians. The Jesuits, Schall, Verbiest, Buglio and Magalhaes were freed with most of the Christian civil servants, but tragically the remaining five of the Bureau staff were still held and then executed for 'having chosen the wrong date'. The Bureau of the Calendar was handed over to Yang, to his horror since he knew he was no astronomer, and all members of the Christian missionary orders, Jesuit, Dominican and Franciscan were rounded up and imprisoned together in Canton except for the four Jesuits of Beijing who were allowed to stay there. All Christian churches in China were closed and that included the large and beautiful church which Schall had built in Beijing.

The imprisonment of all the missionaries together in Canton allowed them to give long and careful consideration to the differences over the Riccian tradition between the Jesuits and the other Orders; a conflict we will consider in detail in the next chapter.

On 15 August 1666, Fr Johann Adam Schall von Bell died and several hundred Chinese Christians were allowed to accompany his body to its grave beside that of Li Madou. The Church in China remained in a state of limbo for two more years until 1668 when the young Kangxi Emperor took power into his own hands. He was very unhappy that even with the help of the Muslim Astronomical School Yang had not been able to produce a satisfactory Calendar for him. In the months of December 1668 and January 1669 the Emperor set a number of tests to be carried out by Verbiest and by Wang and his staff at the Bureau. Verbiest won these tests. In March 1669, Verbiest and his colleagues were put in charge of the Bureau of the Calendar again. In August that year Schall was posthumously restored to all his old ranks and privileges as were the five Christian astronomers who had been executed, and their families suitably compensated.

Yang was now sentenced to death for making false charges but because of his old age he was allowed to retire to his home village. In the event he died on the journey home. However, Yang's book the *Budeyi* remained of long-term importance. It became the basis of the late eighteenth and nineteenth-century rejection of Christianity by Confucian intellectuals. Although it was completely wrong in the chapters in which Yang tried to prove the Jesuit mathematics and astronomy were inaccurate, it was a powerful assertion of neo-Confucian orthodoxy and was particularly strong in its demolition of the attempt by Buglio in his *Tianxue Chuangai* to relate a very literalist Biblical chronology to China's past.[17] It is also a major source for Professor Gernet's study *China and the Christian Impact*, in which Gernet asserts the essential incompatibility of Christianity and Confucianism.

THE KANGXI EMPEROR AND VERBIEST

When Kangxi sent a special marble tablet inscribed with words of praise for Schall to be laid on his grave the previous close relations of the Qing Dynasty and the Christian mission seemed to have been restored. Verbiest took Schall's place as head of the Calendar Office which again came to be staffed by Chinese Christians trained in modern mathematics and astronomy.

In 1670 the Emperor was petitioned to allow the missionaries in Canton to return to their previous residences and in 1671 an imperial edict granted this request. However the proscription of Christianity made during the Regency was not specifically rescinded. In this situation the Christian Church was in practice free to operate because of the relationship of the Beijing Jesuits with the Emperor and so long as they conformed to the ways of Li Madou. At the Canton 'Conference' the Dominicans and Franciscans had agreed to do so, but when Fr Navarette who had been in Canton returned to Europe he withdrew his agreement and continued a campaign against the Ricci tradition.[18] However the Mendicants who were working in China as opposed to their leaders in Europe, accepted the Jesuit way in general. Indeed some of them became articulate defenders of Ricci's approach, the most notable of these being the Chinese Dominican, Fr Gregory Lopez (Lo Wenzao), later the first Chinese to be consecrated a bishop of the Roman Catholic Church. The seventies and eighties of the seventeenth century saw a period of growth and prosperity for the Church similar to that during the reign of the Shunzhi Emperor.

Verbiest, whose Chinese name was Nanhuairen, became a close friend and adviser of the Kangxi Emperor. He, together with Philippe-Marie Grimaldi and Thomas Pèreira acted as tutor in mathematics to the Emperor. Verbiest had a translation into Manchu made of Ricci and Xu Guangqi's Chinese version of Euclid for the benefit of the young Emperor. Verbiest was made a mandarin of the second rank of the First Division and in addition to his duties as President of the Board of Astronomy he was also made Vice-President of the Ministry of Public Works. He was involved in the recreation of the old observatory and laboratory on the Eastern Wall, he built new astronomical instruments, he planned improvements in the canal system and like Schall before him designed and cast new artillery pieces for the imperial army. He also introduced to China the thermometer and developed a primitive form of steam power which could drive a small cart or a small paddle boat. This use of steam was unknown in Europe and remained as a sort of quaint toy in China.[19]

With his astronomical instruments in his luggage, Verbiest went on two long and exhausting field trips with the Emperor and his senior Manchu military officers north of the Great Wall. They were meant to toughen up the officers, growing soft by their long stays in Beijing; but he asked the Emperor to be excused from any similar event in the future. He was, after all, thirty years Kangxi's senior. He became, as Schall had been in the previous reign, a close personal friend as well as adviser to the Emperor. Of this relationship, Nigel Cameron, no partisan of the Society of Jesus, says

> He was one of the 'Great Mandareens' (as contemporary English writers called them) of the greatest and most populous and most sophisticated empire of the world − no mean feat for a boy from a Belgian country place. Never before and never after was Jesuit influence in China so deep. This came about because of the conjunction of a brilliant Emperor and a brilliant Jesuit.[20]

In 1688 Ferdinand Verbiest died in Beijing and was given an official state funeral attended by Manchu princes and senior mandarins as well as vast numbers of Christians. He was entombed at the same Jesuit site with Ricci, Longobardo and Schall.

Within a few weeks of his death there arrived in Beijing a group of French Jesuits, all trained in mathematics and astronomy and subsidised by King Louis XIV of France. Their arrival marks the beginning of the new and deeply troubled period of Jesuit history in China but it was also the last act of its most successful period. Together with Pèreira and other companions of Verbiest they settled into the work of the Society in the capital, including the work of the Bureau of Astronomy. So quickly did they assimilate themselves that one of them, Jean-François Gerbillon, was asked to accompany Pèreira as part of the Chinese delegation to meet with representatives of the Tsar in an attempt to resolve the problems that had been growing for twenty years over the expansion of Russian authority closer and closer to the borders of China. The

Treaty of Nerchinsk of 1689 settled the frontier problem to Kangxi's satisfaction. This was perhaps the crowning step that led to the success of the policy of Valignano and Ricci as it had been patiently followed by Longobardo, Schall and Verbiest – the Edict on Christianity issued by the Kangxi Emperor on the 22 March 1692. This edict is of such importance as the climax of Alessandro Valignano's aim of gaining the agreement of the Emperor of the greatest state on earth to the propagation of the Christian faith that it is appropriate that a large section of the text be reproduced here:

> We have seriously considered this question of the Europeans, who, attracted from the extremity of the world by the renown of your remarkable prudence ... have crossed ... the seas ... Since they have been living among us they have merited our esteem and gratitude, by the great services they have rendered us in the civil and foreign wars, by their diligence in composing useful and curious books, their integrity, and their sincere regard for the public welfare. Besides this the Europeans are very quiet; they do not excite any disturbances in the provinces, they do no harm to any one, they commit no crimes, and their doctrine has nothing in common with that of the false sects in the empire, nor has it any tendency to excite sedition.
>
> Since, then, we do not hinder the Lamas of Tartary or the Bonzes of China from building temples, and offering in them incense to their gods, much less can we forbid these Europeans, who teach only good laws, from having also their churches and preaching their religion publicly in them.
>
> We decide therefore that all temples dedicated to the Lord of Heaven, in whatever place they may be found, ought to be preserved, and that it may be permitted to all who wish to worship this god to enter these temples, offer him incense, and perform the ceremonies practiced according to ancient custom by the Christians.
>
> Therefore let no one henceforth offer them any opposition.[21]

This edict of toleration can compare validly with the 'Edict of Milan' of AD 313 issued by Constantine. The Roman Emperor went on to become a Christian which Kangxi did not; but on the other hand the Church did not reject Constantine's gesture, as was to happen to Kangxi's. The 'Edict of Milan' did no more than the edict of 1692, in both instances Christianity was recognised as a 'religio licita', a valid element in society. Of course if one has the ideological belief that Confucianism and Christianity can never really be reconciled and live together then the later fatal split must be seen as inevitable. If the only possible Confucianism is that of Yang Guangxian then as Professor Gernet insists no cohabitation would appear possible. However it should be noted that the same narrowly orthodox neo-Confucianism which Yang represented was equally unhappy about Buddhism, yet Buddhism remained Chinese. Also, as we shall see in the next chapter, it was ultimately the Church's denial of the validity of the way of Valignano and Ricci that led to Kangxi and China's rejection of Christianity.

Within a few months of the apparent victory of the policy of Li Madou, Fr Maigrot, Vicar Apostolic of Fujian issued a formal instruction to all priests in his vicariate banning Christians from taking part in the rites honouring Confucius and those honouring their ancestors. This action began the intense controversy over these Rites which was to bring to an end the assimilation approach of Valignano and Ricci in the moment of their triumph.

In the next chapter we will look at how various political, social, national and religious tendencies in Europe and in the East came together to bring about this disaster for the Christian mission or, in the eyes of some, its deflection in the nick of time from a path leading to a sub-Christian syncretism.

NOTES

1. The White Lotus Society refers to a largely secret movement rooted in both popular Buddhist and Daoist piety which was often a channel for uprisings of common people against injustice.
2. Along with Li Zhizao and Xu Guangqi the most distinguished scholar and administrator to become a Christian.
3. A Chinese but since he was born and raised in Macao we have only a European name for him.
4. Translation of Edict to be found in Dunne, *Generation of Giants*, p. 137.
5. He became, in the view of Dunne and Rule, one of the ablest defenders of the Valignano–Ricci position.
6. Dunne, op. cit., p. 187
7. As we have seen in Chapter Five, Rodriguez was never a convinced supporter of the Valignano approach even in its more limited Japanese form.
8. D'Elia, *Galileo in China*, pp. 22–3.
9. Because of delays, death, disease and other difficulties only 8 of the 22 who set out finally worked in China.
10. See D'Elia, op. cit., for the persistent attempts made by these Jesuits to get help from Galileo even after they had arrived in China.
11. Dunne, op. cit., p. 196.
12. Ibid., p. 202.
13. D'Elia, op. cit., p. 34.
14. Attwater, *Adam Schall*, p. 76.
15. Dunne, op. cit., pp. 340–4.
16. Attwater, op. cit., pp. 119–20.
17. Rule, *K'ung-tzu or Confucius*, pp. 98–100.
18. For a new biography of Navarette see Cummins, *A Question of Rites*.
19. Cameron, *Barbarians and Mandarins*, p. 240–5.
20. Ibid., p. 242.
21. Cary-Elwes, *China and the Cross*, p. 122.

CHAPTER NINE

The Pope, the Bourbon Kings
and the Kangxi Emperor

W e have seen that there was an internal debate within the Society of Jesus, initiated by Longobardo, about the use of Shangdi and Tian for God and to a lesser extent about one or two other terms such as linghun for soul. By 1630 this had been resolved in favour of the original suggestions of Ricci that these were valid usages in the process of Christian apologetic but that Tianzhu should continue to be used in worship and scripture translation. However neither Longobardo nor anyone else in the Society in China was opposed to the fundamental accommodation approach that had been initiated by Ricci under Valignano's guidance and with his authority.

Within a very short time of the arrival of the Franciscans and Dominicans from the Spanish possessions, first from Formosa in 1632 and then, from 1633 onwards, from the Philippines, the Valignano–Ricci missionary strategy was challenged. Strangely enough the very first Dominican was sympathetic to the Jesuit approach and was an Italian, Angelo Cocchi. He set out with another Dominican and some Spanish and Philippino soldiers as an envoy of the Spanish Governor of Formosa to seek trading privileges in Fujian. After adventures with pirates and storms, Cocchi and a few companions were eventually washed up on the shore of Fujian. They were taken care of by the local authorities but were detained in Fuzhou. After a time the local governor decided to send Cocchi back to Formosa since there was no intention of giving the Spanish any trading privileges. Cocchi, who had always intended to begin missionary work in China, did not go but substituted a Japanese Christian who wanted to leave China. Meanwhile, he dressed as a Chinese and got in touch with Fr Aleni who helped him settle as a Chinese in the village of Fuan which contained a large Christian congregation. He reported to the Dominican authorities in Manila that Dominicans must come to China and live as Chinese, learning Mandarin and following the Jesuit way. He specifically insisted that the policy advocated in Manila of Dominicans simply landing illegally on the coast and starting to preach, was not the way. In Manila it was decided to follow up this initiative by Cocchi, and a group of Dominicans and Franciscans were sent to Fujian province. The leading Dominican was Juan Bautista de Morales and the leading Franciscan, Antonio Caballero a Santa Maria. They got to Fuan with the aid of Chinese Christians sent to bring them into the country by Cocchi. Shortly after the Franciscans moved on to make their centre at Dingdou. All of these missionaries were in China illegally, they were not there with government permission as were all the Jesuits. It is also clear that, other than Cocchi, they preached in public without magisterial permission and they used the crucifix constantly in public. Their very presence, let alone this form of behaviour, could – depending on the attitude of local magistrates – endanger local Christians who were associated with them. This did not seem to occur to them in this period, indeed they would appear to have seen such trouble as virtuous martyrdom. This is seen very clearly in an incident of which much was made in criticism of the Jesuits.

Antonio a Santa Maria travelled to Nanjing in 1634. As we saw in the last chapter Nanjing had been the scene of the only really widespread and violent persecution of Christians as a result of the actions of Shen Que. The Christians were just emerging from this dark period and their first legal visit by a priest, Fr Simbiasi, allowed to visit only by the authority of the Grand Secretary, Xu Guangqi, was about to take place.

The Nanjing Christians gave hospitality to the Franciscan, but explained he would have to leave since his illegal presence would put them all in danger again because of the still suspicious and antagonistic attitude of the local mandarins. He did not accept this but saw it as a Jesuit plot aimed at hindering the work of his Order. In frustration over his refusal to listen to them, the local Christians bound him and sent him off back home on a river boat. There were other incidents of misunderstanding between Jesuits and Mendicants in these years which have been well described and thoroughly discussed in the literature.[1] The important point is that those who followed Cocchi did not agree with what he had written in his original report but felt that they had to challenge the whole Jesuit approach.

The challenge to the Jesuits from the Spanish Mendicants came under three heads. The first was that the Jesuits did not insist on the positive precepts of the Church, such as were imposed on the Indians in 'New Spain' and in the Philippines. The second was the issue of the Chinese terms used for God, soul, angels and other Christian theological terms. The third was the participation by Christians in the rites for honouring the dead and, in the case of literati, the rites honouring Confucius.

The process of challenge began with the preparation of two documents by the recently arrived Dominican and Franciscan Fathers which they sent to their respective authorities in Manila. On the basis of these the Archbishop of Manila and another bishop in the Philippines formally condemned the Jesuit 'customs' in China and wrote to Rome in these terms, though on hearing a Jesuit explanation they formally withdrew the charges subsequently. This action was followed up in 1639 by a series of twelve questions presented by Morales to the Jesuit Provincial, Manoel Dias. Historians sympathetic to the critics of the Jesuits insist that he only went on to send his complaints to Rome because of the delay in getting a reply from Dias.[2] He sent his questions to Dias on 3 June 1639 and certainly Dias took a very long time in replying. This was primarily because he wanted to consult Vagnoni, the leading scholar of the Society, who was in far-away Shaanxi. However, whatever the reason for the delay, not only did Morales not wait for the answer, he had already sent a long letter on the subject to the Congregation of the Propaganda Fide in Rome on 15 February 1639.[3]

Morales was then sent to Rome by his Dominican superiors in Manila to present his complaints about the conduct of the Jesuits in China. Fr Francisco Furtado, the Jesuit Superior in China, after careful consultation with Vagnoni, wrote two important defences of the Jesuit position.[4] One was a letter to Pope Urban VIII, 5 November 1639, and the second a set of specific answers to Morales' twelve questions. This latter document was sent to Rome on 8 February 1640, though the original is no longer extant.

The accusations he was trying to deal with, other than those insisting on the idolatrous and superstitious nature of the rites for the dead and for Confucius, can be briefly summed up as follows. The Jesuits did not impose upon Chinese Christians the positive laws of the Church such as obligatory fasts or abstaining from work on feast days. They did not use the prescribed forms in the baptism of women. They did not proclaim that Confucius was in hell nor insist on the monogamy of converts, and they failed to proclaim the crucifixion and its role in humanity's salvation.

The contrast between the attitude of the Jesuits and that of the Mendicants towards the issues such as that of fasting and abstention from work on certain feast days on pain of mortal sin brings out more clearly than almost anything else why Valignano did not want, in China or Japan, missionaries from the Spanish dominions even if they were Jesuits.[5] In New Spain or the Philippines the lands were under Spanish rule. Society was organised by Catholic Spain so it was possible for people to abstain from work on feast days because society was organised around these feast days exactly as it was in old Spain. The conquistadores had made sure of that. The friars from the Spanish milieu – and it was the milieu that was important rather than what particular Order missionaries came from – did not seem to appreciate that in the Chinese empire society was not so organised. To abstain from work on the many feast days of the Church would mean clashing with the Chinese authorities over a matter that was not central to the Christian Gospel in the eyes of the Jesuits. Furtado pointed this out and further insisted in his two reports that the fasting rules had been ordered with European society in mind. As he pointed out, because so many Chinese lived on a very low level of subsistence with a diet which consisted of rice and herbs and did not even contain many vegetables, to order fasts in these circumstances was to go against Gospel charity.

Furtado admitted that the Jesuits had had to reduce the ritual of baptism for women to the very minimum of pouring water 'in the name of the Father and the Son and the Holy Ghost'. It was simply not permitted in Chinese society for a man, other than husband or father, to touch a woman's breast, ear, mouth or hand as were all necessary if the fully developed liturgical action was to be carried out. Indeed, as we have already seen when discussing the growth of the Christian community within the imperial palace in the last twenty years of the Ming Dynasty, baptism in its minimum but valid form had often to be carried out by a eunuch or by other women.

In his reports Furtado also pointed out that the Fathers had always insisted on monogamy for Chinese Christians, indeed it had been and still was the most common barrier to conversion on the part of many Chinese men. However he agreed that the missionaries of the Society had never expressly condemned the ancient sages and kings of the Chinese historic past for not being monogamous and he insisted the Society was not wrong for so doing.

Lastly he insisted that the missionaries of the Society had never suppressed the importance of the crucifixion of Jesus. They did not use the crucifix in the constant and public way that the Mendicants did because of Chinese susceptibilities, but converts were always carefully instructed about this. A clear example was the recent publication by Aleni of a life of Christ, *Tian zhu Jiangshing Chuxiang Jingjie* liberally illustrated with drawings which included some of the crucifixion and in which the Passion story was explicitly told.[6] He agreed that they did not proclaim that Confucius was in hell since it was clearly possible according to Catholic theology that gentiles like Confucius who followed carefully the light God had given them in their day might very well be saved through God's mercy.

Furtado's answer to these accusations are all-important because they have continued to be repeated by writers well into the twentieth century. However, most important for the future of the Christian Church in China was Morales' challenge to the way the Jesuits had allowed Christians to continue to perform most of the rites associated with funerals and the honouring of the dead, and their allowing Scholar Christians to take part in most of the rituals associated with honouring Confucius.

When Morales reached Rome he submitted his objections to the Congregation of the Propaganda Fide which transmitted them to the Holy Office who appointed an official board of theologians to report on the matter. The Board discussed simply what was put to them by Morales, and they did so very carefully and thoroughly. As a result of their deliberations Chinese Christians were forbidden to take part in the ancestral rites, in most funeral rites and the rites in honour of Confucius 'in so far as they have been correctly described'.

This last was very carefully inserted because the theologians were well aware that they might have before them distorted evidence about a culture of which they knew little. That they took this doubt very seriously can be seen by their judgement on Morales' attempt to have them condemn the calling of Confucius 'sheng'. Did it mean 'saint' or 'honoured teacher' or what? The theologians insisted that since they had no means of knowing all that this word might signify in Chinese they could not condemn its use in reference to Confucius. These recommendations were then promulgated by the Propaganda Fide with Papal authority on 12 September 1645.

The Jesuits in China were astonished when they eventually got word of this Papal ruling. It was decided to send Fr Martino Martini to Rome to present to the Pope and the Holy Office what they believed to be a more accurate description of the various Chinese ancestral and funeral rites together with those honouring Confucius, and so plead for a Papal decision that would allow the Christians under their care to continue as they had been doing since the time of Fr Ricci.

Martini insisted in his presentation on how the Jesuit approach was that of Fr Ricci – by this time well known in intellectual circles in Europe because of the popularity of Trigault's translation of his *Journal* – and the result of many years of close relations with the literati of China, while the complaints were based on that of a few missionaries none of whom had been as long as three years in China and who had all been together in the one small corner of one province. The burden of his case to the theologians of the Holy Office appointed by the Pope to listen to his plea, was that Morales' descriptions of so many of the rites both of the family and of the literati were distorted by the Latin words that Martini had chosen to use in his descriptions. For example Morales had used 'templum' of what was better translated as 'aula' because worship did not take place there. What happened there only appeared to be worship if one did not understand that the 'kou tou' was not 'genuflectio' but a gesture also used to honour the living, as was the burning of incense with which Morales had made great play. Again and again he insists that what is described as an 'altar' in Morales statements would be more appropriately called a table. Certainly it is clear that the newly arrived Mendicants were ready to see altars where there were none. When Gaspar Alenda and Francisco de la Madre de Dios visited Adam Schall in Beijing they later reported that there had been an altar to the Emperor in the Jesuit chapel. This was in fact a plaque on which some ideograms were painted in gold; it was a plaque honouring the Emperor who had paid for the building of the chapel.[7] It differed in physical form but not in intention from the very common equivalent dedications in many a Church throughout Europe, but it was a difference which skewed the judgement of the two new and very nervous young missionary priests.

After long and careful consideration, the theologians of the Holy Office came to the only conclusion they could, which was that if all was as described by

Martini then Christians could participate in the various rites as described by the Jesuit procurator. It should be noted that the Jesuits insisted that there were certain aspects of certain funeral rites and some for honouring the ancestors which Christians had to modify somewhat for performance in a Christian family and there was one form of rite honouring Confucius which Christian graduates had to avoid; but with these noted, Christian participation in the rites was permitted. This decision was promulgated with the authority of Pope Alexander VII on 23 March 1656.

When, as we have seen, all the missionaries other than the Jesuits in Beijing were imprisoned together in Canton during the persecution of the Church in the later years of the Regency, the missionaries of all Orders agreed to follow the ways of Ricci. Despite having agreed with the others in this conference, Fr Domingo de Navarette later disassociated himself from this agreement, saying this was because two alterations were made to the text in Macao by the Jesuit Superior there, who it should be noted was very much a priest of the Padroado and not a member of the China mission. Navarette left China soon after and continued to spend a great deal of time and effort in attacking the whole Jesuit policy in China.[8]

During the Canton imprisonment a list of rules for Christians was drawn up and distributed among the people by catechists and other Christian lay leaders. This gives us, as Professor Minamiki has pointed out,[9] a better picture of what was happening at the grass-roots of the Jesuit led congregations – and in the congregations of the other Orders also, most scholars now agree – than the formal documents being presented at Rome. This pastoral guide included instructions about how the ancestral tablets in a Christian home should indicate that the tablet was the 'seat' ('wei') of the ancestor and should not have on it the ideograms 'shen' or 'ling' which imply that which Christians would mean by soul. It goes into great detail about funeral ceremonies, including various modifications from the strict traditional pattern in some; about the cleansing of the graves in spring and autumn, insistence on the making of the kou tou, and the offering of flowers and incense at the grave and before the tablets to indicate the Christian adherence to 'xiao' (filial piety), the basis of all Confucian morality. All of which could also be offered to a living senior, thus confirming that so-called 'worship' of the ancestors was really a matter of continuing after death the symbols of 'xiao' that were offered in life.

The Dominicans, in Manila it should be noted not China, made a last effort to challenge what was going on in China and asked the Holy Office to make a judgement as to whether the 1645 or the 1656 decision was binding. The Holy Office advised Pope Clement XI to reply that both were binding, which he accordingly ruled in November 1669. This is not as peculiar as it appears at first. If the Chinese rites were as described by Morales, then Christians were not permitted to take part; if however they were as described by Martini, then they were rightly so permitted. It was left, in other words, to the wisdom and consciences of the clergy on the spot in China. In turn, the clergy in China, of all the Orders, appeared at this time to be able to agree to work together amicably and, as we have seen, the first Chinese Dominican priest, later to be the first Chinese bishop, Antonio Lopez, explicitly commended the way of Li Madou.

The Dominicans continued to work primarily in Fujian, but the Franciscans were more widespread in their efforts and by 1692 had set up congregations in Fujian, Jiangxi and in Shandong. In the latter province they had been enabled to begin work, as they willingly acknowledged, through the good offices of Verbiest.

However, these last thirty years of the seventeenth century which were in China a period of quiet and steady development and growth, were the lull before a terrible storm which was to come, not from Chinese opposition to Christianity nor from the often suggested ultimate incompatability of Christianity and Confucianism,[10] but from events and developments in Europe. The rapid decline in power of the Bourbon monarchs of Spain and Portugal in comparison with France and the severe pressure put upon them in the East by the Protestant powers, the Netherlands and Britain, the bitter quarrels in France between Jansenist and Jesuit, between Gallicanism and Ultramontanism, all played their part in the destruction of the Jesuit mission built on the Valignano–Ricci perception of Christianity and of Confucianism.

THE PROPAGANDA FIDE AND THE FRENCH CONNECTION

As we saw in the last chapter, it was the edict issued by Fr Maigrot, Vicar Apostolic of Fujian and a missionary of the Société des Missions Étrangères de Paris (MEP) that began the storm. We have to look at the creation of the Vicars Apostolic in China and of the MEP to see how this came about.

Many in the Papal curia and elswhere in the Church were aware, by the early seventeenth century, that the Padroado and the Patronato were hindrances rather than aids to the Church's world-wide mission. The Patronato maintained royal rather than ecclesiastical authority over all the Churches in the vast Spanish territories in the Americas. The Padroado was somewhat different because the Portuguese empire was not one of vast colonial conquests but key bases from which to dominate commerce and trade, though intended to achieve the same ends of royal control of all ecclesiastical affairs in the Portuguese sphere. Portuguese power was diminishing far more rapidly and visibly than Spanish power, though with hindsight we know that it was soon to follow in decline. The Portuguese collapse was the result of the constant pressure from the Dutch and the English (after 1707 the British). They were less and less able to fulfil their obligations to the ecclesiastical institutions in the East, yet became more and more jealous of their dignity, of which the Padroado was an important symbol. As the most modern and fullest history of Catholic missions expresses it,

En moins d'un siècle, on s'aperçut à Rome que les deux couronnes mettaient l'accent sur leurs droits et déjà déclinaient leurs devoirs…Le plus grave était la prétention des souverains à donner à leurs décrets en matière ecclésiastique la valeur et la caractère de brefs apostoliques, tandis qu'ils exigeaient que les actes du Souverain Pontife et des supérieurs ecclésiastiques obtinissent l'approbation de leurs chancelleries pour devenir exécutoires.[11]

Over against the Patronato and Padroado, the Church authorities in Rome attempted to develop an autonomous jurisdiction over its world mission. In 1622 there was established the Sacred Congregation for Propagation of the Faith, most usually known by its abbreviated title, the Propaganda Fide. Many figures within the Society of Jesus had advocated such an office. From the beginning, their Generals had been committed to developing the mission of the Church from the Church's perspective rather than that of the Iberian royal authorities. This attitude of commitment by the Jesuits to serve wherever it helped spread the faith is symbolised by the famous Fourth Vow of the 'professed' of the Society. Indeed the spirit of the Congregation appeared in the first decades to be one close to that of the Jesuit missions in India,[12] Japan and China. The peak moment of this apparent conjunction came in 1659 when the Propaganda issued a famous 'Instruction', parts of which could almost have been written by Valignano:

Do not attempt in any way to persuade these people to change their customs, their habits and their behaviour, as long as they are not evidently contrary to religion and morality. What could be more absurd, indeed, than to transport France, Italy or some other European country to the Chinese? Do not bring them our countries but the faith, which does not reject or harm the customs and habits of any people, so long as they are not perverse; but, on the contrary, wishes to see them preserved in their entirety.

And since it is as it were written into human nature that every man, in his judgement and in his heart, puts his customs and his country above all others, there exists no more powerful motive for hatred and revulsion than changing ancestral customs, especially those that men have always practised as far back as the memories of their forefathers go, and even more so if, in place of the practices abolished, one substitutes from outside those of another country.[13]

There could be no more clear-cut condemnation of the whole Europeanising pattern of mission that had been practised throughout the Portuguese and Spanish dominions and with which Valignano had specifically and deliberately broken in Japan and even more profoundly in China.

The 'Instruction' was drawn up for the new Vicars Apostolic to be appointed to Indo-China and China. The Vicar Apostolic was a legal device for appointing bishops while bypassing the Padroado, Patronato and other similar traditional concordats with a state. Such an appointment brought the Churches under the authority of the Vicar into direct relations with the Papacy. A Vicar Apostolic had the same authority as a bishop but was appointed directly by the Pope, an appointment which, technically, was not covered by patronage agreements.

A second element in the perceived requirement for this development was the need for an indigenous clergy. It was felt that a much more numerous indigenous clergy in Japan might have preserved the Church there better. Also the brilliant Jesuit missionary in Indo-China, Alexandre de Rhodes, had made a deep impact in Rome with his pleas for an episcopate free from the Padroado and for a 'native' clergy which he believed were the two necessities for the long term survival of the Church in east Asia.[14]

So much then seemed to point, in 1659, to the initiative of the Propaganda Fide as a welcome support to the Jesuit China mission. Admittedly the 'Instructions' of 1659 said that missionaries should not be involved with kings, magistrates and other persons in authority and they should refuse any preference for themselves in the host state. Since these instructions were such as could not possibly be adhered to if a missionary wished to stay in China, other than in hiding, the new Vicars Apostolic would soon learn. What is important is that the paragraphs on 'Accomodation' already quoted appeared as an endorsement of Valignano's 'modo soave'.

Yet it was the action of a Vicar Apostolic, Monsignor Charles Maigrot, in 1693 that began the so-called Rites Controversy which ended in the condemnation by the Church of the Valignano–Ricci tradition of missionary activity. Indeed, only ten years after the 'Instructions' of 1659, we find in a document of the Propaganda an unambiguous attack on the Jesuit approach to mission in China. There is no mention here of the validity of indigenous custom; that element in the 1659 document appears to have gone for good. However, this important text was the volume prepared for the missionaries of the Propaganda going to the East. Fathers François Pallu and Lambert de la Motte, who were the authors of this work, were members of the MEP. In the third chapter they condemn as heresy any involvement by missionaries in commercial transactions; they condemn what they refer to as 'purely human means' in the work of conversion; and warn of the dangers of the corruption of missionaries through too much concern for the sciences and the arts. They do not specifically mention the Jesuit mission in China, but this document is unambiguously a condemnation of their work there, the roots of which can be seen in the 1659 document, despite its interesting paragraph on customs.[15]

It is not possible to investigate what was going on within the Catholic Church in Europe only ten years later that might explain the disappearance of those elements in the 1659 'Instructions' in sympathy with the Valignano approach, together with the development of other elements in that document into an outright condemnation of that approach. Was it the turning to the MEP to staff the missions of Propaganda that was decisive or was it simply the fuller expression of an antagonism towards the Jesuits on the part of the leadership of the Propaganda that was there almost from the beginning?

In 1653 when Alexandre de Rhodes was seeking, on behalf of the Propaganda, suitable men to be appointed as Vicars Apostolic in Siam, Indo-China and China, he met François Pallu in Paris where the latter was at the centre of a religious community living under a rule which Pallu had composed. De Rhodes was so impressed with these men that he invited the group to provide the personnel for this new venture in the East. They responded warmly to de Rhodes' appeal and Pallu, La Motte and a third who never reached his field, Cotolendi, were appointed in 1659 as the first Vicars Apostolic to Indo-China and China.

Meanwhile, in Paris Pallu had already begun the planning of a seminary to train secular priests to serve in the missions in China and Indo-China. In 1663 the seminary was opened in Paris with a sermon by Bossuet, the great intellectual spokesman for Gallicanism.[16] It was from within this seminary and with the support of the powerful ecclesiastics and royal officials who had founded it that the MEP was created. It was the secular priests of this Society that helped the Vicars Apostolic staff the missions of their areas of responsibility in the East.

Pallu and La Motte did not get to operate in China. This was because of obstruction by the Portuguese authorites, ecclesiastical as well as royal, in both Goa and Macao, who saw the Vicars as illegal interlopers. Indeed the Goan Archiepiscopal Inquisition at one time excommunicated La Motte for defying the authority of the Archbishop. The Chinese imperial authorities were not helpful in this period of the regency so there was no hope of getting into China with imperial permission while bypassing Macao. Pallu and La Motte were able to establish themselves in Siam, and in the royal capital there they founded a seminary for the training of indigenous clergy in Siam, Indo-China and China.

Pallu, according to Launay's old but 'official' history of the MEP, kept in close touch with Colbert, Louis XIV's chief minister because of his firm belief in the usefulness to the mission of the Church of the expansion of French colonial and mercantile interests in the East. It is not surprising that when in 1674 he was making another attempt to enter China and his ship was blown off course and he landed in the Philippines, the Spanish authorities held him in custody until they could ship him back to Europe via Mexico. The doyen of the twentieth-century historians of Christian missions, Kenneth Latourette, pictures Pallu as the heroic pioneer of the missionaries of the Propaganda Fide attempting to undercut the nationalist orientation of so much of missionary activity hitherto.[17] In fact he was, apparently, attempting to substitute a different national connection, that of France, rather than trying to break the mould. Heroic and determined he certainly was, and in 1684 he finally reached Fujian – part of the vast area he was meant to administer as Vicar Apostolic – and where within a few months of his arrival he died. His companion at his deathbed was Charles Maigrot, the first of a small but steady stream of MEP priests who now began to enter China, and who succeeded Pallu in his Vicariate.

Maigrot and his French priests of the MEP were to be the spearhead of the challenge to Confucianist Christianity but, oddly enough, France now came to the aid of the Jesuit mission in China. Or perhaps not so odd if we see this as a time when Bourbon France was replacing Spain and Portugal as the great Catholic kingdom in the world.

Verbiest towards the end of his life had become more and more unhappy about the inability to get new Jesuits of the quality necessary to keep the Society in charge of the Calendar Office and so close to the throne. He wrote a number of letters to the General about this, as well as others to be circulated throughout the Jesuit houses in Europe. He was careful not to scorn or criticise Portugal but he was trying to escape the restrictions of the Padroado as the Society's missions in Japan and China had done since Valignano's famous clash with the Portuguese Jesuit authorities and the Portuguese hierarchy over his attempt to take his 'Great Mission' to the East.[18] What appears to have been happening in the years since he arrived in China was that the Society had ceased to be able to find as many volunteers from Italy, Germany and the Netherlands as it had done hitherto in order to keep the mission, although linked to the Padroado, independent of Portuguese control.

Louis XIV and Colbert were both taken up with the idea of French Jesuits answering Verbiest's appeal. It appears that Colbert's death in 1683 held up any action being taken. However in 1685 six Jesuits who had all taught science and mathematics were chosen to go to join the Jesuit residence in the imperial capital. They arrived on the Chinese coast, not at Macao, in July 1687 and were allowed to enter the empire through arrangements made by Verbiest in his role as the senior mandarin in both the Calendar Office and the Ministry of Works. The five Jesuits, Fathers Fontenoy, Gerbillon, le Compte, Visdelou and Bouvet – one had been left behind in Siam to help the Society's work there – arrived at the capital in time to see the massive state funeral accorded their patron, Ferdinand Verbiest.[19] Verbiest died on 7 February 1688 and they arrived in the capital on the 17th.

Louis XIV financed this new venture and insisted formally that these Jesuits were mathematicians and scientists sent by him to aid the work of the Calendar Office. Thus their going to China had nothing to do with the Padroado or indeed the Propaganda Fide. The Jesuits themselves were quite clear that they were missionaries sent to work in the China mission of the Society of Jesus. Gerbillon and Bouvet continued Verbiest's work as teachers of western science to the Emperor and served him in many of the technical capacities that Verbiest had done in his role as a mandarin of the Ministry of Works. They also carried out their duties as priests in the churches of the capital. Others of the French Fathers worked in parishes in the provinces at intervals as well as in the capital. One of them, as we have seen, helped with the successful negotiations with the Russians at Nerchinsk.

The rest of the Jesuits, referred to – in essence I believe wrongly – by historians like Cary-Elwes as the 'Portuguese mission',[20] were sometimes at odds with them because of their rather unusual entry and French royal support. These minor differences were soon forgotten as it became clear that Maigrot's local rulings had had such repercussions in Europe as to threaten everything that the work of the Society stood for in China.

CHINA IN 1700

Despite Maigrot's decree and its impact in Europe which we will consider a little later, the 1690s were, as Latourette says, a decade of peace and growth for Christianity in China. The constant abrasive clashes between Papal authority and the Padroado were settled in 1696 as far as the Papacy was concerned and were so in practice despite the Portuguese verbally insisting on the rights of the Padroado for some time to come. In 1696 the three bishoprics previously conceded by the Papacy as being within the gift of the Padroado – Nanjing, Beijing and Macao – were restricted in their sphere of authority and the rest of China divided among eight Apostolic Vicariates. Some of this was a legal fiction since in four provinces there were still no Christians. It should be noted that despite some grumbling and unease, the Jesuits and the Spanish Franciscans had all accepted the authority of the Vicars.

It is difficult to know exactly how many missionaries and Christians there were in China but reviewing the many sources, some of which are contradictory, a picture does emerge which can be accepted as reasonably accurate. There would appear to have been sixty Jesuit priests, six of whom were Chinese; twenty-nine Franciscans, eight Dominicans, two Lazarists, six Augustinians and fifteen French secular priests of the MEP. These figures do not include Brothers of the various Orders. The Chinese Church was somewhere between two hundred thousand and half a million Christians and existed in all but four of the provinces. There was a widespread network of lay organisations both for evangelism and for the care of the sick. There were no longer Christians among the very top rank of the scholar administrators as there had been in the days of Xu Guangqi but there were still literati Christians. This change would appear to have come from a more widespread support for Sung neo-Confucian orthodoxy among the literati than there had been before, partly perhaps as a conservative reaction to rule by a foreign Dynasty.

That is as may be, but the Christian Church appeared secure under the protection of the Kangxi Emperor who had even allowed the building of a Jesuit house within the imperial palace enclosure and had subsidised the building of the famous 'North Church' of the Jesuits in Beijing as well as two in Hangzhou and Nanjing. In all three there were plaques engraved with messages composed by the Emperor himself. At the opening of all three the Emperor sent a personal representative to be present during the Mass of consecration.

There was one large problem internal to the Church which was still pressing for a solution. This was the matter of the use of literary Chinese in the liturgy.

We have seen how in 1615 Fr Trigault had obtained from Pope Paul V a ruling that Chinese priests could use Chinese as their liturgical language. Fr Buglio dedicated a large part of his life to translating the Missal and the Bible into literary Chinese to make this advance possible. Alexandre de Rhodes in his campaigning journeys in Europe had also advocated this development. Nothing happened for a time because there were difficulties with the Jesuit authorities in Rome over the promotion of Chinese to the priesthood. Then the chaos of the period of the end of the Ming Dynasty and the final establishment of Qing authority also interrupted plans for training indigenous clergy by the Jesuits. However, in 1658 Father Rhodes and in 1660 Fr Fabri of the Jesuits formally petitioned the Propaganda for it to put Paul V's permission into action in China; Buglio's work was done by this time.

What was extraordinary was the fact that the Propaganda managed to stall the whole matter. Again this shows of how little import the paragraphs on accommodation in the 1659 'Instructions' were. It then was decided that the Vicars Apostolic, once firmly established in China, should consider the matter and report back to Rome for a final decision. Even after this happened nothing was finally decided. So in the 1690s Chinese priests varied in practice, some like Bishop Lopez used Buglio's translations, others agonisingly ploughed their way through a Latin text they did not fully understand. The decision had to be finally made and carried through effectively from Rome, but Rome by this time had other things to worry about.[21]

THE RITES CONTROVERSY

When Monsignor Charles Maigrot published his famous Instruction of 26 March 1693, it appeared to many in China as a local difficulty which could be resolved as the conflicts between the Jesuits and Mendicants had been. It certainly raised great difficulties in his own vicariate and he had to suspend from duty two Jesuit priests who refused to accept it; there are even stories that Chinese Christians mobbed him after the suspension of their priests. The other bishops and Vicars Apostolic in China were divided over whether to accept it for their own jurisdictions as were the heads of the various Orders.

The key issues in his Instruction were the banning of Christians from attendance at various ceremonies in honour of their own dead and, in the case of literati, of Confucius; and, what was perhaps even more important, an attack on the intellectual basis of the whole Valignano–Ricci tradition. This was the assertion that the 1656 decree of Alexander VII was based on false information so it should not be invoked. In its sixth paragraph the Instruction declared to be false and scandalous the following assertions:

> That Confucianism, properly understood, contains nothing contrary to the Christian faith.
>
> That the term 'taiji' when used in the classical period was referring to a Creator God.
>
> That the term 'jing tian', 'worship heaven', on all the scrolls presented by the Emperor and hung in the principal Jesuit Churches, is not idolatrous.
>
> That the book *Yi Jing* represents an excellent system of science and morality.

In the last paragraph Maigrot went on to condemn all the Classics as atheistic and superstitious, not just the commentaries of Sung neo-Confucianism.[22] The emphasis on the *Yi Jing* was not one that Ricci had made, but it had become the emphasis of some of the French Jesuits in Beijing.

Maigrot and his colleagues in the MEP were not at all willing for this to be a matter for local discussion. Fr Nicolas Charmont was sent to Rome to reopen the whole issue that had been dormant if not settled since the decree of 1669. It was 1697 before the Holy Office took up the task of investigating Maigrot's claims on Innocent XII's instructions. After a few months of study they were assisted by the Vicar Apostolic of Huguang, Fr Giovanni F. N. a Leonessa. He compiled a long guide for the Fathers of the investigating board. Paul Rule points out that it was a very fair and accurate description of Confucian practices. However, Leonessa had to make certain key decisions about the Latin words to use in translating certain terms and he made decisions that were disastrous from the perspective of the Jesuits. He translated 'sheng' – applying to Confucius – as 'saint' not 'master'; again 'miao' was translated by him as 'chapel' not school or hall; 'kou tou' as genuflection and so on. This gave a deeply religious slant to all Confucian rites for funerals, for the ancestors and for Confucius, which the Jesuits always denied on behalf of the literati although always agreeing that there was superstitious religiosity associated with them among the uneducated. What was extraordinary was that Leonessa also took the line that Maigrot had done following Navarette, that the Confucian literati were atheists, while still insisting that if one were present at their rites one was guilty of worshipping false gods!

The key issues were essentially those of interpreting the meaning of Chinese words, concepts and actions. Yet when the appeal of Maigrot began to be considered by the Holy Office an explosion of pamphlets and books for and against the Jesuits appeared in Europe. These were all written by Europeans about what the Chinese meant by their own actions and words. None of them added anything to the argument on either side. What this enormous literary activity did do was to allow many people with deep feelings about the Jesuits for reasons that had nothing to do with the Christian mission in China to attack and to defend them. Remarkably it led a leading Protestant intellectual, Leibnitz, to write a book defending these leading figures in the then current and later Protestant popular demonology. In France, the home of the MEP, two powerful strands of Catholic piety were deeply opposed to the Jesuits: the Jansenists and the Gallicanists. Both groups seized on what was for them a golden opportunity to attack the Jesuits as those who deviated from Christian and Catholic truth. Charmont, Maigrot's representative in Europe, who could not be unaware of the many enemies of the Jesuits in French ecclesiastical circles, brought Maigrot's complaints to the Archbishop of Paris, who, in classic Gallican style, placed it before the Theological Faculty of the Sorbonne even before the Holy Office had published any kind of ruling. This may very well have been an attempt to pressure Rome into acting with greater speed over the issue. The Faculty was already in bitter conflict with the French Jesuits over a number of issues and were delighted to be able to rule in favour of Maigrot and condemn the whole style of Jesuit mission. They did so, however, by discussing two books written by Jesuits in Europe to defend the Chinese mission. One was a brilliantly written, popularised, and therefore less than accurate version of the Riccian position. Both books, as Paul Rule and George Minamiki have pointed out,[23] defended the mission in terms of a speculative theology which had nothing to do with the Riccian position on Confucianism or on Christianity, but had to do with theological conflicts in Europe.

The Jesuits in China, who had taken a long time to waken up to the seriousness of the threat, now thought they could produce the master stroke that would once and for all settle the issue. They asked the Kangxi Emperor for a ruling. We must be clear as to what they were doing. They were asking the Emperor for a ruling on their traditional understanding of various Confucian ceremonies and of the meaning of a number of key terms in the Classics. They were not asking the Emperor to rule on any matter of Christian theology or belief.

The Kangxi Emperor, who prided himself on loyalty to the Confucian way, consulted the leading Confucian scholars of the day and then wrote his report for the Jesuits to send to Rome. The form of the imperial report was a specific endorsement by the Emperor of a series of statements by the Jesuits about the meaning of ceremonies and of terms. The Jesuits also sent back copies of writings by various Confucian scholars, Christian and non-Christian, both contemporaries and the writings of men from the past like the great Xu Guangqi and Li Zhicao, all confirming the judgement of the Emperor.

The Kangxi Emperor issued his official declaration on 30 November 1700. It was sent off along with all the accompanying testimonies to Rome immediately. There are many summaries of what the report contained; the best, by Paul Rule, reads as follows,

> He approved their statements that Confucius was honoured as a teacher; that 'performance of the ceremony of sacrifice to the dead is a means of showing sincere affection for members of the family and thankful devotion to ancestors of the clan'; that the tablets of deceased ancestors were honoured as a remembrance of the dead rather than as an actual residence of their souls; that t'ien [tian] and shang-ti [shangdi] are not identified with the physical sky but are 'the ruler and the lord of heaven and earth and all things'; and that ching t'ien [jing tian] in the inscription bestowed on the Jesuit Church meant 'revere Heaven' in this sense.[24]

These reports of the Jesuits arrived in Rome in the autumn of 1701 and at about the same time a letter in support of their position came from a completely independent source. A long report reached Rome in favour of the Jesuit position sent by the senior Augustinian in China, Alvaro de Benavente, Vicar Apostolic of Jiangxi.

All of this was to no avail. Indeed it was worse than to no avail, it hurt the Jesuit cause since many senior ecclesiastics expressed their shock that the Jesuits had gone so far astray from the Christian way as to submit an issue of Christian truth to a pagan prince.

In the bitterness of the conflict at the time, both the antagonism felt by many Churchmen in Europe against the Jesuits and some of the unfair and prejudiced pro-Jesuit productions make this misunderstanding of what the Jesuits in China had done and what the Emperor was saying perhaps understandable – though still a tragic error. What is more difficult to explain is the way that a number of twentieth-century historians have repeated the accusation. That scholars as different as the Franciscan A. S. Rosso, J. S. Cummins,[25] a professor of Hispanic studies, and the Protestant mission historian A. H. Rowbotham[26] could all take this line would seem to indicate that the issue of the Valignano tradition of mission is still capable of being profoundly disturbing.

Even before the theologians of the Holy Office had come to a final decision on the issues, the new Pope Clement XI (Innocent XII had died in 1700) appointed a Papal Legate to visit the East. The sending of a Legate was primarily to deal with the problems in India over the Jesuit pattern of mission in southern India as well as to create a more direct link between the Papacy and the new Churches of the East.[27] The situation of the Church, which at that time was undergoing a struggle between the Papacy and the Bourbon monarchs for control, so bizarre to modern eyes, is highlighted by the fact that the Legate de Tournon sailed in a French ship and missed Lisbon, Goa and Macao altogether. The situation might have been retrieved had he paid a careful diplomatic visit to the Archbishop and Governor-General at Goa. Instead he infuriated the Portuguese ecclesiastical and secular authorities beyond measure by visiting India to deal with the Jesuit mission in Madura via the French colony of Pondicherry, while paying no formal attention to the Archbishop of Goa whatsoever.

It is not clear what the Legate's instructions with regard to China were, since no decision had as yet been made when Charles Maillard de Tournon was appointed. However, the decisions of the Holy Office were formulated and turned into a Papal decree by Pope Clement XI on 20 November 1704 and despatched post-haste after de Tournon. Meanwhile the decision was not published in Europe but was held back to enable de Tournon to put it into effective operation in China first. This was the point of sending a Papal Legate. It was to make the final resolution of the Rites issue effective in the field by having someone with full Papal authority there to make it so.

Up till then the sheer problems of distance, taking up to four years to send a letter and get a reply, plus the filter of the Portuguese Padroado coming between Rome and China, had all conspired to make it possible for instructions to be set aside till further appeals to Rome; and then sometimes, with the support of the Portuguese, not to have them implemented. The Padroado had, in the early days, been seen by Valignano and Ricci as a threat to the work of the Society. Later, in the second half of the seventeenth century Portuguese weakness lessened its threat and it had become a useful tool to use selectively for the maintenance of their mission and its particular style. A Papal Legate on the spot cut through all of these difficulties.

Although de Tournon had not seen all the details of Clement XI's decree he knew of its essential points. These were that the use of Shangdi or Tian were forbidden and all tablets in churches bearing the characters Jing Tian were to be removed. Christians were not to take part in any of the ceremonies honouring Confucius or the ancestors. Ancestral tablets in any of the traditional forms were absolutely forbidden, though a simple board with the name only might be permitted in Christian homes.

De Tournon arrived in Canton in April 1705. Clearly many missionaries in China still hoped that he was there in some sort of fact finding capacity or at least with the authority to negotiate which would not be unusual for a Papal Legate. So, while he was still waiting in Canton for imperial permission to travel to Beijing, he was visited by the Augustinian Vicar Apostolic of Kiangxi, Fr Alvaro de Benavente. This persistent non-Jesuit supporter of the Jesuit way placed before the Legate the treatise defending the Jesuit position which, we have already noted, he had sent to the Holy Office in Rome. The Legate was delighted to meet, in this same period, Fr Claude de Visdelou. The only Jesuit of standing to oppose the Jesuit position, he was of enormous help to the Legate and supplied him with much intellectual ammunition. It would appear that it was at this time that de Tournon said that the China mission would have to be destroyed before it could be reformed.[28]

The Legate was invited eventually to come to the capital and ordered to stay in the Jesuit residence. He was visited by mandarins who discussed the reasons for his visit and asked him a number of questions all in preparation for a formal imperial audience. De Tournon was not able to reveal the real reasons for his visit and his statements about why he came were not taken very seriously. Much more important and clearly showing that the Emperor at least suspected why he was there, the mandarins told him that the Emperor wanted to know how the Pope had received the Emperor's decree of 1700 on the Jesuit understanding of the Rites? Again de Tournon had to dissimulate. Negotiations were entered into via meetings with mandarins about the possible setting up of a permanent Papal diplomatic mission in Beijing. Meanwhile de Tournon continued his review of the Chinese Church. He clashed with a delegation from the Beijing congregations and then went on to make the mistake of calling Maigrot to join his staff in Beijing. Maigrot was someone who had already annoyed the Emperor deeply because of his circular of 1693. It really was a misjudgement of massive proportions to bring him to the capital and to the attention of the Emperor, or it was a sign that de Tournon by this time did not care about what the Emperor thought. However, it had been Maigrot's actions based on his judgement on the central issues of the relationship of Christianity to the Confucian tradition that had reopened the whole issue and begun the process that led to de Tournon being in Beijing in the first place, so was it not logical and appropriate for him to be by the Legate's side as his expert adviser on matters Chinese?

De Tournon told the Emperor that he needed Maigrot with him to explain the difficulties presented by the Classics to Christianity since he, de Tournon, did not read Chinese. The Legate told the Emperor so at their last formal meeting on 30 June 1706. The Kangxi Emperor then went north of the Wall to the Manchu capital of Jehol for the summer and Maigrot was summoned there. Maigrot was first interrogated by senior mandarins in Beijing and then apeared before the Emperor himself at Jehol. Even according to Rosso, an historian sympathetic to Maigrot's position, Maigrot's performance was a disaster. He showed that he had little knowledge of literary Chinese, had no direct knowledge of the Classics and confessed to the Emperor that he had never read Ricci's *Tianzhu shiyi*.[29]

The Emperor had had enough by this time. In August 1706 he ordered Maigrot back to Beijing, instructing him to tell the Legate to prepare to return to Europe. De Tournon now left the capital and moved south towards Canton, stopping for a time at Nanjing with its substantial Christian community. The Emperor decided that matters could not be left in the air and that he should end any confusion as to what the situation was. In December he ordered Maigrot and two other missionaries associated with him to be expelled immediately from the empire. More important, he now issued an order that all missionaries who wished to stay in the empire had to receive an imperial 'biao' which would only be issued after the missionary had been examined by officials and had assured them that he would follow the ways of Li Madou.

In Nanjing de Tournon now acted in reply to the Emperor's initiative. He issued a guide to all missionaries as to how to answer the questions that were to be asked in connection with the granting of a 'biao'. The answers were totally negative in accordance with the Papal condemnation of 1704; but his instructions went further by insisting that all discussion of the issue was to cease as the decisions had been finally and infallibly made in the matter of the Rites.

Many missionaries applied for and receieved their 'biao', hoping that de Tournon had misunderstood what had been intended by the Holy Office since no one had yet seen the Papal constitution of 1704. Some Jesuits and other Mendicants used the Padroado as a defence, saying that de Tournon had no legal standing in China. Meanwhile, the Emperor had not yet given up on the Christian Church entirely, as he was to do later, and he actually paid for Jesuits to travel to Rome to attempt to bring about what he considered a rectification of the errors made by Maigrot and de Tournon.[30]

All was to no avail. While held captive by the Portuguese authorities in Macao at the request of the Emperor, de Tournon received, early in 1710, his biretta as a new cardinal of the Church and died soon after in June. The honour made it clear to all that de Tournon had the Pope's support. In 1710 Clement XI rejected the Jesuit appeals and confirmed the terms of de Tournon's Nanjing instruction. Worse was to follow, on 19 March 1715 Pope Clement XI issued the Bull *Ex illa die* which not only repeated in clear and unambiguous detail all the previous condemnations but laid down a strongly worded oath to be taken by all missionaries that they would obey all the instructions exactly and completely. Of this Bull it has been said,

> there is not one among all the decrees of the Holy See so accurately and cautiously worded or so minutely guarded against possible exception and evasion.[31]

The Jesuit missionary approach initiated by Valignano in Japan and developed under his supervision by Matteo Ricci, devout Christian and Confucian Zhunzi, was over. There was still some activity that needs our attention but this served merely to convince the Kangxi Emperor that the Church, having rejected the ways of Li Madou, no longer deserved imperial toleration of its activities in China.

It was the visit of a second Papal Legate, Jean Ambrose Charles Mezzabarba, that finally convinced the Emperor of this. This Legate came to the East via the approved Padroado route and was reluctantly received by the Emperor in the capital in December 1720. His visit and the special concessions he promulgated – with Papal authority he asserted, at least while in China – are often seen as a genuine attempt to find a via media.[32] These concessions allowed modified ancestor tablets; funeral ceremonies and those in honour of Confucius were permitted in certain circumstances, the kou tou and food offerings were allowed at these ceremonies.

The Jesuits and some others welcomed this and proclaimed the 'exceptions' to the Christian community, which Mezzabarba had not intended; but other clergy and religious, including many of the Vicars Apostolic, denied the validity of these 'exceptions'.

The reality was, however, that the decisive events of Mezzabarba's visit were his meetings with the Kangxi Emperor, not the very ambiguous promulgation of his 'exceptions'. In many ways it is quite extraordinary that this great Emperor gave so much of his valuable time and energy to this very small sect among his people. However the honour in which the memory of Ricci, of Aleni and Xu Guangqi were held, his close youthful friendship with Verbiest and the role of subsequent Jesuits as senior mandarins in the imperial administration did make it a special sect. It is important to note this clear proof of the Emperor's concern about Christianity and the memory of Ricci because later, disgusted with what had happened to Christianity of which he had approved and to which he had given such attention, the Kangxi Emperor was dismissive of Christianity, for example in his self portrait made known to the non-Chinese world in Jonathan Spence's *Emperor of China*. Again, later Qing historical revision played down the role of the Jesuits in Chinese history for obvious reasons, and treated Xu Guangqi as a great civil servant and scholar without mentioning that he was a, if not the, leading Chinese Christian of his age.

Among Chinese Christians today there is a popular tradition, which a number of scholars believe probable, that the Kangxi Emperor composed this poem:

> With his task done on the Cross,
> His blood forms itself into a streamlet,
> Grace flows from West Heaven in long patience:
>> Trials in four courts,
>> Long walks at midnight,
>> Thrice denied by friend before the cock crew twice,
> Six-footer hanging at the same height as two thieves,
> It is a suffering that moves the whole world and all ranks,
> Hearing His seven words makes all souls cry.

His authorship of this poem would be in keeping with his many years of intimacy with Verbiest, and with his extraordinarily patient efforts to preserve the Christian tradition of Li Madou.[33]

The decisive meetings between Mezzabarba and the Emperor took place between the third week of December 1720 and 3 March 1721. There are in the records of the Legate's visit all kinds of accusations about Jesuit plotting to prevent the Emperor from coming to an agreement with him. Whatever the Jesuits were or were not doing mattered little, for the Emperor was conducting this affair and had his own very firm ideas.

On 10 January the Emperor said that the quarrel was one among Europeans who were in no position to judge anyway about Chinese matters because they could not read literary Chinese and had not spent their life studying the Classics.[34] Again the Emperor specifically defended Matteo Ricci as one who did understand the Classics and the Confucian way, and insisted on the correctness of Ricci's use of 'Tian' and 'Shangdi' and the honouring of the ancestors.[35] At last when he was presented with and read a Chinese translation of *Ex illa die* his patience was finally exhausted and he wrote (and this personal autograph note on the Chinese text of the Bull has been preserved),

> Now I have seen the Legate's proclamation, and it is just the same as Buddhist and Taoist heresies and superstitions. I have never seen such nonsense as this. Henceforth no Westerner may propagate his religion in China. It should be prohibited to avoid more trouble.[36]

Back in Rome the Propaganda mounted a campaign against the Society of Jesus. In September 1723, on the basis of information given to him by the Propaganda Innocent XIII accused the the Jesuit General of not having acted firmly enough to obtain obedience to the instructions from Rome, and threatened that if action was not forthcoming the Society would be forbidden to accept any new novices. The General bowed before the storm which Rowbotham refers to as the 'high-water mark in the vituperation in the quarrel' over the Rites and attempted to make sure that the Fathers in China were suitably obedient. But to what were Christians to be obedient? What was the status of Mezzabarba's exceptions?

The Congregation of the Propaganda Fide took up the matter for the last time and the result of its deliberations, which began in 1739, was the Bull of Benedict XIV, *Ex quo singulari*. This confirmed the prohibitions of Pope Clement made in 1704, Maigrot's edict of 1710 and of the Bull *Ex illa die* of 1715, and added that all missionaries unwilling to swear an oath of obedience to these instructions, which included a specific rejection of Mezzabarba's exceptions, should be withdrawn from China.

Although Jesuits were to be tolerated as scientific assistants to the imperial Government in Beijing until the suppression of the Society in 1773, the China mission of Valignano and Ricci was over. With the exception of certain famous literary families like that of Xu Guangqi, Christianity ceased to be an option for people in the mainstream of Chinese life. The Catholic Church did not die in China, but it became a harassed sect appealing to people at the periphery of society. Christianity was no longer a Chinese but a foreign religion associated essentially with foreigners and foreignness. Even before this was driven home by the alliance of Protestant and Catholic nineteenth-century missions with European military and diplomatic domination of China, the eurocentric mental attitude which produced *Ex quo singulari* had made it so.

It has been said by many authorities, even by someone as sympathetic to the Riccian tradition as Paul Rule, that the Catholic Church would not have prospered in China under the two immediate successors of the Kangxi Emperor no matter what. Clearly no one can be sure about 'what would have happened if...' yet historians are, quite appropriately, called on to make judgements on this kind of issue. Would the Yongzheng Emperor have been so unsympathetic if his father had not been so thoroughly disillusioned by the Rites Controversy and the ultimate rejection by the Church of Li Madou, and more importantly, through him the Confucian tradition. Had the Church accepted the Riccian tradition, then Christianity would have remained an officially recognised Chinese form of religion certainly until the death of the Kangxi Emperor in 1722. What would have been the attitude of his successor then? Even had he been antagonistic it would have been towards a Church in a very different situation, a more Chinese Church and one with a literati leadership capable of surviving with real vigour some imperial displeasure exactly as Buddhist and Daoist groups often had to do. The Yongzheng and Qianlong Emperors were insising on their orthodox Chineseness despite their Manchu origins and so any kind of sympathy for Christianity would have weakened this, it has been argued.

The real issue, it would seem, is why the Riccian tradition was rejected by the Church. Was it in the end because western Christianity was so inextricably linked to European culture that it simply could not shake itself free from the identification of Christianity with European culture with no remainder? Was the insight that enabled Valignano to produce *Il Ceremoniale* and to work so closely with Ricci towards his goal of the acceptance of Christianity as a respectable possible faith for a Confucian Scholar a temporary aberration in the tradition of western Christianity? Aberration or not, where did this Jesuit vision come from?

NOTES

1. By J. S. Cummins in numerous articles and most recently in *A Question of Rites*; and Rowbotham, *Missionary and Mandarin*; and very thoroughly by G. H. Dunne, *Generation of Giants*.
2. Cummins, *Jesuit and Friar*, p. 400.
3. For founding of Congregation see Delacroix, *Histoire Universelle des Missions Catholiques*, vol. 2, chp. 6.
4. Rule, *K'ung-tzu or Confucius*, pp. 89–94.
5. J. S. Cummins in none of his works appreciates this point. In a number of places he chides Valignano for not recognising that some Jesuits in the Philippines and Mexico also wanted to use Spanish arms to aid the spread of Christianity in Japan and China. He does not appreciate that Valignano wanted no one from the Philippines and New Spain because he had seen that even Jesuits from there were tainted by the conquistador mentality.
6. Ricci's *Tianzhu shiyi* still caused this kind of misunderstanding.
7. Dunne, op. cit., p. 248.
8. Cummins, *A Question of Rites*, passim.
9. Minimaki, *The Chinese Rites Controversy*, pp. 34–5.
10. Both sides of this argument are thoroughly discussed in Young, *Confucianism and Christianity*, and Gernet, *China and the Christian Impact*.
11. Delacroix, *Histoire Universelle des Missions Catholiques*, p. 110.
12. Fr de Nobili SJ had begun a mission attempting acculturation in the area of Madura in south India.
13. Rule, op. cit., vol. 2, p. 126.
14. Cary-Elwes, *China and the Cross*, pp. 126–30.
15. Rule, op. cit., p. 127.
16. Gallicanism was a strongly held position among many French Catholics, which was a firm insistence on the fundamental autonomy of the French Church over against the Papacy. For obvious reasons, Gallicanism was anti-Jesuit, as was the powerful Jansenist Augustinian tradition which bitterly opposed what it saw as Jesuit Pelagianism.
17. Latourette, *A History of Christian Missions in China*, pp. 117–19.
18. See Chapter 3 above.
19. Vissière, *Lettres Edifiantes et Curieuses*, pp. 117–19.

20. Cary-Elwes, op. cit., pp. 138–61.
21. The most careful discussion of this strange story of the Chinese liturgy is in Dunne, op. cit., pp. 162–75.
22. Rule, op. cit., p. 130.
23. Ibid. pp. 134–7. and Minamiki, *The Chinese Rites Controversy*, pp. 39–40.
24. Rule, op. cit., p. 132.
25. To be fair to Cummins, he gives some examples of the almost hysterical anti-Jesuit bias among some Churchmen in chp. 1 of *A Question of Rites*.
26. Rowbotham, op. cit., pp. 145–6.
27. The Malabar Rites issue created by the work of de Nobili.
28. Rule, op. cit., chp. 3, n. 85.
29. Rosso, *Apostolic Legations to China*, pp. 168–9.
30. The Emperor financed two such delegations, one in 1706 and another in 1707.
31. Rowbotham, op. cit., p. 165.
32. Ibid., p. 170.
33. A copy of this poem in Mandarin, together with this literal translation into English, was presented to the author by Bishop Wang of Jinan, Shandong Province, in 1990.
34. Rule, op. cit., p. 144.
35. Rosso, op. cit., pp. 357–60.
36. Ibid., p. 376; and Rule, op. cit., p. 144.

CHAPTER TEN

Whence Came the Vision?

The expansion of the Christian Church in the early centuries of its existence was a process by which the core belief in a resurrected Messiah rooted in the Jewish scriptures adapted itself to, while also modifying profoundly, a number of non-Jewish cultures. This happened in the Graeco-Roman world but also in Armenia, Nubia, Ethiopia, South India and, in its Nestorian form, also among the Mongol and Alan peoples of Central Asia. A somewhat later example is the christianising of the Russian peoples in which Christianity was also 'Russified' with Moscow as the 'Third Rome' at the centre of Holy Mother Russia.

In the Latin Christian areas of the West that remained after the massive expansion of the military and political power of Islam, this flexibility appeared to die away. Western Europe was Christendom and what was European was Christian and what was Christian was European. This became most explicitly so among the Iberian kingdoms during the experience of the re-conquest of the land from the power of North African Islam. Even when Christendom appeared to be broken up by the shock of the Reformation, Calvinists in Massachussetts and Connecticut were no less confident of the identity of their culture as the only possible Christian culture as any Catholic conquistador in Mexico. Again when eventually Protestantism became dynamically orientated towards mission in the closing decades of the eighteenth century, it followed the same pattern of understanding Christianity and Civilisation as being inextricably linked and that Civilisation meant the culture of Protestant northern Europe or North America. It has only been in the late nineteenth and then increasingly in the twentieth century that some real cultural flexibility has returned to Christianity.

It is in this context that we must see the work of the Society of Jesus in Japan and China. The missionary approach was so different that it presents a puzzle that has to be explained. It is so different that it cuts across any neat attempt to present a coherent model of the history of the outreach of western Christianity.

The result is that it is sometimes ignored by historians, or its differences are played down and ironed out.

As we have seen, when Pope Alexander VI promulgated the Bull *Inter caeterae divinae*, he divided the newly 'discovered' lands and those yet to be discovered between the crowns of Portugal and Spain. In the normal way of Medieval Europe, the kings received the authority to make all ecclesiastical appointments in their new dominions which were to be christianised at their expense. Some have said this was simply an extension of the Crusades; it is more accurate to say it was an extension of the re-conquest, which is so neatly reflected in the name which the Spanish settlers and soldiers gave to themselves, conquistadores.

In the highly acclaimed and most recent general study of the history of Christian missionary expansion, the late David Bosch's *Transforming Mission*, the author says that it was at this period that the Latin word 'missio' was first used of this activity. Bosch sees this use coming from the sending out to their new dominions of clergy by the Iberian monarchs.[1] The word had up till then only been used in narrowly theological discussions about the sending of the Son by the Father and so on in discussions of the doctrine of the Trinity. However, Bosch asserts, with some measure of authority, that the first person to use 'missio' about the sending by the Church of persons to carry out special tasks was Ignatius Loyola.

But of what was Ignatius using the word? It was of the availability of the members of his new Society of Jesus to be sent forth by the Pope to carry out any task, any where, at any time for the greater glory of God. The new Society was specifically organised to serve Christ through his servant on earth the Pope, and not the ecclesiastical structures which were so carefully controlled by royal authority as to make the Church simply the spiritual aspect of royal power.[2] From its very inception then, the Society of Jesus was a challenge to the traditions of Medieval Christendom with its close alliance of throne and altar and where, in the Iberian kingdoms, the throne was the senior partner. As we have seen, the Inquisition in Spain was a royal institution and a powerful tool of royal authority which did not, in practice, pay any attention to Papal authority.

Bosch goes on to develop the idea that this domination of Christian activity outside Europe by the Portuguese and Spanish thrones became increasingly disturbing to thoughtful Churchmen. As a result of this the Sacra Congregatio de Propaganda Fide was set up in 1622 in an attempt to get the direction of Christan missionary activity out of royal hands and into the hands of a Church organisation acting free from royal control.[3]

However, the initial response to royal control of the Church as opposed to ecclesiastical autonomy was, I suggest, the creation of the Society of Jesus. The fourth vow of its senior members is the key to this. As we noted above, this is a vow to be available to be sent anywhere at any time. Part of the Constitutions of the Society of Jesus reads,

> It should be observed that the vow which the Society made to obey him [the Pope] as the supreme vicar of Christ without any excuse, meant that members were to go to any place whatsoever where he judges it expedient to send them for the greater glory of God and the good of souls, whether among the faithful or the infidels.[4]

It is to this activity which is specifically set up over against the sending forth and appointment of ecclesiastics by royal authority, that Ignatius applies the word 'missio'.

Already then in the very Constitutions of the Society of Jesus we have the beginnings, at least, of something different from the simple identification of European political power and Christianity.

Potential was there, but it was potential that could be stifled as we have seen it was in the Lisbon headquarters of the Portuguese province of the Society at the time of Valignano's appointment as Visitor to the East. Yet the potential was there and it was exploited by the very first Jesuit to go on a 'mission' outside Europe, Francis Xavier. As we have suggested he began to exploit the difference by his insistence on translation,[5] so that, in the first instance, the Paravas learned the basic elements of the faith and of prayer and worship in their own language and were exempted from changing their appearance and diet to conform to Portuguese norms. By the end of his life, he was clear that the Church in Japan and possibly China was not to be simply an extension of the Portuguese Church, but what that meant in detail he had not worked out. Indeed he had withdrawn somewhat from an initial bold form of translation which he believed had gone badly wrong.

It was Alessandro Valignano who clearly and unambiguously created the approach to the spread of Christianity in Japan and China that finally leads to the crisis of the Rites controversy. His ideas can be found in his *Il Ceremoniale per i missionari del Giappone*, in Schutte's two-volume study of his principles and in the life and work of Matteo Ricci with which he was involved every step of the way.

Before we go further with the developments in the East it is worth noting that the fundamental principles of the Society were certainly part of what made the difference. This can be seen in what happened in South America. A. D. Wright in his study of the Counter-Reformation[6] points to the constant clash between the Society and the royal authorities about the creation of an indigenous priesthood, and how they sought a place free of royal control which eventually they created among the Guarani in what are referred to as the Paraguay 'reductions'.[7] These covered a much larger area than modern Paraguay and extended into what is now Brasil, Uraguay and Argentina. This story had as bitter an end as the Jesuit 'experiment' in Japan and China.

What the story in South America shares with that in the East is the Jesuit hostility to European, particularly Spanish, conquest. In the East the Portuguese were a lesser threat, they were more of a social or psychological threat than a physical one. They restricted their empire to a series of key bases and their hinterland from which they tried to monopolise the trade of the area. However, wherever they had bases they believed the Portuguese Padroado existed, and christianisation should still mean conforming to Portguese ways. But it was at least possible to get round their authority since they had no real power in Japan and China, though they did control the way there. The truly great fear that Valignano had was the threat from the expansion of Spain across the Pacific to the Philippines. The Spanish empire was very different from that of Portugal, it was one of actual conquest, occupation and forced hispanicisation on the ground. The Spanish presence was not simply one of a crusading mental attitude, but of crusading conquest. Until his death Valignano, who had after all grown up under Spanish colonial rule, continued to warn the authorites in Manila that Japan and China were not to be seen as places where the faith was to be spread by conquest.[8]

So far so good. The reaction in South America as in China and Japan was to insist that it was better to spread the Christian faith in a situation as free as possible from any relation to Portuguese or Spanish imperial authority. The issue is, however, that in Japan and China the Jesuits went much further than that and tried to integrate Christianity and the indigenous culture so that there developed a pattern of Christian life which was Chinese or Japanese and not a replication of European Christianity.

The attempt to disassociate Christianity from European political authority is rooted in the very foundations of the Society but that does not explain the further step the Jesuits took of attempting what has in the second half of the twentieth century been called indigenisation, assimilation or acculturation, and what has been challenged both in the past and in the twentieth century as a falling away from Christanity into syncretism.

The Constitutions of the Society of Jesus were the platform upon which this effort was based but there were other important contributions. These additional contributory elements were, first, Italian Humanism, second, the personality produced by the *Spiritual Exercises*, third, the judgement of the Jesuit pioneers that Chinese and Japanese cultures were like those of the old Roman world, truly civilised though alien; indeed many insisted that Chinese society was clearly superior to that of the old Graeco-Roman world. This was often expressed by insisting that the Japanese and Chinese were 'white'.

Let us look at the third factor first. Valignano has been accused by many of arrogance and prejudice.[9] He certainly believed that Africans, Indians and the peoples of Indonesia were inferior to Europeans. It is clear that he did not see his pattern of missionary indigenisation applying in India or Indonesia or Africa, where in fact in the twentieth century it has happened more thoroughly and on a wider scale than anywhere else; and de Nobili did attempt this style of mission in India after Valignano was dead, though the latter would not have thought it possible or wise. The Visitor was firmly convinced that these two peoples, the Chinese and the Japanese, were 'white' and had to be approached differently from other peoples, not simply in a situation free from Iberian imperial pretensions, but in an intellectually and spiritually different way. This was a situation, he insisted, where the missionary had also to learn as well as teach. In many ways it was his regrettable prejudices against the other peoples that helped him see the Chinese and the Japanese as different.

The second factor was the nature of person the Jesuit was when he had been shaped by the basic spiritual training given in the Jesuit novitiate, centering on Loyola's *Spiritual Exercises*. The whole process was one of stripping down and then rebuilding the emotions, the will and the intellect. One very specific part of the experience was and is to help the person undergoing the *Exercises* to be able to make correct decisions in difficult and confusing situations. The whole process should lead to a person emerging who is not the automaton so often referred to by those who misunderstand the process, but someone with immense confidence. The fully formed temporal or spiritual coadjutors, the professed of the Fourth Vow were men who had been trained to act and work in the world for the glory of God and the salvation of souls in all kinds of situations. They were trained to have, and they did have, confidence in their ability to choose the right way to carry out whatever 'mission' they had been given.

However it also freed the Jesuit from the wrong kind of confidence. This spiritual training gave them the ability to reflect on any situation in ways that could and did challenge conventional wisdom whether in Church or state. That good and devoted man, Caballero de Santa Maria, was only too typical of so many of the missionaries of the day and of the Catholic and Protestant missionaries of later times. They would sympathise with his famous insistence that it did not matter whether the ancient Chinese had known God or what they had called Him, it was a matter of indifference. Missionaries were there to proclaim the Gospel and that they were going to do. The *Spiritual Exercises* did not allow such lack of self-reflection and self-critical awareness.

The third element was Italian humanism. When one considers the key figures in the initial period of the shaping and carrying out of the Jesuit approach to Japan and China, one thing is clear; other than Francis Xavier, whose family were perpetual Basque rebels against the Spanish state, they were all Italians. Alessandro Valignano, Organtino Gnecchi-Soldi, Francesco Pasio, Michele Ruggieri, Matteo Ricci, Nicolo Longobardo and Giulio Aleni were the most prominent.

Most of them were also intellectually prepared in the Roman College of the Society, the future Gregorian University, in the same period. This is not to claim some kind of ethnic element as necessary to the Jesuit vision for Japan and China. Jesuit Fathers from other parts of Europe came to help the cause and some of them were Spanish and Portuguese. What can be said however is that it was difficult for anyone growing up in Spain or the Spanish empire or in Portuguese territory not to be deeply affected by the whole 'conquistador' understanding of Christianity and of the world. The Italians of the period were free from this infection and they also grew up in the cultural golden age of a specifically Catholic humanism.

Again and again those who were critical of the approach, and those who misunderstood it within the Society, were Portuguese or Spanish. Examples are Vice Provincial Coelho and his aim of fortifying Nagasaki; or the new Visitor of 1614, Valentim Carvalho, who, never having been in China, attempted to ban on his arrival the Jesuit involvement in teaching mathematics and science and the study of Confucian philosophy; or again Rodriguez 'the Interpreter' who could warn against the inadequacy of the quality of Japanese Jesuits only days after seeing some die for the faith! It is also worth noting that some of the leading European missionaries, not Jesuits, who supported the ways of Li Madou were also Italian, notably the first Dominican, Cocchi, in Fujian, and the leading Augustinian, Vicar Apostolic of Jiangxi, Alvaro Benavente. Spanish, Portuguese, French, German and Flemish Jesuits all followed the Valignano–Ricci approach to mission, but that does not change the fact that the originators were Italians – it was they who had the vision and passed it on.

The vision that inspired the work of Alessandro Valignano and guided perhaps the most intellectually brilliant of all missionaries, Matteo Ricci, drew on a combination of sources. Being an Italian did not guarantee that one had it, being Spanish did not stop one from following it with commitment, simply being a Jesuit was in itself not enough, though that did produce what Professor Lugon calls 'La République Chrétienne des Guaranis'.[10] However it would appear that it was the coming together of the impact of the *Spiritual Exercises* with the very fundamental aims of the Society of Jesus and with individual Italians formed in a particular moment of Italian history that created the vision that shaped the Christian century in Japan and the Confucianist Christianity of Li Madou.

To say that the vision was betrayed is perhaps too harsh. What is certain is that the Europe of the eighteenth century, whether Catholic, Protestant or Deist, was not ready for it and could not understand it. To the arrogant imperialist expansionism of nineteenth century Europe it was nonsense.

NOTES

1. Bosch, *Transforming Mission*, p. 228.
2. Ibid., p. 226–8.
3. Ibid., p. 229.
4. Ganss, *Ignatius of Loyola*, p. 307.
5. See Chapter 2 above.
6. A. D. Wright, *The Counter-Reformation*, p. 32.
7. Ibid., p. 34.

8. Moran, *The Japanese and the Jesuits*, pp. 46–9.
9. Even by a sympathetic commentator like Moran, op. cit., p. 192.
10. Delacroix, *Histoire Universelle des Missions Catholiques*, vol. 2, p. 268.

Bibliography

For a reader who wishes to pursue any aspect of the Jesuit story in Japan and China in depth the necessary basic collections of manuscript documents in Rome, Paris, London and Lisbon are listed in Rule, *K'ung-tzu or Confucius* and Boxer, *The Christian Century in Japan*. In September 1983 an international academic symposium was held in commemoration of the 400th anniversary of the arrival of Matteo Ricci in China. The papers presented at that symposium have been published in a massive 900-page vol ume in Chinese and English, *The International Symposium on Chinese–Western Cultural Interchange*, Taipei, University of Taiwan, 1983.

This bibliography is primarily of printed material in English, though some important works in French and Italian are also listed.

Attwater, Rachel, *Adam Schall: A Jesuit at the Court of China, 1592–1666*, London, Geoffrey Chapman, 1963.
Bernard-Maître, Henri, *Aux Portes de la Chine*, Tientsin, 1934.
―――― *Le Père Matthieu Ricci et la société chinoise de son temps (1552–1610)*, Tientsin, 1937.
Berry, Mary E., *Hideyoshi*, Cambridge, Harvard University Press, 1982.
Boxer, C. R., *The Christian Century in Japan 1549–1650*, Berkeley, University of California Press, 1967.
Braga, J. M., 'The Panegyric of Alexander Valignano sj', *Monumenta Niponica*, v, 1942, 523–35.
Cameron, Nigel, *Barbarians and Mandarins: Thirteen Centuries of Western Travellers in China*, Chicago, University of Chicago Press, 1970.
Carey-Elwes, Columba, *China and the Cross*, London, Longmans Green, 1957.
Cieslik, H. J., 'The Case of Christovao Ferreira', *Monumenta Nipponica*, 29:1, 1974, 1–54.
―――― 'The Great Martyrdom in Edo, 1623', *Monumenta Nipponica*, 10:1, 1954, 1–44.
Cohen, Paul A., *China and Christianity*, Cambridge, Harvard University Press, 1963.
Coleridge, H. J., *The Life and Letters of St Francis Xavier*, 2 vols, London, 1902.
Cooper, Micheal, *Rodriguez, the Interpreter: An Early Jesuit in Japan*, New York, Weatherill, 1974.
Covell, Ralph R., *Confucius, The Buddha and Christ*, Maryknoll, Orbis Books, 1986.
Cronin, Vincent, *The Wise Man from the West*, London, Rupert Hart-Davis, 1956.

Cummins, J. S., *A Question of Rites: Friar Domingo Navarette and the Jesuits in China*, Aldershot, Scolar Press, 1993.
—— *Jesuit and Friar in the Spanish Expansion to the East*, London, Variorum Reprints, 1986.
Dehergne, J., *Répertoire des Jésuites de Chine, de 1552 à 1800*, Paris, Letouzey at Ané, 1973.
Delacroix, S., *Histoire Universelle des Missions Catholiques*, vols I and II, Paris, Librairie Grund, 1966.
D'Elia, Pasquale M., *Galileo in China*, Cambridge, Mass., Harvard University Press, 1947.
—— *Fonte Ricciane*, 3 vols, Rome, The State Library, 1942–49.
Delplace, L., *Le Catholicisme au Japon*, 2 vols, Brussels, 1909–10.
Drummond, R. H., *A History of Christianity in Japan*, Grand Rapids, Mich., Eerdmans, 1971.
Dunne, George H., *Generation of Giants: The Story of the Jesuits in China in the Last Decades of the Ming Dynasty*, London, Burns and Oates, 1962.
Ebisawa, Arimichi, 'Irmao Lourenço: the First Japanese Lay-Brother of the Society of Jesus', *Monumenta Nipponica*, 30:2, 1975, 225–33.
Elison, George, *Deus Destroyed: The Image of Christianity in Early Modern Japan*, Cambridge, Mass., Harvard University Press, 1973.
Friede and Keen, *Bartolome de las Casas in History*, De Kalb, Northern Illinois University Press, 1971.
Fujita, Neil, *Japan's Encounter with Christianity: The Catholic Mission in Pre-Modern Japan*, New York, Paulist Press, 1991.
Gallagher, Louis, *China in the Sixteenth Century: The Journals of Matteo Ricci 1583–1610*, New York, Random House, 1953.
Ganss, G. E., *Ignatius of Loyola: The Spiritual Exercises and Selected Works*, New York, Paulist Press, 1991.
Gernet, Jacques, *China and the Christian Impact*, Cambridge, Cambridge University Press, 1985.
Harris, G. L., 'The mission of Matteo Ricci, SJ', *Monumenta Serica*, XXV, 1966, 1–168.
Hay, Malcolm, *Failure in the Far East*, London, Neville Spearman, 1957.
Jennes, J., *A History of the Catholic Church in Japan*, Tokyo, Oriens Institute, 1973.
Kitagawa, J. M., *Religion in Japanese History*, New York, Columbia University Press, 1966.
Latourette, Kenneth S., *A History of Christian Missions in China*, London, SPCK, 1929.
Laures, J., *The Catholic Church in Japan: A Short History*, Tokyo, 1954.
—— *Two Japanese Christian Heroes*, Tokyo, 1957.
Malatesta, E. J. (ed), *'The True Meaning of the Lord of Heaven', Ricci's classic translated with notes by D. Lancashire and Peter Hu Kuo-chen*, St Louis, Institute of Jesuit Sources, 1985.
Minamiki, George, *The Chinese Rites Controversy*, Chicago, Loyola University Press, 1985.
Moran, J. F., *The Japanese and the Jesuits: Alessandro Valignano in Sixteenth Century Japan*, London, Routledge, 1993.
—— 'Letters from a Visitor to Japan, 1579', *Proceedings of the British Association of Japanese Studies*, 1979, part I, ed. G. Daniels.
Murdoch, J., and Yamagata, I., *A History of Japan during the Century of Early Foreign Intercourse*, London, 1949.

Mungello, D. E., *Curious Land: Jesuit Accommodation and the Origins of Sinology*, Stuttgart, Steiner-Verlag, 1985.

Needham, Joseph, *Science and Civilisation in China*, Cambridge, Cambridge University Press, 1954.

Pagés, Leon, *Histoire de la Religion Chrétienne au Japon depuis 1598 jusqu'à 1651*, 2 vols, Paris, 1868–70.

Panikkar, *Asia in the Era of European Domination*, London, Allan and Unwin, 1953.

Pfister, Louis, *Notices biographiques et bibliographiques sur les Jesuites de l'Ancienne Mission de Chine (1552–1773)*, 2 vols, Shanghai, 1932–4.

Reinstra, M. Howard, *Jesuit Letters from China*, Minneapolis, University of Minnesota Press, 1986.

Rosso, A. S., *Apostolic Legations to China in the Eighteenth Century*, South Pasadena, Cal., ed. P. D. and Ione Perkins, 1948.

Rowbotham, Arnold H., *Missionary and Mandarin: The Jesuits at the Court of China*, Berkeley, University of California Press, 1942.

Rule, Paul, 'Jesuit and Confucian? Chinese Religion in the Journals of Matteo Ricci SJ 1583–1610', *Journal of Religious History*, v, 1968, 105–24.

—— *K'ung-tzu or Confucius, The Jesuit Interpretation of Confucianism*, Sydney, Allen and Unwin, 1986.

Sansom, George, *Japan: A Short Cultural History*, Stanford, Stanford University Press, 1952.

Schurhammer, Georg, *Francis Xavier: His Life and Times, vol. IV: Japan 1549–1552*, Rome, The Jesuit Historical Institute, 1982.

Schutte, Johannes F., *Valignano's Mission Principles for Japan*, vol. I, parts 1 and 2, St Louis, Institute of Jesuit Sources, 1983.

Sebes, J., 'A "Bridge" between East and West: Fr Matteo Ricci SJ, his Time, his Life and his Method of Cultural Accommodation', in *The International Symposium on Chinese–Western Cultural Interchange*, pp. 555–616; Taiwan, University of Taipeh, 1983.

Spence, Jonathan, *Emperor of China: Self-Portrait of K'ang-hsi*, London, Book Club Associates, 1974.

—— *The Memory Palace of Matteo Ricci*, New York, Viking Penguin, 1984.

Standaert, N., *Yang Tingyun, Confucian and Christian in late Ming China*, Leyden, E. J. Brill, 1988.

Tacchi Venturi, P. (ed), *Opere Storiche*, 2 vols, Macerata, 1911–13.

Valignano, Alessandro, *Il Ceremoniale per i Missionari del Giappone*, Roma, Edizione de Storia, 1946.

Vissière, I. & J. L., *Lettres Edifiantes et Curieuses de Chines par des Missionaires Jesuites 1702–1796*, Paris, Garnier-Flammarion, 1979.

Wright, A. D., *The Counter-Reformation: Catholic Europe and the non-Christian World*, London, Weidenfield and Nicolson, 1983.

Xavier, Francis, *Monumenta Xaveriana*, Madrid, 1899–1912.

Young, John D., *Confucianism and Christianity: The First Encounter*, Hong Kong, Hong Kong University Press, 1983.

Index